Latin American
Rebels and the
United States,
1806–1822

ALSO BY GORDON S. BROWN

The Norman Conquest of Southern Italy and Sicily (McFarland, 2003)

Latin American Rebels and the United States, 1806–1822

GORDON S. BROWN

McFarland & Company, Inc., Publishers
Jefferson, North Carolina

LIBRARY OF CONGRESS CATALOGUING-IN-PUBLICATION DATA

Brown, Gordon S., 1936–
　　Latin American rebels and the United States, 1806–1822 / Gordon S. Brown.
　　　　p.　　cm.
　　Includes bibliographical references and index.

　　　ISBN 978-0-7864-9899-4 (softcover : acid free paper) ∞
　　　ISBN 978-1-4766-2082-4 (ebook)

　　1. Latin America—History—Wars of Independence, 1806–1830.　2. United States—Foreign relations—Latin America.　3. Latin America—Foreign relations—United States.　4. United States—Foreign relations—Spain.　5. Spain—Foreign relations—United States.　I. Title.
F1412.B818　2015
327.730809'034—dc23　　　　　　　　　　　2015007974

BRITISH LIBRARY CATALOGUING DATA ARE AVAILABLE

© 2015 Gordon S. Brown. All rights reserved

No part of this book may be reproduced or transmitted in any form or by any means, electronic or mechanical, including photocopying or recording, or by any information storage and retrieval system, without permission in writing from the publisher.

On the cover: *inset* Luis de Onís; *background* 1816 map of the United States (Library of Congress)

Printed in the United States of America

McFarland & Company, Inc., Publishers
　Box 611, Jefferson, North Carolina 28640
　　www.mcfarlandpub.com

Table of Contents

Preface 1
Timeline 5
Introduction 11

1. Uneasy Neighbors 17
2. Contested Loyalties 32
3. The First Rebel Agents Show Up 45
4. Filibusters, American and Émigré 58
5. Bringing American Privateers into the Fight 74
6. More Rebel Schemes for Armed Intervention 89
7. The Rise and Fall of the Republic of the Floridas 103
8. Hindering the Privateers 115
9. Recognition or Neutrality? 130
10. Agreement with Spain 143
11. Success Is a Matter of Fact 159
12. The End of the Beginning 172

Chapter Notes 183
Bibliography 193
Index 201

Preface

Recent, and continuing, international problems provided the stimulus for this study. Some five years ago, the United States was faced with a policy dilemma: how to react to rapid and revolutionary changes in the Arab world, where popular revolts against autocratic rule were gradually morphing into armed struggles challenging the stability of an entire region. Those revolts had begun as popular movements, inspired by a desire for liberty from oppression, and the sentiments of the rebels resonated strongly with American public opinion as well as our national ideals. But as the revolts turned into contests for local and even regional power, the situation became considerably murkier, while American interests were much less easy to identify. In Syria, Libya, Egypt and elsewhere, new and unfamiliar contestants for power emerged, including factions both unfriendly to democracy and to the United States. Our American dilemma was simple to pose, but extremely difficult to answer: whom, if anyone, to support in this rapidly-changing set of circumstances—ones which could profoundly affect our interests in the region, but which we only marginally understood and had only limited ability to influence?

The basic dilemma is not new. The United States government faced a similar challenge in its earliest days, when it had to respond to a revolution in nearby Haiti. Our response in that case was vacillating, at first supporting the revolutionaries because of immediate strategic and commercial interests, then backing away, and eventually turning hostile. Domestic American politics had also played an important part in that policy vacillation, which I enjoyed writing about a number of years ago. And then the Haitian revolution was then followed, some ten later, by a broader-scale set of interlinked revolutions in Spanish America that, when I thought about it (even though I had never studied it in depth), might provide a better and more useful parallel by which to compare and judge the current developments.

The Spanish American revolts broke out in the early 1800s, in the vast territories of Spain's nearby South and North American colonies. Soon, the region was aflame with overlapping struggles for independence from Spain and for leadership of the revolutionary movement. The stakes for the United States were great. In an international climate dominated by the Napoleonic Wars, the young, militarily weak and untested American government had no stronger strategic imperative than to remain neutral with respect to Spain and the other combating European powers. Yet it was inevitably drawn, both by proximity and a shared desire for freedom from European colonial rule, into sympathy with the struggles for independence being fought next door in Spanish America. But Americans at the time only marginally understood the region and its people, and had serious doubts as to the prospects, long-range intentions, or reliability of the revolutionary groups that soon began to appeal to the North American republic for aid. Should the United States support the movements for change, stand with the status-quo forces, or try to straddle the divide in a posture of neutrality, real or professed?

The similarities between our current dilemma in the Arab world, and the situation in revolutionary Spanish America almost exactly two centuries ago, are strong enough to have given me hope that a study of our connections to the revolutionaries during the earlier period would be interesting, and perhaps even useful.

As I explored the issue, I found that there are no recently published books that cover the specifics of America's contact with the revolutionary governments and the agents they sent to seek our assistance. In the decades before World War II, a significant number of scholarly articles and books had been published on the diplomatic history of early U.S.–South American relations, as well as on specific incidents involving the deeds or misdeeds of the Spanish American patriot agents. More recent articles have covered limited aspects of the subject, while a number of excellent books have covered the politics and diplomacy of America's expansion into Spanish territory. The earlier works, in particular, drew heavily and thoroughly on original sources, particularly the Spanish and Latin American ones concerning the early contacts with the United States. They provide a rich scholarly foundation for this work, but, today, are both incomplete and out of date.

My intent in this study, then, has been to bring together the substantial body of previous scholarship on the separate aspects of the subject into a single, concise, coherent narrative for a current audience. The study is centered on the activities of the agents, formal and otherwise, sent by the revolutionary juntas to the United States, and the corresponding activities of U.S. agents sent to the rebelling provinces. It does not focus on the diplomatic history of the period more than is necessary to describe the concerns of the American administrations, their constraints in dealing with both the Spanish American revolutionaries and the Spanish government, as well as Washington's incentives to maintain a neutral stance in a rapidly changing and dangerous environment.

Because the story unfolded on three continents, with numerous actors and much of the activity concentrated in the key years 1816–1820, it has presented some difficulties in presentation. As spelled out in more detail at the end of the Introduction, this has required some shifting back and forth between a chronological and a thematic presentation, which I trust will allow a reader to keep clear track of developments in their various aspects while at the same time maintaining a sense of how they fit together. A timeline has been included to help in that process.

I could not have put together this story effectively without the cooperation and help of a number of colleagues who guided me in my efforts to understand more of the Spanish American situation at the time, as well as helping me avoid errors in describing the flow of the many often interconnected events. While their advice has been invaluable, any errors of interpretation, translation of the Spanish texts, or presentation of the facts are, of course, mine. I am particularly grateful to Professor James A. Baer for his general guidance, Edward A. Bradley for collegial sharing of manuscripts, Robert and Karol Service for their support and also meticulous editing, and Julio Hang for helping to dig out some items from the basically inaccessible archives in Buenos Aires. My thanks go once again to the staff at the Library of Congress and National Archives for their help in accessing the treasures of those two great institutions.

Timeline

1806

Feb. **U.S.:** Francisco Miranda expedition leaves New York to liberate Venezuela

July Aaron Burr accused of conspiracy to provoke rebellion in Spanish Texas

Ogden and Smith acquitted of aiding Miranda in violation of neutrality law

Nov. United States and Spain establish Neutral Ground on disputed Louisiana-Texas border

1807

Nov. **Spain:** Napoleon sends French army into Spain; popular resistance develops

1808

May **Spain:** King Ferdinand forced to abdicate; Joseph Bonaparte named king

Insurrections against French spread; local pro–Ferdinand juntas formed

1809

Mar. **U.S.:** James Madison inaugurated as president, replacing Thomas Jefferson

Oct. Luis de Onís arrives as Spanish regency's envoy, is denied full recognition

1810

Jan. **Spain:** Regency Council established in Cádiz to rule in name of King Ferdinand

Timeline

Apr. **Venezuela:** Caracas Fernandista junta formed; national congress called for

May **New Granada:** Cartagena establishes Fernandista junta; other cities follow

Argentina: Buenos Aires establishes Fernandista junta, not all provinces follow

June **U.S.:** First rebel envoy arrives: Telésforo de Orea, from Venezuela

Aug. First American agent arrives in New Spain: William Shaler in Havana

Sept. **Mexico:** Revolution breaks out under Miguel Hidalgo

U.S.: American settlers create Republic of West Florida in disputed territory

Dec. United States annexes West Florida, dissolves republic

1811

July **Venezuela:** First Republic declared; Francisco Miranda one of its leaders

Sept. **U.S.:** Representative of Mexican rebels, Bernardo Gutiérrez, arrives in Louisiana

Oct. Rebel delegation arrives from Buenos Aires, headed by Diego de Saavedra

Nov. **New Granada:** Cartagena declares independence; issues privateer commissions

1812

Feb. **Spain:** Cádiz Cortes passes liberal constitution

Mar. **U.S.:** Filibuster into northeast Florida creates Republic of Florida; rapidly suppressed by U.S. government, which occupies Amelia Island

June War declared against Great Britain

July **Venezuela:** First republic falls; Miranda imprisoned

Aug. **U.S.:** Gutiérrez and U.S. citizen Augustus Magee launch filibuster into Texas

1813

Aug. **U.S.:** Gutiérrez-Magee filibuster defeated at San Antonio by royalist troops

Venezuela: Simón Bolívar returns; establishes Second Republic

1814

Apr. **Spain:** Following Napoleon's defeat and exile to Elba, Ferdinand returns as king; abolishes 1812 constitution the following month, orders pacification of colonies

July **Venezuela:** Second Republic defeated by earthquake, royalist forces

Dec. **U.S.:** Treaty of Ghent signed, formally ending War of 1812 before battle of New Orleans

1815

Apr. **Venezuela:** Royalist army under Pablo Morillo lands, aiming to crush colonial rebellions

July **U.S.:** Ports declared open to ships of all flags, even of non-recognized governments

Dec. **Mexico:** Rebel leader Morelos killed, but his envoy, José Herrera, active in New Orleans

1816

Jan. **U.S.:** Onís finally fully accredited as royal Spanish minister to U.S.
Deposed Chilean leader José Carrera arrives, seeking to recruit naval force

Feb. Informal Buenos Aires agent issues first privateer commissions to Americans

May Émigré general Xavier Mina arrives with plans to reinforce rebellion in Mexico

New Granada: Morillo captures Bogota, having also subdued Caracas and Cartagena

July **Argentina:** Congress of Tucumán declares Buenos Aires (Argentina) independent

Sept. **U.S.:** Mina, with assistance from émigrés and Americans, sails for Gulf coast

Venezuela: Bolívar returns to Venezuela, establishes rebel base at Angostura

U.S.: Chilean leader Carrera departs with purchased ships and small force

Privateer Louis Aury establishes base at Galveston to serve New Orleans market

Nov. **Mexico:** Mina expedition arrives in Galveston, joins Aury's fleet

Timeline

Dec. **U.S.:** New Venezuelan envoy, Lino de Clemente, arrives with arms buying mandate

1817

Feb. **Chile:** José San Martín's army crosses the Andes, defeats royalist army at Chacabuco

U.S.: Pro-patriot Gregor MacGregor arrives in Baltimore, aiming at raid into Florida

Mar. President James Monroe inaugurated

Neutrality Act passed, attempting to strengthen anti-privateer measures

June MacGregor filibuster seizes Amelia Island in Florida from Spanish

Group of Argentine patriots arrive to oppose current Argentine ruler, Pueyrredón

July New Argentine envoy, Manuel de Aguirre, arrives, seeking arms and recognition

President Monroe envisages sending fact-finding commission to South America

Aug. John Quincy Adams becomes secretary of state

Sept. Privateer Aury assumes command of Amelia filibuster under Mexican flag

Nov. **Mexico:** Mina expedition defeated

Dec. **U.S.:** U.S. Navy seizes Amelia from filibustering group, held "in trust for Spain"

Fact-finding commission departs for South America

1818

Jan. **U.S.:** Andrew Jackson leads punitive force into Florida, against Seminole Indians

Minister Onís receives authority to negotiate all outstanding issues with U.S.

Apr. Congress debates recognition of new South American governments

Neutrality Act of 1818 passes; codifies and strengthens neutrality measures

Chile: San Martín's victory at Maipú liberates Chile

May **U.S.:** Jackson seizes Spanish Pensacola; Cabinet supports his controversial action

New Argentine envoy, David DeForest, arrives

July	Mission headed by Baptis Irvine arrives in Venezuela to seek end to privateering
Sept.	Venezuelan envoy Aguirre departs with New York–built ships
Oct.	United States and Britain sign London Convention, fixing Canadian and Oregon borders
	Onís receives more flexible instructions for border negotiation with Adams
Nov.	Fact-finding commission returns from South America
Dec.	Government loses key anti-privateering court case in Baltimore

1819

Feb.	**U.S.:** Adams and Onís sign Transcontinental Treaty fixing U.S.–Spanish borders
Aug.	**New Granada:** Bolivar, having crossed the Andes, wins decisive battle at Boyacá

1820

Jan.	**Spain:** Mutiny in Cádiz; King Ferdinand obliged to accept liberal constitution in March
Mar.	**Argentina:** Juan de Pueyrredón deposed
Oct.	**Spain:** Government finally ratifies treaty with U.S., over king's veto
Dec.	**Colombia:** Venezuela and New Granada merge to form independent Gran Colombia

1821

Feb.	**Mexico:** Plan de Iguala brings together insurgents and royalists on path to independence
Mar.	**U.S.:** Treaty ratified; Congressional debate ends with mild resolution on recognition
June	**Venezuela:** Bolívar's defeats last major royalist force at Carabobo
Sept.	**Peru:** San Martín captures Lima
	Argentina: Government agrees to stop issuing privateer commissions

1822

Mar.	**U.S.:** President Monroe's message to Congress proposes recognition of new governments
May	Act of recognition passes Congress
July	Manuel Torres of Gran Colombia is first accredited South American diplomat

Introduction

The government of the United States, just over a decade old at the beginning of the nineteenth century, was as yet untested in the international arena. While Europe was racked by the titanic struggles of the Napoleonic era, the United States was at peace and booming; the coastal cities were prospering from trade with the warring Europeans, and a flood of ambitious settlers were opening up new lands in the Mississippi and Ohio river valleys. Clearly, a thriving America had no interest in getting involved in the great struggle going on among the European nations. Indeed, a brief undeclared naval war with France had shown how divisive it could be domestically to be seen as taking sides among the major powers. The policy of neutrality set out by President George Washington was a good, indeed essential, fit for the nation's prosperity and security.

And yet North America was inevitably a strategic arena in which the major powers might chose to expand their competition. The United States was bordered on the north and northwest by British Canada, and on the west and south by Spanish Louisiana and Florida, while Napoleon had ambitions to restore France as a North American power. It was Spain's precariously-held colonies, though, that were of greatest concern to the new Jefferson administration. They were only weakly defended by a corrupt and feckless monarchy, and it was entirely possible that either Britain or France might attempt to change the balance of power by seizing them. The thought of having either of those two powerful combatants become an immediate and ill-disposed neighbor was a frightening possibility, and yet one that the practically unarmed United States government had neither the power nor the gravitas to stave off—except through artful diplomacy. And that meant, in practical terms, that the price of avoiding any British or French intervention was to support Spain's continued but unpopular and unsatisfactory hold on its North American colonies.

But there was another complication. Many Americans, including Jefferson, coveted the same neighboring Spanish colonies for national expansion. This was not new. Once the flood of American settlers had breached the barrier of the Appalachian Mountains, the next political obstacle to expansion had become the borders with Spain. The neighboring Spanish colonies were tempting—weakly defended and largely unsettled except by Native Americans. Incidents such as the Blount Conspiracy of 1795 inevitably occurred, exposing the conflicting interests at play: American settlers and their political representatives who wanted to push the Spanish aside, while the federal government needed to maintain a neutrality that respected—at least as long as the European wars continued—Spain's interests.

Within a few years Spain had lost the huge territory of Louisiana, first to France and then to the United States, but that had only moved the tension along the U.S.-Spanish borders farther to the west, in addition to the always-troublesome border with Florida. The administration of another president from expansionist-minded Virginia, James Madison, claimed and even tried to acquire sections of Florida, as well as parts of Texas, but could not risk any overly aggressive moves while war raged in Europe. Indeed, when America's own war with Britain broke out in 1812, the policy of neutrality toward the other European powers continued to protect America's interests and needed to be maintained, even if not always scrupulously.

The growth of independence movements in Mexico and South America after 1810 only put a new twist on the policy, when Madison's government took the position that the struggle between Spain and its breakaway colonies was simply a civil war in which the United States would treat the belligerent parties equally. James Monroe, the next president, and also from Virginia, would continue that policy, coupled with a pressing desire to settle the borders with Spain on terms that would allow a continued expansion of American settlement and trade. The rights and wrongs of the struggle between Spain and its rebellious provinces were subordinated to Washington's primary aims, which were to stay out of the European struggle while protecting its expansionist ambitions.

The present study is an effort to describe some of the pressures put on America's policy of neutrality as a result of the arrival in the United States of refugees and activists from the rebellious Spanish colonies. The

Introduction

rebels, inspired in many cases by the ideals of the American revolution, tried from their very early days to establish lines of communication with the northern republic, and sent both official and unofficial agents to procure arms and, if possible, obtain official American support. Intent on furthering their fight for self-rule in their home provinces by any means, they put the U.S. policy of neutrality to a series of tests as they bought arms, commissioned American privateers to fight as their proxies, conducted filibustering expeditions from American territory, and gathered Congressional support and favorable public opinion. The rebel agents' activities were in turn followed closely by an active Spanish diplomatic mission that insisted that the United States follow a strict interpretation of its policy of neutrality, while Spanish spies and agents did all they could to counter the rebels' activities. The United States had, in effect, become another theater of the Spanish American independence struggle.

The U.S. administration, for its part, started the period with a poor understanding of Spanish American developments and aspirations. Moreover, it not surprisingly had significant apprehensions about dealing with the suddenly-arrived and often over-zealous representatives of little-known revolutionary councils, or juntas, whose intentions, capabilities, and potential for long-term stability were little understood. And while successive administrations had considerable sympathy for the rebels' anti-colonialist stance, they could not afford to aggravate imperial Spain, or Europe's other monarchical powers, in a manner that could endanger American security and territorial ambitions.

The book aims to describe the sort of dialogue, halting and full of misunderstandings and mistakes, in which the U.S. government and the rebels tried to find rules of acceptable revolutionary activity that would not overtly compromise Washington's need for neutrality. That dialogue was by no means static, consisting as it did of official exchanges, media campaigns, domestic politics, espionage, piracy, court cases, and armed filibusters. The study will deal with the wider aspects of the policy debate—the reactions of the major powers and particularly the diplomatic ramifications of the negotiations with Spain—only as they are necessary to clarify aspects of the contacts with the South American patriots.

A word as to the organization of the study may be appropriate. It begins with a look at the background to the issues involved. It then describes the first contacts with the agents sent to the United States by the revolutionary juntas, followed by an account of the first rebel efforts, during our 1812–15 war with Great Britain, to use the United States as a launching pad for filibustering raids into Spanish territory. Then, looking at the years immediately following the end of that war as well as the war in Europe, when a multiplicity of rebel-sponsored activities were spawned in and from the United States, the presentation becomes thematic. The next four chapters are focused on the rebel successes in enlisting American privateers to their cause, the resulting legal and policy controversies, and the various patriot-led armed incursions into both Mexico and Florida. The remaining chapters return to a chronological treatment, studying the policy issues, political debates and diplomatic steps that led to recognition of several patriotic regimes, and the opening of a new page of normal diplomatic relations with those new and proudly independent countries, bloodied but no longer parts of Spain's American empire.

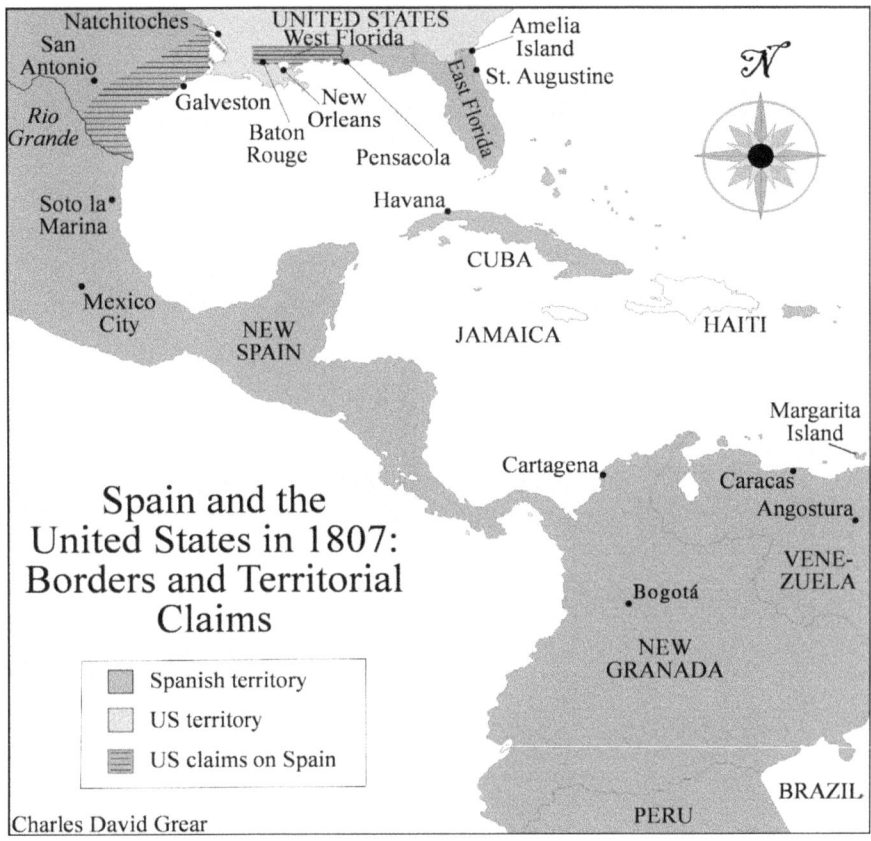

This map shows the Caribbean-area borders between Spain's American colonies and the United States in 1807, after the 1803 purchase of the still largely non-demarcated Louisiana Territory. The U.S. claims on Spanish territory were based on Washington's interpretations of the various prior agreements between France, Britain, and Spain concerning the possession and borders of Louisiana and Florida.

Chapter 1

Uneasy Neighbors

By all accounts, Tennessee senator William Blount was an astute politician. As territorial governor, he had led the territory's rapidly growing population to statehood in spite of opposition in Congress, and was recognized as the leading political figure in the region. And yet, he had now made a serious political blunder, putting aspirations for his western region above the interest of the nation. Fomenting an attack on Spanish Louisiana, after all, was scarcely controversial in his part of the country. And yet, back in Philadelphia, the administration and most of his colleagues in Congress were determined to make him pay for his error.

Blount's record of public service was not in question. The North Carolina native had served with the state militia during the Revolutionary War, afterwards in the state's legislature, and then the Continental Congress. As a delegate to the 1787 Constitutional Convention in Philadelphia, he had signed the constitution on behalf of his home state. Several years later, when North Carolina relinquished to the new federal union its claims to lands west of the Appalachian Mountains, President Washington appointed Blount as governor of the new Southwest Territory that was created from the ceded land, covering most of what soon became the state of Tennessee.

His move to Tennessee suited Blount's purposes very well, for he—like many others in those early days of the new republic—envisaged the western territories as vital to both his, and the nation's, future. He speculated heavily in Tennessee land, of which he came to own more than a million acres. As governor, he worked assiduously to make those investments pay off, establishing the capital at the new town of Knoxville, encouraging a steady flow of settlers into the new lands, and obliging the Cherokees to sign a treaty in which they ceded still more land to the newcomers. His master coup in politics, however, came in 1796, when he forced the hand of a reluctant Congress to raise the territory to statehood. Having realized that the Federalist controlled national legislature was opposed to giving the vote to the territory's Democratic-Republican leaning citizens, Blount hastily organized a territorial convention that drafted a state constitution, elected its representatives (including him as senator), and applied to Congress under the terms of the Northwest Ordinance. Congress, finding no way out of the position Blount had put them in, was obliged to admit Tennessee as the sixteenth state in the union. Blount consequently was a hero in Tennessee, if not in Philadelphia.

In spite of this political success, Blount was not doing well. Cash was short, his credit was overextended, and the vast tracts of land that he had bought on that credit were not appreciating fast enough to hold together his speculative house of cards. Part of the problem, in his view, was the fact that Tennessee shared a Mississippi River border with the Spanish-owned but unstable Louisiana territory. That vast, loosely defined and thinly populated area had been in Spanish hands since 1763, surrendered by France as a cost of having lost the French and Indian War. As far as Spain was concerned, the territory was a useful strategic buffer between its silver-rich colony of Mexico and the ambitious and expansionist Americans. But it was a weak buffer. Indifferently, indeed poorly, administered by Spanish governors in distant Havana, it attracted few Spanish settlers and was a drain on the Spanish treasury. Moreover, its defenseless condition made it a potential prize in the European struggle that had broken out following the French Revolution. A potentially rich and strategically important prize in that struggle for global supremacy, Spanish Louisiana was ripe to be seized, either by the British or the French.

In the circumstances, Blount preferred the British as potential neighbors. His preference however was linked to his pocketbook more than his patriotism, as he thought that British rule would help protect his investments far better than that of the revolutionary French or even the feckless Spanish rulers. But his preference became his downfall, at least as far as national politics was concerned. Sometime during 1797, Blount became involved in a murky scheme that would have involved him in recruiting frontiersmen, plus Cherokee and Creek Indians, to support a British seizure of Louisiana and Western Florida from the Spaniards. Though the plot fell apart when the British backed off, Blount's role in it was exposed when an incriminating letter of his was intercepted and handed over to the government.

1. Uneasy Neighbors

Had the plot been put into effect, it would have resulted in a breach of America's neutrality policy and a violation of its 1795 treaty with Spain, thus possibly dragging the United States into the European war. At a time fraught with concern for the nation's security, disclosure of the plot gave the Adams administration reason to make an object lesson of the senator's indiscretion. Blount was charged with conduct "inconsistent with his public trust and duty as a senator," impeached by the House of Representatives, and rapidly thereafter expelled from the Senate. Although the impeachment motion itself was later dismissed by the Senate, Blount's career in national politics was at an end.

But the decision in Philadelphia had by no means hurt Blount's political standing in Tennessee and the west. Whether or not he had been involved in a serious plot, neither his motivation for plotting against Spain's vulnerable colonies, nor his actions, were much questioned by his fellow westerners. Spain's rule over Louisiana and Florida had few friends west of the mountains, and Blount continued to serve with honor in the Tennessee legislature until his death in 1800.

Westerners, quite simply, saw the world differently from their eastern brethren. Separated from the original colonies by the mountains, and thus largely dependent on the Mississippi river system for transportation and sale of their produce, and on themselves for their security, many western settlers had come to consider that their fate was in their own hands rather than that of the distant federal government. Separatism was in the air, encouraged by the British from Canada and the French and Spanish from Louisiana or Florida, all of whom wished—regardless of their own bitter rivalry—to limit the power of the new American republic in the region west of the Appalachians. Embittered frontiersmen and Indians were easy recruits for separatist or anti-settler agitations.

But beyond the unacknowledged common goal of holding back American expansion, the European powers saw western North America as just another theater in which to fight their own struggle for supremacy. Ambitious Americans, too, could take advantage of the ambiguous situation for their own purposes. It was a climate which provided opportunity for adventurous men, and where the political and diplomatic niceties that might be honored in Philadelphia and the eastern coast could be set aside by restless settlers or disaffected politicians ready to take a chance for personal gain.

Blount's conspiracy had by no means been the first. The most egregious attempt had occurred some four years earlier, when that hyperactive diplomatic representative of revolutionary France, Edmond Charles Genêt, compounded his other differences with the administration of President Washington by attempting to raise an army of Kentuckians, under the leadership of the broke and disaffected General George Rogers Clark, to capture New Orleans and other points from the Spaniards. The resulting scandal brought about not only Genêt's dismissal and Clark's bankruptcy, but major legislation designed to avoid such imbroglios in the future. Anxious to stay out of the European struggle, President Washington asked Congress to pass the 1794 Neutrality Act, which among other things barred both American citizens and aliens from taking part in any expedition directed against the territory of a nation at peace with the United States. On the face of it, that should have relieved the domestic threat against Spanish possessions in North America. But it should be noted that Blount was expelled for misuse of his public office, not for violation of the neutrality law. As he had not yet recruited a force or actually participated in a raid on a friendly country, he was not culpable under the law. That was an important loophole, and there were others. In effect, then, the 1794 legislation stopped neither the Burr conspiracy of 1805, nor the various real and imagined filibustering attempts of the coming decades, some of which will be discussed in these pages.

The basic fact was that the Spanish territories were an attractive target, while the Americans who lived in the area known as the western waters held enough grievances against the Spaniards, real and concocted, to justify resentment, hostility and even aggression. When the settlers had flowed over the mountains following the revolution, they found rich lands to farm, but also that the access to market of their goods was, or could be, blocked by the Spaniards. All the rivers—which were the vital means of transport in the region—flowed west or south, and across their mouths onto the sea lay the territory and trade barriers of the unloved Spaniards. Spain periodically threatened to close the Mississippi and actually did so once, in 1784, while the Spanish customs barriers at Natchez also posed a troublesome potential hindrance to American exports. The settlers were determined that their goods should have free access to the sea, and if that could not be guaranteed by diplomatic means then they had no problem with schemes to dislodge Spain from Louisiana, the Florida panhandle, or both. (The panhandle then extended westward up to the Mississippi River; its western section, or West Florida, ran between the Mississippi and the Apalachicola rivers and was governed from Pensacola, while the eastern end was joined with the main peninsula to form the separate province of East Florida, governed from St. Augustine.)

1. Uneasy Neighbors

The boundary between the two Spanish Floridas and what would become the Mississippi Territory had been set at the 31st parallel by the 1795 Pinckney Treaty with Spain, which also provided a limited right for Americans to export their goods freely through New Orleans. But Spanish colonial authorities were unpredictable and, as far as the American settlers were concerned, not trustworthy. Moreover, the entire border was porous, the Spanish side only lightly garrisoned and, in the Floridas, a haven for hostile Indians, runaway slaves, and British and Spanish agents or adventurers who had agendas that generally clashed with American settler interests. Border disputes and incidents were frequent, and any resolution required the cooperation of Spanish colonial administrators who were generally seen as disinterested, arbitrary, or corrupt.

There was, in America of the time, a general disdain for the Spaniards. Most Americans were Protestants (the western settlers disproportionately so) who had absorbed some, at least, of the anti-Spanish propaganda which had been circulating in England and elsewhere since the colonial and religious wars of the sixteenth century. In the popular imagination, Spaniards generally came to be characterized as cruel, tyrannical, superstitious, intolerant, or corrupt—or even all of those. Few Americans had first-hand contact with Spaniards, and those who did—East coast merchants or settlers living near the border—rarely found the experience positive. A few important merchants in Philadelphia, Baltimore, and New York (many of them Catholic) prospered through having gained inside positions in the Spanish mercantile system of trade monopolies. But those outside the system found the Spaniards infuriating trade partners, while the western settlers generally found the colonial administrators to be haughty, unresponsive, arbitrary or corrupt in settling border and trade problems. The Spanish officials, for their part, saw in the American settlers' freedom of action and thirst for land a serious threat to the security, indeed the very existence, of their provinces, and one can understand their unwelcoming response to the settlers. The two parties were not good neighbors.

And yet, as seen from the viewpoint of the national government, the Spaniards were preferred as neighbors. The Spanish state under the decadent and corrupt rule of Charles IV was weak, unable to project power or even to maintain it convincingly in such marginal provinces as Florida and Louisiana. Spanish rule in those provinces, in short, presented no strategic challenge to the United States. Rather, it was fear that the provinces might fall into the hands of one of the more ambitious powers, specifically France or Great Britain, that concerned presidents Washington,

Adams and Jefferson. Blount's real error, in their view, was that he had envisaged replacing a weak and malleable neighbor with a strong and troublesome power.

As much as a decade earlier, Jefferson counseled one of his friends who had voiced the separatist and anti-Spanish feelings typical of Kentucky that "we should take care ... not to press too soon on the Spaniards. These countries [the Spanish provinces in North America] cannot be in better hands. My fear is that they are too feeble to hold them till our population can be sufficiently advanced to gain it from them piece by piece."[1] That sentiment expresses the kernel of a long-standing but undeclared American policy toward the Spanish in North America: that their very weakness played to America's growing strength, and that over time American pressure—demographic, economic, diplomatic, and military—would lead to absorption of most of Spain's North American holdings.

It follows that there was consternation in Washington in 1802, when it was learned that France had bullied and bribed the Spaniards into surrendering their rights to Louisiana. Revolutionary and expansionist France simply could not be a comfortable neighbor, the more so as it was clear that Napoleon aspired to re-establish the French empire in the Americas. In his vision, Haiti and the other sugar islands would finance his wars, and Louisiana would provide the goods to sustain their operations. French occupation of Louisiana would, at the same time, frustrate Great Britain or America's hopes to be the dominant regional power. President Jefferson, normally a friend of France, was quick to realize that Napoleon would be a very dangerous neighbor, but his only available response was to engage in crisis diplomacy. The history of the negotiations undertaken to forestall or mitigate the French takeover have been covered in many other books, and it is enough to note here that the Louisiana Purchase eventually took place in early 1803, thanks to a number of factors including luck, the tenacious resistance of the Haitian revolutionaries who upset Napoleon's game plan, and Napoleon's own frustrated decision making. In making his snap decision to sell the territory to the Americans, it should be noted, Napoleon had sold out the Spanish: he had promised them not to transfer to any other power the territory they had just ceded. And then he had done just that.

In buying Louisiana from the French, America had suddenly become a continental power, no longer hemmed in by a Mississippi River border or sharing a long western border with a potentially hostile European neighbor. The Mississippi border with the Spanish colonies had been moved far to the west and also southward, toward the Mexican Internal Provinces and their borderland of Texas. The possibilities for American expansion westward had suddenly increased dramatically. The Spanish of course were alarmed: added to their anger over Napoleon's abandonment of their interests was a deep concern over American intentions. They had lost their buffer zone; the Americans were now much closer to their key continental possessions, and the border much less defensible. Jefferson's next action only increased their concern. In keeping with his policy of putting pressure on the weaker neighbor, the American government rapidly put forward claims that the purchase agreement with the French, though vaguely worded, properly included both Spanish West Florida as far as the Perdido River, and Texas up to the Rio Grande. As Jefferson confided to a friendly senator, "These claims will be a subject of negotiation with Spain, and if, as soon as she is at war, we push them strongly with one hand, holding out a price in the other, we shall certainly obtain the Floridas, and all in good time."[2]

America's possession of Louisiana and the important port of New Orleans had suddenly made it a Caribbean power. America now had strategic responsibilities and vulnerabilities in an area with which it was not very familiar. Outside of the few Philadelphia and other merchant houses that had benefitted from access to Spanish trading licenses to sell grain to Cuba and Mexico, few Americans were at all familiar with the Spanish possessions that bordered the sea. South America was even less well known. A few learned Americans corresponded with South American scholars through the American Philosophical Society, historical societies and library companies, and those exchanges fed a slowly growing understanding of South America's culture, environment, and history. But the general public was satisfied with its hazy preconceptions, and even on the eastern coast, where merchants scoured the world for markets in which to place America's growing food surpluses, South America was little known.

American merchants had largely been frozen out of Spanish colonial markets, in spite of chronic food shortfalls there, by Madrid's monopolistic trade restrictions. Or at least until the outbreak of war in the 1790s, when Spain's naval weakness made it impossible for her merchants to supply the overseas provinces. Neutral carriers like the Americans were then allowed periodic access, but the trade was all the same tightly controlled by a system of permits rationed out by the Spanish consuls in Philadelphia. The rules for access were both complex and frequently changing, varying with the fortunes of war among the major powers and the whims of the officials. For merchant houses not previously part of the circle of favored Spanish clients, entering the trade faced them with the risks of instability, corruption, and arbitrary rules.

And yet, American traders were used to risks. Responding to the opportunity and to the fact that British naval superiority had driven off most privateers, American traders began to venture to South America, particularly to the markets in Caracas and Buenos Aires. They carried not only American exports—flour, wheat and tools were the most important—but also goods transshipped from West Indian ports, with the result that by the end of the century the trade had more than doubled from what was admittedly a modest beginning level. The growth in trade, and its accompanying problems, prompted the Adams administration in 1800 to appoint the first U.S. consul to South America—Augustine Madan, who was appointed to La Guaira, the port of Caracas.

With the exception of a period around 1802 when the European powers were in a truce and the Spanish monopolies at least partially restored, American trade with the Spanish colonies in the Caribbean and South American continued to grow until 1807, when the Jefferson administration installed a general trade embargo. Along with the increase in trade came an increase in awareness, at least in the merchant cities of the East coast, of the general political and economic situation in those provinces.

Even so, there was little awareness in the United States of the internal political situation in Spanish America or the potential in some provinces for revolutionary activity. Anti-colonial incidents that had taken place in distant Peru under Tupac Amaru and in Colombia under the Comuneros in 1781 had scarcely registered in America. But then, in 1783, a young and charismatic Spanish army officer from Caracas, Francisco Miranda, visited with a message that conditions in South America were indeed turning in the direction of revolt against rule from Madrid. Well referred by the Spanish governor general of Cuba, Miranda was introduced around Philadelphia by the Spanish consular agent, Francisco Rendón, until the latter learned to his embarrassment that Miranda was in fact a dissident as well as a fugitive from disciplinary charges in Cuba. Nonetheless, armed as he was with a commanding personality, an interesting story, and a profound interest in the achievements of the American Revolution, Miranda was widely received in both political and intellectual circles, and made a lasting impression for his intelligence, energy and passion. More importantly, he made some important connections with persons attentive to his story, with many of whom he remained in contact as his ideas and plans evolved.

1. Uneasy Neighbors

Among these were Alexander Hamilton, Thomas Paine, Henry Knox, Rufus King, and William S. Smith. He would engage many of them again. In early 1785, Miranda left the United States for England, entertaining hopes that he might be able to return to Spain, where—in spite of his ever more vocal arguments in favor of rebellion—he sought to obtain relief from the charges of his accusers.

Miranda was a precursor, entirely premature in his hope that revolution in his country was imminent. Discontent with rule from distant, corrupt, and grasping Madrid was indeed growing in the Spanish American provinces, but was still limited. The local merchants and creole gentry were dissatisfied over their treatment by the royal court, but not yet rebellious, and the liberal ideas of the Enlightenment had not yet penetrated much beyond the reading groups of the elite. The monarchy was still unchallenged, and any open expression of disaffection was still largely underground, or like Miranda, abroad and beyond the reach of Spanish punishment.

An interesting example of the reach of Spanish authority can be seen in the work of Santiago Filipe Puglia, a Spanish critic of his government who had fled to Philadelphia in 1790. Earning his living as a language teacher, he was the first of his countrymen to take advantage of Philadelphia's situation as a center of the publishing business, in an attempt to distribute anti-regime propaganda. His major work, *Desengano del Hombre (Man Undeceived)*, a Rousseau-inspired attack on the Spanish monarchy, was published in 1794 only because of a grant from that inveterate rabble-rouser, the Frenchman Edmond Genêt. But most copies of the screed were lost, and the rest were banned by the ever-alert Inquisition, so that the book had no practical effect. Like Miranda, Puglia was ahead of the time.

In Spanish America and even Spain, discontent with Madrid's rule gradually grew. American-born creoles were aggrieved economically by the taxes and monopolies imposed by the decadent royal court, and also highly resentful over the second class status to which they were relegated by the imperious peninsular Spaniards. Inevitably, the various threads of dissent began to crystallize into political action, and a number of liberally inspired conspiracies were unearthed by the authorities. Among them were the anti-monarchical San Blas Conspiracy of 1795 in Spain, involving Juan Bautista Mariano Picornell, and the subsequent anti-colonial Guaira conspiracy, which involved Picornell, Manuel Gual, and José Maria Espana. Those names will show up again.

For twenty years following his departure from America, Francisco Miranda sought support for his goals in Europe. Arrived in London, he tried to interest the British—who were at the time at war with France's ally Spain—into intervening in South American affairs. He gained a sympathetic hearing from senior British officials, but his idea of enlisting their support for a group of unknown foreign revolutionaries never rose to the top of the government's priority list, and his schemes remained in limbo. So too did his relations with the Spanish, who kept him on a string concerning his possible appeal. All the while, they spied on his every move, describing him as having "exalted imagination, accomplishments more than moderate, fervor and impetuosity in his bearing, and above all an extraordinary activity."[3]

Demonstrating his preference for activity, Miranda traveled to a number of European capitals while awaiting answers to his requests. He was accompanied part of the way by William Smith, who was serving at the time as secretary to his father-in-law John Adams at the American mission in London, but had decided for his own purposes to support Miranda's efforts. On his return to London in 1789, Miranda learned that he would have to face justice, if at all, in Spain—where he feared the court would not give him a favorable hearing. Still without a positive answer to his appeals to the British, he thus found himself without prospects in London. As a result, he left for France in 1792 and joined the enemy. There, he was welcomed at first, given the rank of general, and command of French troops on the Netherlands front. His military career however was not a success; he was accused of incompetence and treason, and landed in prison and then house arrest for a time. Five years later, he was able to negotiate his return to England where the authorities, once again at war with Spain, were prepared to listen to his latest schemes for a joint military-revolutionary expedition to liberate Spain's colonies in South America.

Miranda, who had continued to cultivate his contacts in the United States, increased that correspondence in 1798 as his prospects for British support were beginning to look somewhat more promising. He kept Rufus King, the current American minister in London who was both a sincere proponent of South American liberation and anxious to harm France and its ally Spain, informed of his talks with Prime Minister William Pitt. With King backing him in his own reports to Philadelphia, Miranda hoped to secure some sort of American endorsement that might help convince the British to actually implement his schemes. Miranda wrote to President Adams, Hamilton, and General Knox, as well as to William Smith and

1. Uneasy Neighbors

other more regular correspondents, but only Hamilton[4] among the Americans chose to answer him directly—even though they took notice of the schemes and admitted, in their private correspondence, some possible advantages from them. In the end, the American government chose to ignore his appeals, the British backed down, and a truce was negotiated among the warring powers. With Spain and Britain at peace, at least temporarily, Miranda was left in the unpleasant role of a British pensioner who was kept around London because he might someday be useful, yet not trusted enough to be given his passport and freedom to travel.

For a man with energy and ambition to spare, Miranda's situation must have been frustrating. Yet he had other irons in the fire. His home had become a center for Spanish expatriates and would-be rebels, and he was also helping build an international clandestine network. In 1797, he and his friends had founded a quasi-Masonic lodge in London, the Gran Reunion Americana. Both it and a sister organization in Spain, the Sociedad de Caballeros Racionales, had informal links with the masonic movement and adopted masonic schemes of organization. This allowed members to take advantage of masonry's international brotherhood and its liberal political outlook, as well as its traditions of discipline and secrecy, while at the same time allowing good Catholics to join in spite of the Church's prohibitions. Over the coming years, "Mirandista" lodges of this nature, whether known as Lautaro Lodges as in Argentina and Chile, or Sociedad Patriótica as in Venezuela, became key elements of dissident organization in South America, and evolved into a loose revolutionary network linking London, Spain, a number of key South American cities, and even Philadelphia.

When war broke out again in 1804, with Spain once again allied to a dominating France, Miranda saw a chance to encourage the British to brush off old plans and look at new ones. But, even though Pitt was once again prime minister, Miranda soon realized that he would never get the degree of support he needed in London. He began to envisage independent action, based from America, and sought financing and support both in London and through his remaining friends in America, among whom he still had a small number of hopefully influential supporters—Rufus King (who had returned from London), and Colonel William Smith. Having finally received his passport from the British, he sailed for New York, arriving in November 1805.

Determined that the time for action was right, Miranda must have been pleased to note that the mood in America was more than peevish toward the Spaniards. Spain's action of closing off trade access to New Orleans in 1802, even though temporary, had inflamed public opinion, and when added to the damages caused to American commerce by Spanish privateers, gave the Jefferson government arguable reason to demand reparations from Spain. Which they did, repeatedly. The Americans had even ratcheted up the dispute, pushing their claim that the boundaries of the Louisiana Purchase rightly included not only much of Spanish Western Florida, but coastal Texas as well, down to the Rio Grande. The Spanish, already angered at Napoleon's perfidy in reselling their old possession, naturally bridled at these American pretensions to still more territory. Their minister in the U.S., Carlos Maria Martínez de Irujo, had become so incensed at the American demands, and vented his indignation so repeatedly and publicly, as to have severely prejudiced his relations with the administration. All in all, the climate was favorable for anti-Spanish action; there was even talk of war. Miranda was not the only schemer seeking to seize the moment. Aaron Burr's inchoate conspiracy, suspected to be a raid into Spanish Texas, was also in the air, and speculation was rife about the official position of the administration toward the various plots that were more or less openly bruited about.

His way paved by introductions from Rufus King and the administration's keen interest in his views on British policy, Miranda soon traveled to Washington. A short stop in Philadelphia brought him into contact with Aaron Burr, but the two did not hit it off, possibly seeing each other as rivals. Miranda did however renew some acquaintances from his earlier visit and pick up some other letters of introduction, all of which further smoothed his reception in the nation's capital.

In Washington, he was received cordially by both Jefferson and Madison, and in long conversations with the latter laid out his aspirations, if not his actual plans—which were still unformed. In a much later justification of his actions and non-actions, Madison wrote that Miranda had informed him of his hopes to bring revolution to South America, but that he had given no reason to suspect that he would organize a military force in the United States. Moreover, Madison claimed, he had told Miranda that the United States and Spain were at peace, and that if the two countries did go to war, it "would take place not in an underhanded and illicit way, but in a way consistent with the rules of war."[5] America's neutrality law, he reminded Miranda, prohibited citizens from engaging in any hostile actions against nations at peace with the United States.

Miranda had a different recollection of the conversations, or at least he chose to tell his potential supporters his version of the truth. He claimed that his friendly reception, plus the tenor of the responses he had received in Washington, amounted to a sort of wink at his proposition, as long as his actions were kept masked and discreet. Given the nature of the political climate at the time, and Miranda's native enthusiasm and charisma, it was not long before his contacts in New York and elsewhere believed that he indeed did have some sort of go-ahead from Washington.

Back again in New York, and through the good offices of William Smith, Miranda was introduced to a number of enterprising businessmen who might give him the wherewithal to launch his project. The key one was Samuel Ogden, a Pearl Street merchant who had a substantial business which included four armed merchant ships, one of which, the *Leander*, he was ready to make available to the expedition. His motives were, it seems, a combination of enthusiasm for Miranda's objective, and the prospect of a good profit if the venture succeeded. The ship would carry the adventurers, but also a cargo—most of it bought on credit—that Ogden hoped to sell dearly in Venezuela.

Confidence in the project, and that there was some sort of official acquiescence in it, pervaded the city. The involvement of Smith, son-in-law of ex-president Adams and official surveyor of the port of New York, as well as that of U.S. Naval Agent John Swartwout, gave it still another layer of apparent legitimacy. Smith had even agreed to have his son, another William, accompany Miranda as his aide. Many other individuals were informed or brought into the affair, including ex-senator Jonathan Dayton, who it turns out was also an informant for Spanish minister Irujo. The latter, probably reflecting his own distrust of the Jefferson administration as well as the reports he was getting from Dayton and the Spanish consulate in New York, reported to Madrid that he was convinced the expedition had official sanction. He also alerted the Spanish officials in Venezuela of Miranda's expected raid. Miranda, with Smith's help and his own money plus what he had raised in London and New York, set about obtaining the necessary arms and recruits to flesh out the military force with which he proposed to free his country from Spanish rule. In the end, it was a motley group of American adventurers, foreign soldiers of fortune, and overoptimistic idealists, numbering about 200, who boarded the *Leander* in early February along with their arms—but only after it had very properly cleared the port as an innocent merchant ship headed for Haiti. Just before leaving but too late to be stopped, Miranda wrote to Madison, announcing his departure and stating that he believed he had acted "conforming in everything with the intentions of the government"—to which Madison subsequently added a marginal notation "not true."[6]

The expedition was a disaster; the time was not yet ripe. After stopping in Haiti and Jamaica to obtain reinforcements, the party set sail for Venezuela, but was driven off by Spanish warships which had been on the lookout for them. Two small supply ships were captured; sixty crewmembers were imprisoned and ten of them executed. The diminished group then retired to Barbados, where Miranda's leadership was questioned and disputes broke out. Eventually, the expedition regrouped and sailed to Trinidad, where Miranda gained enough support from freewheeling British Navy commanders to proceed once again. In early August, they finally launched their invasion, and succeeded in seizing the small Venezuelan port city of Coro. But after a short two weeks they were driven off by the army and the loyalist population. The expedition dissolved; Miranda withdrew to the British islands, where he stayed until his return to England in 1807. The *Leander* was eventually confiscated and sold in Trinidad to pay off the remaining soldiers and crew; however many of them never were paid, and Ogden and his creditors lost their investments.

On his return to London, and in spite of the fiasco, Miranda oddly enough had gained increased credibility in British government circles, as a man who had taken on the Spanish empire.

For the American government, however, the expedition proved to be a serious embarrassment. Spanish minster Irujo's complaints over what he considered the U.S. government's lack of reaction to Miranda's open preparations for war against his country soon became so strident that he was told that his presence in Washington had become "dissatisfactory." He was virtually declared persona non grata; Madison would no longer meet with him. Nonetheless, he stayed in Philadelphia with his American wife until 1808, and kept up his pressure on the administration through the press, the good offices of his colleague the French minister, and acid dispatches to his government in Madrid. In the face of Irujo's public charges, which were taken up with glee by the Federalists in opposition, Jefferson and Madison protested their and the government's innocence. They had indeed been aware of Miranda's general plans, they argued, but in no way had they officially sanctioned or sponsored them. Jefferson went so far as to pledge his honor to the Spanish consul general, Valentin Foronda (who was a personal friend) that, although Irujo may have

> wished it to be believed that we were in unjustifiable cooperation in Miranda's expedition[,] I solemnly, and on my personal truth and honor, declare to you,

that this was entirely without foundation, and that there was neither cooperation, nor connivance on our part. He informed us he was about to attempt the liberation of his native country from bondage, and intimated a hope of our aid, or connivance at least.... We had no suspicion that he expected to engage men here, but merely to purchase military stores. Against this there was no law, nor consequently any authority for us to interpose obstacles. On the other hand, we deemed it improper to betray his voluntary communication to the agents of Spain. Although his measures were many days in preparation at New York, we never had the least intimation or suspicion of his engaging men in his enterprise, until he was gone.[7]

Jefferson tried to make amends by showing his displeasure at what had happened in New York. He dismissed Smith from his position as port surveyor, and had him and Ogden brought before the district court on charges of violating the neutrality act. Those trials took place in July 1806, even as Miranda was preparing to invade Venezuela. Smith claimed that he had acted in accordance with government wishes and was being used as a scapegoat; the prosecution charged that such a defense was immaterial; he had still broken the law. The juries sided with the defense, and Smith was acquitted, Ogden a few weeks later. Jefferson, in his letter to Foronda, blamed the acquittals on "the protection given them by private citizens at New York, in opposition to the government, who, by their impudent falsehoods and calumnies, were able to overbear the minds of the jurors." Sour grapes.

No amount of explanation or rationalization could solve the underlying problem; the damage had been done. The Spanish were already highly suspicious of American intentions toward their vulnerable colonial possessions; the Blount affair had been only one demonstration of American hostility, and exposure of the yet more dramatic conspiracy of Aaron Burr in 1806 would raise their distrust still more. The Miranda affair had exposed the difficulty of enforcing America's neutrality law, and the administration's willingness to even try to do so had been put into question. The Spanish had reason to ask if they could trust either the American administration's word, or its protestations of neutrality.

The two sides had developed mirrored, distrustful, images of each other.

Chapter 2

Contested Loyalties

It was Napoleon's ambition that opened the door for an independent Spanish America. In 1807, the French emperor was the master of most of Europe, having crushed Prussia and Austria at the battle of Austerlitz, cowed the Russian czar, and reduced the Spanish monarchy to a fawning ally. Determined by his recent successes to bring his major remaining foe to heel, Napoleon then declared a complete stoppage of trade from continental Europe to Great Britain. He would starve Britain into yielding. But, to his anger, the trade blockade was not fully effective, in part due to the fact that Britain's long-time ally Portugal had kept its ports open. As far as the Emperor was concerned, that was cause for war. He bullied the Spanish court into allowing free passage for a French army, which then proceeded to occupy substantial areas of Spain before launching a successful attack on Lisbon at the end of the year.

Portugal's royal Braganza family, led by Prince Regent João VI, managed to escape just in time, avoiding capture and disgrace. With the help of the British Navy, and accompanied by a thousand members of his court, the prince sailed off to the rich and loyal colony of Brazil. In Rio de Janeiro, the court was reestablished, and royal rule over the trans–Atlantic empire resumed.

Spain's royal family was not so lucky. Beset by the country's military humiliation, economic collapse, and popular anger, the royal court had no coherent answer. King Charles IV and his son Ferdinand struggled with each other for control over policy, a family feud that was ended only when a popular uprising in March 1808 obliged Charles to abdicate in favor of his son. Unfortunately, this played directly into the hands of Napoleon, who saw a chance to get rid of these troublesome and vacillating allies. Sending still another French army into Spain, ostensibly to restore order, the emperor invited the king and his son to France—for their own protection, of course. The still mutually alienated Charles and Ferdinand, unable to ignore the emperor's summons, travelled separately to Bayonne. There, they were obliged in early May to accept the further humiliation of renouncing their claims to the throne, in favor of Napoleon's brother Joseph Bonaparte. When the royal father and son were also placed under house arrest, Bourbon royal rule was, at least on paper, finally over.

The Spanish people however were made of tougher stuff. Although the royal court meekly acknowledged Joseph Bonaparte as their new king, and some liberal thinkers at first welcomed the new French-directed regime in Madrid, uprisings against the occupation broke out throughout the country. Loyalist provincial juntas were established in many areas, and sporadic fighting soon proved that the Spanish and their provincial armies could effectively contest French rule, well enough indeed to push the French armies back into the north of the country. The Bayonne abdications were declared void by the Council of Castile, and the imprisoned and absent Ferdinand proclaimed king once again, in August. The Peninsular War, a long and bloody struggle for control of Iberia in which the British and Portuguese would join the Spanish in driving out the French, had begun.

It was a rough beginning. The loyalists were soon on the defensive, struggling to organize their decentralized and often feuding juntas, even as Napoleon himself led still another huge army into the country to crush them. A Supreme Junta was established late in 1808 to serve as a surrogate for the absent royal government and to coordinate the activities of the various provincial juntas and armies, or at least as much as possible in view of the fractured condition of the country. It also called for the convocation of a general parliament (Cortes) for the entire nation. This Cádiz Cortes was to include representation from the colonies, and was expected to draft a new constitution. But, even as the Spanish loyalists tried to get their house in order, their control over the country was slowly being reduced by the inexorable pressure of the French armies. From the redoubt in the north into which they had retreated after their initial defeats, the French pushed relentlessly south, recapturing Madrid at the end of the year and pushing the Spanish forces further south and west throughout 1809 and much of 1810. By the time the Cortes was convoked in September of 1810, the royalist government—now in the form of a Regency Council for the absent Ferdinand—had retreated to Cádiz, its last foothold on Spanish soil.

Such momentous events in the homeland were of course avidly followed and debated in the vast Spanish colonies in the Americas. King Joseph's court had its adherents among royal officials from Spain, as well as some support from those liberal and reformist thinkers who were attracted by the ideals of the French revolution, which they hoped to see applied in Spain and the colonies. But that support was both limited and non-cohesive, while the general population in Spanish America both resented and feared the Napoleonic takeover. Nor was the new regency council an obvious option for the loyalty of the colonists, tainted as it was by the failings of the old court and its own tenuous grip on power in besieged Cádiz.

In this situation of contested loyalties, the leading merchants and civic leaders, many of them native-born creoles, began to find their political voice. In a number of provinces the *cabildos*, or town councils, began to assert a claim to greater self-rule in order to meet the pressing challenges. Two premature juntas actually tried to assume local power in Peru, but were quickly put down by royalist authorities. And most provinces did chose to send representatives to the national Cortes in Cádiz, seeking to have their voice heard in a new, and it was hoped, more liberal and inclusionary regime for the Spanish empire.

In a situation where everybody was in control, nobody was really in control, and when so much depended on the outcomes of an experimental Cortes and the Peninsular War, the pressures for increased autonomy that had been suppressed for years in the American provinces began to grow. In 1810, the first open revolt broke out in Dolores, Mexico under Father Miguel Hidalgo y Costilla, but after initial successes it was crushed within a year, and Hidalgo executed. In South America, events moved at first in a more peaceful manner. Following the example of the provincial juntas that had been set up in Spain, and sometimes in opposition to the rump viceroys or other officials of the royalist court, sometimes in cooperation with them, cabildos set up ruling juntas in several South American provincial capitals. During 1810, juntas were set up in New Granada (a larger version of present day Colombia and Ecuador), Venezuela, Rio de la Plata (Argentina), and Chile. Those juntas claimed to exercise local power in the name of the still imprisoned Ferdinand, and stated their intent to defend the provinces against French subversion. In Rio de la Plata, in fact, a local cabildo had already organized a successful defense against British attempts to occupy the province in 1806 and 1807, providing the local leaders with a heady sense of having earned a leading voice in their own future. Change was not just in the air, it was inevitable, but what direction it might take was entirely unclear.

2. Contested Loyalties

Shortly after its April 1810 coup, the junta in Caracas, Venezuela, was in trouble. Although it professed its loyalty to Ferdinand, it had deposed and expelled the royal captain general and declared that the besieged regency in Cádiz could no longer govern the colony effectively. That act posed a direct challenge to the regency council's putative authority, and made it likely that the junta (and other separatist provincial juntas) would have to fight a civil war against the royalist forces in country. Faced with that probability, the French menace, and fear of civil unrest or slave rebellion in the plantation belt that surrounded Caracas, the junta, headed by well to do creoles, needed to take control before the region fell into disorder. To do so it needed arms, and, if possible, allies from outside.

The junta decided to send two missions to capitals where it hoped to find a friendly reception. A wealthy young liberal, Simón Bolívar, along with Andrés Bello and Luis Lopez Mendez, were sent to Great Britain, while Bolívar's brother Juan Vicente, along with the Caracas merchant Telésforo de Orea, went to the United States. Their tasks would be difficult. While Britain was opposed to the extension of French revolutionary influence into South America and therefore a potential supporter of the junta, it was at the same time allied to the regency government in Cádiz, which it could not alienate by openly supporting the separatists. As for the United States, the Venezuelan delegation held hopes that America's anti-colonial history and liberal ideals would lead to ready support for a fellow breakaway colony. That hope would be tested.

Neither American public opinion nor the administration had given much thought to the questions that would be posed by this suddenly arrived delegation. Newspapers had speculated on the prospects opened up for American trade by Spain's loosened grip on its colonies, and trade with Spanish America had indeed picked up somewhat following the expiry of Jefferson's hated trade embargo in 1809. But the trade as yet had no impact on policy, even though there was growing awareness of its potential, or at least of a need to contest a growing British dominance in the South American market. Much more significant in its impact was the large and lucrative trade which was being conducted with the Iberian Peninsula, where American grain was feeding the British, Spanish and Portuguese armies fighting the French.

The new administration of James Madison, too, was focused largely on the situation in Europe. Angry over British arrogance in its challenges to America's neutrality, the administration continued Jefferson's policy of leaning cautiously toward the French—the caution augmented by concern over Napoleon's autocratic ways, plus fear about the export of radical Jacobin ideas into the slaveholding states. As far as Spanish American affairs were concerned, the administration remained fixated on obtaining possession of West Florida from Spain, or at least keeping it from falling into the hands of Britain. While recognizing that the collapse of the Bourbon regime in Spain might mean turmoil in Spanish America, possibly even revolts, the administration as yet had seen no reason to focus on the diplomatic or practical implications of those contingencies.

Communication with the Spanish government was, in any case, in a state of suspended animation. America had no diplomatic representative in Spain, the latest envoy having departed, conveniently, in 1808 before the establishment of the Bonaparte monarchy made a choice between the two rival Spanish kings necessary. Jefferson and Madison had then taken the position that, Spain being in a civil war, the United States would remain neutral and recognize neither of the contesting monarchies. But, given that there were a large number of points of contention between the two countries, a dialogue needed to be maintained. King Joseph, prudently and realistically, had never nominated a minister to the United States. Spain thus would be represented by the existing, *fernandista,* mission.

The Spanish mission, still in Philadelphia, had been under interim management since the unlamented minister, Carlos Irujo, had left in July 1808. The mission had been entrusted to the consul general, Valentin Tadeo de Foronda, a learned man who was friendly with Jefferson and an active member of the American Philosophical Society. But, even though Foronda had been granted full negotiating powers by the old Spanish regime of King Charles, his ideas were far too liberal for the new regency regime, or for that matter the pro-royalist crowd of Philadelphia merchants who supported the mission's activities. The result was that he was given little to do, and the regency attempted to check his suspected Bonapartist tendencies by appointing José Ignacio Viar, a previous consul general still resident in Philadelphia, to co-head the mission. As might be expected, the result was a mission seriously divided internally, criticized by its usual local supporters, with limited entrée in Washington and, in effect, incapable of performing its job.

In June 1809, the Cádiz regency appointed a trusted and experienced diplomat, Luis de Onís, to head the mission to the United States. His formal instructions were ambitious: he was to get American recognition of the regency as the legal government of Spain, to obtain supplies for the fight against the French, to counter Bonapartist propaganda in the Americas, and to monitor any separatist attempts in the colonies. Arriving in Philadelphia in October, Onís quickly put his stamp of strong leadership, ceaseless activity, and intense patriotism onto the mission. He abolished the job of consul general, dismissed Foronda[1] and Viar, rearranged assignments at the various consulates, and reinforced the mission's ties with its local supporters.

But, much to his chagrin, Onís failed to gain his first diplomatic objective. Received in Washington by Secretary of State Robert Smith, Onís was firmly but politely told that he would not be officially recognized as the minister of Spain; that American policy was to remain neutral in Spain's civil war, and to recognize neither party. But, Onís was also told, the administration had no problem with his remaining in the United States to perform other official functions, even though his mission's formal contacts with the administration would remain at the consular level. For Onís, a proud Spanish nobleman acutely sensitive to the honor of his nation and himself, the rejection was a blow. He had already groused that the Spanish frigate that had carried him to New York had not been accorded the proper honors upon arrival; now he was to be treated as a sort of second class envoy—by a government that he already suspected of being partial to the Bonapartist enemy. He started his mission with a chip on his shoulder.

The setback, however, did not slow down Onís. He arranged to have his consul in Baltimore, Juan Bautista Bernabeu,[2] recognized as the channel for official communication between the mission and the administration, and also tried to develop a sort of back channel for communication with the secretary of state, through the local district attorney Alexander Dallas. (The effort was not very rewarding, even though Dallas later became secretary of the treasury.) Onís also considered approaching American officials indirectly by offering gifts to the ladies Madison and Smith, but was turned down in that attempt at gaining influence by his superiors in Cádiz. Another effort, to employ a relative of Dolly Madison as an agent of influence in Washington, also came to naught. But those clumsy efforts to buy access were out of sight. In public, Onís was received cordially into Philadelphia and Washington society, and was feted by Spain's friends and supporters during visits to Boston and New York. He established himself in a grand Philadelphia house with an equally impressive carriage, and even brought a Spanish circus company to town to further burnish Spain's image. Although dealt a weak hand, Onís fully intended to make Spain's voice heard in the United States.

The less conspicuous aspects of the Spanish mission's job were pushed forward as well. His visits to New York and Boston gave Onís the opportunity to firm up contacts with the pro-Spanish merchants who had benefitted from Spain's monopoly trading system in the past, and who were now urged to cooperate in meeting the regency's urgent supply needs. Onís used the visits to evaluate, and then retain, Spain's consuls in the two cities: Thomas Stoughton in New York and his brother John in Boston. The two brothers were American Catholics and strong supporters of Spain (John's daughter Matilda was even married Josef de Jáudenes, who had been the Spanish diplomatic representative to the United States 1791–96), but the ever-suspicious Onís initially had doubts about their loyalty. In New York and Boston, Onís also had a chance to meet distinguished members of the Federalist party, whom he saw as potential allies in pursuing anti-Bonapartist measures via public opinion as well as in Washington.

Particularly eager to monitor potential French revolutionary or dissident Spanish activity in the hemisphere, Onís reenergized his consulates concerning their political reporting tasks[3]—which included the recruitment of informers and secret agents. All members of the consular staff were required to swear their loyalty to Ferdinand. By the end of the year, the consulate in Baltimore was busy gathering information on the rather blatant operations of a Captain Desmolard, who had arrived on a French warship and set up operations in a large rented house; Onís reported that Desmolard controlled some fifty revolutionary agents operating in the Spanish colonies and the United States. To share this kind of information and provide a warning system for threats to the regency's rule, Onís expanded communications with the royal representatives in Havana, Mexico, Venezuela and elsewhere in the Spanish provinces.

In short, by the end of the year, Luis de Onís, even though not fully accredited in Washington, had reinforced the Spanish anti-Bonapartist presence in the United States. He was beginning a tour of duty that would be marked by prodigious reporting, effective clandestine operations, active consular pursuit of Spain's interests, and repeated, forceful, and more than occasionally strident presentations of Spain's views to Washington and the general public.

In one of his earlier dispatches to Cádiz, in November 1809, Onís reported that he had learned that a group of four Spaniards in the city were engaged in suspicious, possibly pro-Bonapartist, activities. In this case, Onís had just discovered the obvious. Philadelphia had for some time had been the destination of choice for dissidents from Spanish America, who were drawn by the city's central location, cosmopolitan air, and the propaganda platform offered by its numerous publishing houses, but above all by its liberal tradition and the aura created by the Philosophical Society, Franklin, and the historic Continental Congress and constitutional convention. As the Ecuadorean dissident (and subsequently president of his country) Vicente Rocafuerte wrote during his stay in Philadelphia a decade later: "And where can I find memories more sublime, lessons more heroic and worthy of imitation, or examples more like our present political situation than in famous Philadelphia? Yes, in this very city, asylum of the oppressed, center of knowledge, bulwark of liberty."[4]

On a more practical level, a good reason for going to Philadelphia was that there was already a small nucleus of a Spanish dissident community in that city. Santiago Filipe Puglia, mentioned earlier, had been there since 1790, but his one act of dissidence had come to naught, and he apparently led a quiet life as translator and teacher. It is not clear whether he was one of alleged conspirators identified by Onís, but the city at any time hosted a number of Spanish Americans, either as residents or in transit, such as Francisco Miranda on his two visits, or Simón Bolívar in 1806. Moreover, Onís was not always an accurate reporter, and in his anti–Bonapartist fixation he had a tendency to exaggerate the threat in his dispatches. This particular report though, while perhaps not accurate in detail, was quite appropriate.

There was indeed a budding Spanish dissident community in the city, and its central figure was Manuel de Trujillo y Torres. Torres, born in the Spanish Canary Islands, had emigrated to what is now Colombia in 1778 at age sixteen with his father, the archbishop-viceroy. His education having inspired him with the liberal philosophy of the Enlightenment, Torres eventually became involved in an anti-colonial conspiracy in 1794 and was forced to flee to avoid prosecution. He had been in Philadelphia since 1796, where his intelligence, social talents, his skill in English, and his standing as a gentleman scholar from an area of growing interest soon made him a respected figure in society. As long as he received income from the wife whom he had left behind in Colombia, he lived well, but over time his means diminished, both from bad business decisions and the death of his wife which resulted in confiscation of the family estates. Nonetheless, he continued to live well, one supposes with occasional assistance from the many friends and supporters he acquired over the years.

One of Torres' early acquaintances was the fiery and controversial Irish-American journalist William Duane, who had settled in Philadelphia after having been expelled from British India for his critical writings. Duane, normally a difficult and quarrelsome man, was favorably impressed by the knowledge, skill, and character of the dissident Spaniard, and the two became close friends. Through that friendship, plus his own anti-colonial and anti–British passions, Duane became an early proponent of independence for the South American colonies. When he took over as editor of the newspaper *Aurora* in 1798, he turned it into the leading organ supporting the Jeffersonian democrats. Taking advantage of such an influential platform, Torres worked with Duane, translating or drafting items for the paper and then seeing that they were also circulated in Spanish America. By late spring of 1810, news of the Venezuelan rupture with the regency had reached North America, touching off conjecture in the press that it was the harbinger of a wider independence movement.

The *Aurora* was the leader in reporting news and opinion on developments in South America, regularly stressing the advantages that independence of the colonies would bring to American trade and prosperity. The *Aurora* however was not alone. In Baltimore, the respected *Niles' Register* had begun to report news and generally favorable commentary about developments in South America, as did the *Richmond Enquirer*. In New Orleans, the first Spanish language paper in the United States, the *Misisipi*, had been appearing since September 1808. That paper, actually bilingual, was published for the émigrés from the northern Spanish provinces such as Mexico, and advocated both resistance to Bonaparte's claim to the Spanish throne, and increased autonomy for the American colonies.

This, then, was the situation in the United States, and particularly in the Spanish-speaking community of Philadelphia, when the first representatives from the South American juntas arrived. The city hosted two Spanish-speaking communities: the royalist Spanish mission with its influential friends in the merchant community on the one hand, and on the other hand a tiny group of dissident Spaniards who were opposed to both the regency council and the pretender regime of Joseph Bonaparte—even while sympathizing with some French revolutionary ideals. The second group would grow over time and be increasingly committed to independence for the colonies, a goal to which its de facto leader, Manuel Torres, had long been dedicated. The diplomatic mission, of course, was equally dedicated to thwarting that movement.

The delegates from Caracas, Orea and Bolívar, arrived in Baltimore in early June, accompanied two assistants, Juan Tinoco, and Juan de Iriarte. They had come on the schooner *Fame,* and brought with them a cargo of coffee, indigo, and hides that they intended to sell in exchange for the arms they had been sent to buy. Their arrival was no surprise to the ever-alert Spanish minister. Luis de Onís, it seems, had already received word from Venezuela that they could be expected, and had sent a friend and agent to Baltimore to sound them out as discreetly as possible.

Onís's agent in this situation was Francisco Caballero Sarmiento, a prominent businessman in Philadelphia who was working with Onís out of self-interested patriotism. Sarmiento was Portuguese-born, a man of shrewd enterprises who had made fruitful contacts in his father's home of the Spanish Canary Islands before coming to America in 1787. Through those contacts and the help of Spanish minister Irujo, Sarmiento had obtained a number of the sought-after licenses to trade with South America, which he then used to obtain for himself a notable position in the Philadelphia grain trading community. His marriage to Catherine Craig connected him yet more closely with the prominent merchants John Craig and Robert Oliver, with whom he conducted profitable enterprises in Caracas and Vera Cruz respectively. Sarmiento lived in Caracas between 1805 and 1808, implementing the grain importing monopoly that he shared with Craig. He had strongly opposed Francisco Miranda's 1806 expedition, putting his wealth to the service of the royal governors with loans that enabled them to drive off the raiders. Sarmiento had returned to Philadelphia when the Bourbon regime fell, maintaining a fierce loyalty to the royalist cause that made him one of the principal accusers of the previous consul general, Foronda. Onís quite naturally found him a useful ally, and the two were already collaborating in the task of procuring arms to strengthen the position of royalist forces in South America. Sarmiento, with a career and wealth that had been based on favoritism and monopoly, naturally had enemies. Miranda called him "a fit agent of murders, poisoners, and others of that ilk," while Onís to the contrary defended him to Spanish officials as "invaluable." Onís was obliged to admit privately to his son Mauricio however, that Sarmiento was a "scoundrel," but all the same loyal, and had "a good heart."[5]

Sarmiento, who undoubtedly knew Telésforo de Orea or members of his merchant family from his time in Caracas (the de Oreas too were *islenos*, from the Canaries), made contact shortly after the delegation's arrival. It must have been an interesting conversation. Orea (whose family, like Sarmiento, had opposed Miranda's expedition four years earlier) was now fearful that the regency was all but doomed, and that the colonies, through their juntas, needed to look after their own interests—maybe even through independence. An idealist and admirer of America's successful republican experiment, he believed that common anti-colonial backgrounds and republican ideals would bring about a natural alliance between North and South Americans.

The more experienced and cynical Sarmiento on the other hand wanted simply to dissuade the young man from his rebellious stance. He used an argument which he knew should resonate with this wealthy creole: the race card. Consider carefully, Sarmiento warned Orea, how the junta's separatist steps, initiated by upper class white creoles, could provoke a descent into class and then racial warfare such as had happened in Haiti. Rebellion, once unleashed in the context of Venezuela's rigid class and race distinctions, could lead to a social upheaval, enormous loss of life and property, and the end of the whites as the privileged class. Orea, apparently unwilling to dispute the point, simply rejoined that Sarmiento's history as a grasping monopolist made him vulnerable, too.[6] (Sarmiento, unfortunately, was prescient in his prediction. The liberation struggles—and in Venezuela particularly—would over time be marked by persistent class and race-based conflict, violence, and atrocities, although in the end the creoles did succeed in maintaining their privileged status.)

Not dissuaded from his task by Orea's cold shoulder, Sarmiento turned to see what he could gain from a conversation with one of the junior delegation members, Juan de Iriarte. He came away with the impression that the delegation's priority was to fulfill the needy junta's arms purchasing mission; its political aims if any were unclear. His conversations served as the basis for Onís's subsequent reporting, and probably achieved one local result as well: he had sowed a seed of doubt in a delegation that had a defined task, but an undefined identity. The Venezuelans were still Spaniards, legally and emotionally; their junta persisted in claiming loyalty to Ferdinand. But in a world of rapid and dangerous change they wanted to protect Venezuelan interests as well. They were neither fully loyal nor in full rebellion; it was a conflict in identity that Onís would try to exploit.

After a short time in Baltimore, the delegation proceeded to Washington to announce their arrival and test the official reaction to their mission. Orea and Bolívar met with Secretary of State Robert Smith, whose reception was friendly but whose message was that the American government could not compromise its neutrality by any involvement in their arms purchases. The delegation, he added, was nonetheless free to buy and ship such supplies as they could find on the commercial market. In short, no official hindrance, no official help; a good signal of a sort but not as positive as the delegation may have hoped. While in Washington, they also called on William Thornton, a champion of Latin American independence and a friend (and ex-neighbor) of President Madison, who would prove a warm friend and point of contact for South American patriots, but whose actual political influence was minimal. Thornton, according to Onís's reports home (his source seems to have been the State Department's Spanish translator), offered them an early version of his visionary plan for a Pan American political union. More usefully, he probably gave them an introduction to Manuel Torres in Philadelphia.

Manuel Torres's role, up to this time, had been that of a dissident intellectual and propagandist. He was now being asked to play a more active role, as a facilitator of actual separatist actions, a role that would expand to include purchasing agent, planner, even occasional conspirator, and finally diplomat. While we have no record of his thoughts at the time, they must have included both satisfaction that events were moving forward, and concern that they might be premature, as Miranda's expedition had been.

Stephen Girard, Torres told Orea and Bolívar, was the man to see. French-born Girard was a successful merchant who was familiar with the Caribbean from trade with Haiti, and who had begun to show an interest in the South American markets that his ships could visit on their way to China. A Mason with liberal and anti-monarchical views (his ships were called *Montesquieu, Rousseau, Voltaire,* and *Liberty*) and also financially astute, he would later become the richest man in America. Girard agreed to sell the merchandise the Venezuelans had brought, and try to find suitable arms with the proceeds, plus whatever could be realized from the promissory notes they were authorized by the junta to offer.

It was not an easy deal to put together. Girard found that he could not get the prices he had expected for the Venezuelan goods. Then, he found that the best guns available on the market were being bought up by Minister Onís, who had large orders to fill and ship to South America, plus the clear advantage of good credit with which to buy them. And finally, there was the problem that the credit standing of the Caracas junta was untested; nobody wanted the notes except at a punishing discount. Given the difficulties, the two delegates decided to separate: Bolívar would stay to continue the search for additional quantities of arms, while Orea would return to Caracas with a partial shipment of arms and to report on their progress, such as it was.

The effort, for the Venezuelans, had been neither success nor failure.

They had learned that the Americans of the north were clearly poorly informed about the changing circumstances in the southern hemisphere, unwilling to take much of a chance on supporting the efforts of unknown rebels, and careful not to prejudice their relations with the European powers. As a result, they were likely to refer to their tradition of neutrality toward the disputes of other powers as a rationale to fend off any requests for official assistance. Yet, at the same time, they were basically well inclined, friends of liberty, entirely willing to allow arms purchases from the private sector, and cautiously intrigued about the prospects for their future in the region.

It would take work for the two sides to understand each other's capabilities and limits, but the Philadelphia circle was a useful platform, and the future payoff, both material and political, could be important.

Over the coming years, Orea and other official representatives of the new patriot regimes would continue to appeal to the United States government, as well as the private sector, for assistance. Successive Washington administrations would, in response, justify an official hands-off position by citing their traditional policy of neutrality. Nonetheless, the official envoys and their more militant non-official colleagues resident in the United States would often test, and occasionally exceed, the limits of U.S. neutrality. The experience was often frustrating for all sides, including the Spanish royalists, and in time both royalists and rebels would see the policy as biased in favor of their opponents.

Chapter 3

The First Rebel Agents Show Up

Shortly before returning to Caracas in mid–July, Telésforo de Orea took part in an unusual and interesting meeting. He met with the British minister to the United States, Francis Jackson, but also present at the meeting was a representative from the Department of State, and Luis de Onís. The protocol, if surprising, was entirely proper, as Orea worked for a government that claimed to be loyal to King Ferdinand, and Onís was the royal envoy. But, even if the protocol was correct, the atmosphere must nonetheless have been a bit strained, since Orea represented a rebel regime that had refused allegiance to the very Regency Council that Onís represented. Given how formative and fluid the situation still was, indeed, it appears that the various parties were simply taking occasion to explore each other's views and intentions.

Orea later told the American representative that he had come away with the impression that the Caracas junta could expect little help from the British, who were too closely allied to the regency to be friendly to the rebels—particularly if the junta were to declare independence. Onís, on the other hand, reported after the meeting that he had found Jackson to be entirely too complacent about the rebellion, which in the Spanish minister's excited view was largely the product of a French plot against Spain.[1] (He was wrong; a major motivation of the Caracas junta was to defend the province against French intrigues.) So if both Onís and Orea found Jackson's attitude confusing, it is no surprise. The British wished to have it both ways—supporting their Spanish ally while at the same time seeking commercial advantage in the rebellious colonies. Ambiguity was useful to them.

If the two diplomats in their turn tried to draw Orea out as to the Caracas junta's intentions, the lack of reporting on the point indicates that he must have stuck to his instructions: the junta was loyal to Ferdinand. However, Orea was not firm in that position for the longer term. When he returned to Caracas, he had two major points to make in his report. First, that the delegation had received a warm welcome in the United States and that further arms purchases, though perhaps less extensive than had been hoped, were underway. And secondly, that he was convinced that the U.S. government would not recognize or openly assist the junta (or any other separatists) unless they first declared themselves independent. The first message was favorably received, while the second one hit a sensitive nerve in the divided junta, as it gave support to those more radical and vocal members who had been pushing for independence. To resolve the ongoing debate as to where to take their rebellion, the junta decided to assemble a national congress from the various separatist provinces of Venezuela. When that congress finally convened in March 1811, it was led by a group of independence-minded members such as Simón Bolívar and Francisco Miranda, who had returned from London the previous December.

In official Washington, the visit of the first delegates from a dissident junta had also triggered a response, but not in policy; officially, U.S. neutrality was a given. It was rather in the realization that events in the Spanish colonies had begun to move rapidly, and that an official U.S. presence on the ground would be useful, both to understand the local situation better and to serve American commercial interests in a growing but unstable market. Secretary of State Smith accordingly appointed trade representatives to three key regions: Robert K. Lowry to Guaira, the port of Caracas, Joel Roberts Poinsett to Buenos Aires and Chile, and William Shaler to Cuba and Mexico. In the absence of diplomatic relations with either Spain or the dissident colonies, the three were not given diplomatic or consular titles, but rather appointed as agents for seamen and commerce. Their instructions, however, indicate that Secretary Smith expected political reporting as much as commercial facilitation, and also instructed them to take a friendly attitude to any moves toward independence. The key parts of his June 1810 instructions to Poinsett are clear:

> As a crisis is approaching which must produce great changes in the situation in Spanish America, and may dissolve altogether its colonial relations to Europe, and as the geographical position of the United States and other obvious considerations give them an intimate interest in whatever may affect the destiny of that part of the American continent … you will make it your objective whenever it may be proper to diffuse the impression that the United States cherish

3. The First Rebel Agents Show Up

the sincerest good will toward the people of Spanish America as neighbors ... and in the event of a political separation from the parent country and of the establishment of an independent system of National Government, it will coincide with the sentiment and policy of the United States to promote the most friendly relations and the most liberal intercourse.... The real as well as ostensible project of your mission is to explain the mutual advantages of commerce with the United States to promote liberal and stable regulations, and to transmit seasonable information on the subject.[2]

Shaler and Lowry arrived at their new posts by the end of summer, Poinsett not until early 1811, and they soon gave the Madison administration its first direct (if not necessarily impartial) reporting on the situations in the breakaway provinces. Minister Onís, ever suspicious, and particularly so of the administration's intentions, immediately reported to Cádiz that Lowry was being sent to Venezuela to promote Bonapartist plots. Shaler and Poinsett were equally suspect.

At the same time, Onís had another interesting bit of news to report: that the Venezuelan envoy Juan Vicente Bolívar had asked to pay a courtesy call. Bolívar could shelter behind the stance that he was simply following the precedent set by Orea's earlier meeting with Onís and Jackson, but his request for a meeting was nonetheless unusual. Both knew that the junta's loyalty to King Ferdinand was wavering, and that talk of independence was in the air. Onís correctly sensed that there was more to this than a simple courtesy visit.

Onís used the occasion to sound out Bolívar's views. Presumably he found that Juan Vicente had doubts about the junta's course, since Onís then reported to Cádiz that he had urged Bolívar to remain loyal to the regency, and felt that he might do so. Over the coming months, even as Bolívar continued his arms purchases, he met a number of times with Onís, who continued to try to wean him away from his more radical colleagues in Caracas. But, with the arms sales negotiations going very slowly—Stephen Girard had backed out of further involvement—Bolívar would have to remain in the United States until the following summer.

By the fall of 1810, Onís in any event had a more pressing crisis to deal with. In June, a group of American settlers in the good farming bottomlands of Spanish West Florida had set up a junta-like local administration in response to the situation in Spain and their grievances with the local administration. Taking their movement a step further in September, they seized the Spanish garrison town of Baton Rouge, and declared an independent Republic of West Florida. Onís was appropriately incensed over this violation of Spanish sovereignty. Negotiations concerning the American claim that a major part of the province constituted part of the Louisiana Purchase had been going on intermittently since 1803, and the seizure of Baton Rouge, he believed, was simply a hidden attempt by the administration to take by force what it had claimed, unsuccessfully, through negotiation. The fact that the governor of the so-called republic was Fulwar Skipwith, previously an American diplomat in France and a Virginian like President Madison, simply increased the Spaniard's suspicions. And they were not without basis; while the events in Florida were not orchestrated by Washington, the Madison administration had by no means been caught by surprise. When, only a month later, Madison annexed the territory between the Mississippi and Pearl Rivers by presidential proclamation,[3] declaring that it had always been part of Louisiana, Onís considered his suspicions confirmed.

Following on the administration's action of sending American agents, without a by-your-leave, to areas of Spanish America that were in defiance of the regency, the West Florida charade confirmed to Onís that the Madison administration simply intended to challenge Spanish sovereignty wherever possible. He took his and Spain's case public, publishing a strong attack on the annexation, and a defense of Spain's claim to the territory, in a pamphlet signed anonymously by "Verus"—a totally transparent pseudonym as it had also been used by his predecessor, Carlos Irujo. Not even officially accredited, Onís was venturing onto the same thin ice of anti-administration propaganda that had gotten Irujo into trouble.

William Shaler was the first of the U.S. agents to arrive at his post. As a Connecticut merchant in the China trade, he had spent some time at the turn of the century in the Rio de la Plata area and the Pacific coast of South America, where he had advocated American republican ideas with enough enthusiasm to gain unfavorable attention from the Chilean authorities, leading to a short imprisonment. Arriving now in royalist Havana with an official status that had never been approved by the Spanish authorities, speaking French rather than Spanish, and unable to hide his republican and anti-monarchical feelings, he once again attracted the attention of the security officials. He nonetheless managed to send a number of informative reports to the State Department before being politely but firmly asked to leave somewhat over a year later, in November 1811. He moved to New Orleans, a most effective listening post from which to follow events in his second country of responsibility, Mexico. Although the initial revolutionary uprising there under Miguel Hidalgo had already

3. The First Rebel Agents Show Up

been crushed, there were still many signs of impending change, and Shaler had been told that a representative of the defeated rebels wanted to make contact. Shaler, an expansionist who looked forward to American gains at Spain's expense, settled in to report to Washington, and to await events.

The second agent in position was Robert Lowry, who was in Venezuela by early autumn of 1810. In this case, the local government was more than ready to receive him, but in the end disappointed that he had not come with a diplomatic title that would have been a provided some sort of recognition of their rule. More or less ignored by a junta that was preoccupied during most of the next year with internal politics, and somewhat isolated on the island of Guaira, Lowry busied himself with his commercial responsibilities, reporting regularly on the growing British dominance of the local market and arguing for a stronger American presence, even visits by U.S. warships to show the flag.

Joel Poinsett, the third of this first group of American agents, did not arrive in Buenos Aires until February of 1811. The well-travelled and wealthy South Carolinian arrived just as a change of government took place, one of the many such events (including wars with neighboring provinces) that would plague the early years of the separatist regime. Poinsett, a man of great energy and action, urged the new junta to move toward independence, which he argued would help open the door to U.S. assistance and trade. He at the same time urged his own government to take a more active role in promoting trade, and did get them to agree to name him consul general. But he was unable to influence Washington's stance on non-recognition. The local junta in any event was far too plagued with internal and regional struggles to move away from its relatively comfortable position of virtual autonomy, behind a fig leaf of nominal loyalty to the distant regency council. It did, however, decide in June that it would send a delegation to the United States to test the waters with an arms purchase.

Poinsett's activism naturally annoyed the ubiquitous and influential British in Buenos Aires, one of them describing Poinsett as "particularly diligent and active in propagating doctrines and opinions prejudicial to the British government and subjects."[4] By November, Poinsett, sensing that he had done all he could for the moment, appointed a resident American businessman from Philadelphia, William Gilchrist Miller, to be American consul in his absence, and headed on over the Andes to his other country of responsibility, Chile.

The Buenos Aires junta's decision to send a delegation to Washington came shortly after the government in Caracas had also decided to renew its appeal for assistance. Telésforo de Orea was once again chosen as the Venezuelan representative, to be accompanied this time by a Caracas lawyer active in the movement, José Rafael Ravenga. They would present credentials from the Caracas congress, which was acting as the interim government. Their instructions included the recall of Juan Bolívar, who had fallen into disgrace in Caracas when the news of his negotiations with Onís had come to light. (Juan had already received a caution from his brother Simón, who warned that people were calling him a traitor, and demanding punishment and confiscation of his property.)

Orea and his delegation reached New York at the end of April, their arrival duly reported to Luís de Onís by the local consul, Thomas Stoughton. Onís quickly put his informants on the job of tracking the delegation's movements, but he was generally dismissive of Orea, showing his class prejudice by calling the creole merchant "one of those ill-born villains of the revolution."[5] Onís at the moment was concentrating his attention on other, and possibly more dangerous, foreign agents.

Luis de Onís was fixated on the activities of French agents passing through United States ports on their way to Spanish America. They were, he thought, the real fomenters of revolutionary or separatist activities in the colonies. Onís reported that there were several hundred active agents in the Americas, and exposed a number of operations, although in his zeal he also made a number of inaccurate or false reports. One surveillance operation about which Onís took particular satisfaction was his reporting, and later penetration, of a group of French agents who arrived in Philadelphia early in 1811. Headed by Jacques Athanase D'Amblimont, the group seems to have exercised very lax security, since Onís's operatives were able to steal their instructions, codes, agent identities, and even some of D'Amblimont's and the French minister's correspondence—all of which proved that the group had been sent to infiltrate into Mexico, map out possible invasion routes, expand the French agent network, and sow dissension and resentment against the regency. Onís also succeeded in having the papers stolen of another French agent, Louis Jean Ledresench, who was in touch with the French minister in Washington in early 1811 for the purpose of raising a pro–Bonapartist movement—once again in Mexico, on whose riches the French appear to have had particular designs.

Onís regularly reported his findings to the viceroys in Mexico and Havana, as well as to Cádiz, alerting them to the dangers. He obviously took pride in his efforts, boasting in a letter to his son that "if everyone worked as hard as I, Bonaparte would no longer exist." He had earlier preened himself before the same correspondent, asserting that "it was an act of Providence that I came to this country, as otherwise the Americas surely would have been lost if Foronda had stayed, or someone else had come with less energy and control over these issues."[6]

To Onís's suspicious mind, moreover, the United States was playing along with Bonapartist efforts to separate the Spanish American colonies from *fernandista* Spain. Onís considered the Madison administration to be "servile" to the French, engaged in "scandalous conduct in promoting, by every means in their power, the machinations of Joseph to make himself the master of our colonies."[7] He was also sure that the Americans' real aim was to profit from disorder in the Spanish colonies in order to expand their own sphere of influence or even territory. Nor was he entirely off the mark, either with respect to American long-term intentions, or a French desire to enlist American cooperation in promoting separatism.[8]

While Onís fretted about the French, Orea and Ravenga settled in not far away in Philadelphia, where they had joined up with Manuel Torres. Their arrival began to give form to what would become known as the "Philadelphia circle," a loose group of colonial dissidents and republican revolutionaries and propagandists, coordinated informally by Torres, who would work and scheme together to forward their cause in the breakaway colonies.

The circle of émigré activists had begun to grow in 1810 through the arrival of Manuel Garcia de Sena and his brother Domingo. Manuel de Sena, a young Venezuelan lawyer, who would contribute to the revolutionary cause largely through his annotated translations of the works of Thomas Paine and John McCulloch's history of the United States. Both were published in Philadelphia and distributed widely in South America, the former in particular influencing the constitutional debate underway in Venezuela. They had been preceded in 1810 by a translation of the American constitution, published in Philadelphia by the Caracas native Joseph Manuel Villavicencio. These works, their publication by different printing houses, and their successful distribution in South America, affirmed the position of Philadelphia as the leading American platform for revolutionary propaganda activities.

In an early May 1811 visit to Washington, Orea found that his credentials from the Caracas congress would still not be recognized by the administration. But, in a sort of face-saving gesture, the new Secretary of State James Monroe said that Robert Lowry's title in Guaira would be raised to the more official one of consul. Orea was also received amiably by President Madison, without however any indication that the official stance of distant but friendly neutrality would be altered.

Orea did not immediately replace Juan Vicente Bolívar, whose concern about his status and personal safety if he returned to Caracas must have been acute. In July, though, he received word from his brother that the situation had calmed; on reconsideration his conversations with Onís were no longer seen as treasonous, and that he would be free to return in safety. Bolívar decided to take the advice, but before leaving he had a final conversation with Onís. The Spanish diplomat had apparently taken somewhat of a liking to the rich and aristocratic Bolívar, and had requested a royal pardon for him in case he deserted the separatists. Bolívar told Onís that he still planned to return to Caracas, where he would work for reconciliation with the regency. He sailed at the end of the month, on the brig *Mary*, with the arms and agricultural supplies that he trusted would earn him a good reception in Caracas.

Bolívar's promise to work for reconciliation would never, however, be tested. The *Mary* apparently ran into a deadly storm, was blown off course somewhere near the Bahamas, and was lost at sea along with the all its cargo, crew and passengers.

He would not in any case have been able to change the situation in Venezuela, where the national congress, led by Miranda, the Caracas contingent, Juan Vicente's brother Simón, and others, were in the process of choosing a different course. On July 5, 1811, the congress declared that its participating provinces had formed a fully independent confederation, and set about drafting a liberal constitution and a bill of rights. The first Venezuelan republic had begun. But it was born in the midst of a war with those provinces that remained loyal to the regency, and with some parts of the confederation less than fully committed to the cause.

News of this new independent republic to the south reached the United States within the month, and attracted immediate attention, with most journals taking a positive attitude, both in view of the prospects opened up for American trade, and in pleasant recognition that the new Venezuelan constitution seemed to have been modeled in part on the American. Much of the press commentary had an anti-Spanish cast, however, while concern was also voiced about the course of the ongoing struggle in Venezuela, the dangers of a social upheaval there, and the dictatorial tendencies of some of the republican leaders. America's attention all the same remained concentrated on the European struggle and the growing

3. The First Rebel Agents Show Up

dispute with Great Britain, and tended to see the confusing developments in Spanish America through that lens—initially concerned that the rebellions were French-inspired, yet confused by the obvious British role in profiting from the activities of the separatists.

The U.S. government, particularly after the Venezuelans had declared their independence, recognized that it had to begin developing a policy for potential contingencies. Madison, in his message to Congress of 5 November, noted the issue in a simple paragraph, and urged that Congress recognize the changes in South America with "an obligation to take a deep interest in their destinies, to cherish reciprocal sentiments of good will ... and not be unprepared." Congress appointed a committee of the House, which a month later reported that it had obtained approval of a joint resolution by both houses. The non-binding resolution stated "that they behold, with friendly interest, the establishment of independent sovereignties by the Spanish provinces in America ... the United States feel great solicitude for their welfare and that, when those provinces shall have attained the condition of nations by the just exercise of their rights, the Senate and House of Representatives shall unite with the Executive in establishing with them, as sovereign and independent states, such amicable relations and commercial intercourse as might require their legislative authority."[9] It was a statement that was positive in tone, yet its several subordinate clauses and phrases left more than enough room for deliberate or even dilatory action.

Against this background and favorable climate, other delegations began to arrive from regions in Spanish America that had not yet taken moves toward independence, or even effective control of their regions. The most important of these was the delegation from Buenos Aires, which arrived in early October 1811 on a ship belonging to the American consul in that city, William Miller. The principal member was Diego de Saavedra, son of the latest junta leader Cornelio Saavedra, who favored a federal approach to deal with the region's fractious politics. He was accompanied by Juan Pedro de Aguirre, who had fought against the British in 1806–1807 in the militia that now supported Saavedra; he was currently secretary of the cabildo. Concerned for their security, the two had travelled under false passports, and had come for a limited purpose: to buy arms to strengthen the junta against its external foes as well as its various regional competitors, located in the regions now known as Uruguay, Paraguay and Bolivia.

Saavedra and Aguirre first checked in with Torres and Orea, who put them in touch with Stephen Girard as a merchant who could help them fill their shopping list. They made a trip to Washington as well, to talk to Secretary of State James Monroe and inform the government of their objective. Monroe told them that they were free to buy arms on the open market, but that the government was obliged to still consider their government as if it were a Spanish province, and therefore could not provide, as the Argentines had requested, protection for any shipment of arms they might make.

Back in Philadelphia, the *porteños*[10] found the local merchants unwilling to accept their assurances that there was real value in the special peso appropriation the junta had made for buying arms. Nonetheless, with the help of Torres and Orea, they eventually reached agreement with Girard for the purchase of 20,000 muskets and flints on credit, with Venezuela taking one third of the contract. But the risk-avoiding Girard made the agreement subject to the explicit approval of the American government, writing a letter to Monroe asking for assurances that "the shipment alluded to will not be considered as unlawful or disagreeable to the President ... and that the government will facilitate me the means of obtaining said muskets."[11] Monroe never answered, and the cautions Girard, once again, pulled out.

Discouraged, the Argentines spent the next few months negotiating a credit agreement with William Miller and the Van Beuren merchant house, a face-saving agreement that allowed them to return with a shipment of a thousand muskets with bayonets, hundreds of thousands of flints, and other military necessities. By May, they were back in Buenos Aires, where William Miller, the consul and a promoter of separation from Spain, reported enthusiastically that "the friendly reception given to these gentlemen, the general interest in the success and the enthusiasm in favor of the Liberty of this country shewn by all classes in the U.S., and the partial attainment of their objective, has produced the effect expected: the United States are looked up to as the only sincere friends of their cause, not only by the Government but by the people."[12] In reality, however, the mission was seen as only a limited success.

The Argentines were not the only would-be arms buyers who were disappointed by the prospects of aid from America. The market situation was unfavorable, as good muskets were getting hard to find as America prepared for possible war with England, while the creditworthiness of the Spanish American juntas was unknown and scarcely respected. Likewise, political support (as Telésforo de Orea had concluded and reported home) did not flow freely from shared republican ideals alone; it would take money or solid credit to buy support in America. While Orea continued to buy arms with his available funds, Onís reported that he was probably wasting his money, as the shipments ran a high probability of being confiscated by a Spanish blockade of the rebel ports. Onís also reported that Orea had been disappointed by the official American reaction to Venezuela's declaration of independence; there had been neither recognition nor aid, merely a lukewarm statement looking toward the future. By late 1811, a frustrated Orea was talking to the French minister in Washington, Louis Sérurier, about possible aid from the country his junta had originally sought to keep at arm's length. Now that Venezuela had declared its independence, the regency in Cádiz had become, in a way, their common enemy.

One delegation to the United States did have success, and did so with minimum notice. In July 1811, a small delegation arrived in New York from Cartagena, Colombia to buy arms. The delegation was headed by Pedro de la Lastra, and apparently could pay with the hard currency that was more available in the Andean region than in Venezuela. In Philadelphia, Lastra and his colleague Nicolás Mauricio de Umaña met Manuel Torres who introduced them around, while Spanish informants kept an eye on them for Onís. Little is known of their dealings except that Onís reported, some six months later, that they had left for Cartagena with a cargo of some 1500 muskets plus other materials. The goods were undoubtedly needed in Cartagena, which had just declared its independence, in November 1811.

Early in the new year, the situation changed drastically. The United States was moving rapidly toward war with Great Britain, with the natural result that the situation in South America dropped way down the political agenda. Then, at the end of March, a strong earthquake hit Venezuela, killing fifteen to twenty thousand people and leveling Caracas and other towns. Devastating for the young republic's reputation, the quake somehow had damaged only those areas that had declared for independence, leaving the loyalist areas virtually untouched. Public opinion turned sharply against the republican regime, which in the emergency situation had been turned over to Miranda as virtual dictator. In response to the human disaster and Orea's pleading, the American congress voted to send five shiploads of foodstuffs and other aid to the stricken area, but by the time they arrived the situation had been reversed, and the goods were confiscated by the Spanish.

After the earthquake and its fatal damage to the moral and political image of the Miranda regime, the military situation of the young republic also disintegrated rapidly. When the other provinces held back assistance, Caracas was isolated, and Miranda was forced by the end of July 1812 to negotiate an armistice. Discredited, and either deserted or betrayed by Bolívar, Miranda was handed over to the Spanish forces. He and a few of his supporters were imprisoned, in violation of the terms of the capitulation, and were deported to Spain. There the ambitious, charismatic and brave, but ultimately non-performing revolutionary agitator died in prison in 1816, to be buried in an unmarked grave.

The first Venezuelan republic had been crushed.

With the fall of Venezuela, the leaders of rebellious New Granada had good reason to fear that Spanish forces would soon turn their attention westward, and attempt to reestablish royal control there, too. Needing outside help, they chose a Venezuelan who had fought with Miranda and escaped the Spanish forces, Manuel Palacio Fajardo, to represent them in and seek assistance from both the United States and France. Arriving in New York in October 1812, he stayed there and in Baltimore for some weeks before appearing in Washington at the end of the year. There, Fajardo met with both President Madison and Secretary of State Monroe, who reportedly were intrigued by the information he gave them about the wealth and revolutionary determination of his country. But, in response to his questions about assistance, they disappointed him with chilly reminders that the United States intended to maintain its position of neutrality. Fajardo wasted little time in America after hearing the "pretty words" that he took as a turn-down; he approached the French minister in Washington, Louis Sérurier, for assistance, and before long was in Paris, and subsequently in London, working with the circle of active patriots there.

Other Venezuelan revolutionaries were scattered as well by the fall of Caracas. One of them, Pedro José Gual, had just been designated to represent the republic in the United States, and was still waiting for a ship in Guaira when the republican government fell. Suddenly a diplomatic representative without a country to represent, he nonetheless had a cause to champion, and was determined to pursue it. He arrived in Baltimore in October 1812, accompanied by Juan Bautista Picornell, where they found the United States already at war with Great Britain and distracted from events in the southern hemisphere.

Gual and Picornell were both dedicated to South American liberty.

3. The First Rebel Agents Show Up

Picornell, the elder of the two, was from European Spain, a Mason who had been involved in the 1795 San Blas conspiracy against the monarchy. He was condemned to death, then transported to Guaira, Venezuela when his sentence was commuted to life imprisonment. Even in prison, he maintained his revolutionary propaganda, and was once again involved in a plot, this one the Gual and España conspiracy of 1798. He managed nonetheless to escape, and after a number of years of revolutionary activity in the Caribbean (which included stops in Baltimore and Philadelphia), he joined the leaders of the first republic in 1811. Gual on the other hand was a Caracas creole, the nephew of the 1798 conspirator Manuel Gual, and a lawyer with liberal ideas who had joined the Sociedad Patriótica, the local Mirandista lodge which was headed by Picornell. Elected to the national congress, Gual had served as Miranda's secretary during the period of the first republic.

Both men were at the moment rootless and probably almost penniless, but looking for a way to continue the struggle from the United States. They would, of course, go to Philadelphia. But they would find, during the next few years, that the North Americans had their own crisis to face, and little concern for the events unfolding in the southern continent.

Chapter 4

Filibusters, American and Émigré

The United States went to war with Great Britain in June 1812. Although Congress's declaration of war came after years of acrimonious dispute with the British over trade restrictions, violations of American neutral rights, and incitement of Indian insurrections, the Madison administration found itself ill-prepared to actually wage war. Early military defeats, plus the persistence of strong opposition to the war from the trading interests on the East Coast, made the war a divisive issue that would dominate American policy discussions for the next three years. In such circumstances, the struggle between the Spanish regency and its colonies could no longer attract much attention, and the question of recognizing the rebel juntas dropped from public view. The defeat of the first Venezuelan republic, moreover, had discouraged those few Americans who were inspired by the anti-colonial nature of the separatists' efforts.

Regardless of the level of American attention, the struggle would of course go on, and North America would inevitably become a theater of conflict. And since the Spanish American rebels could no longer hope for assistance from a U.S. administration preoccupied with its new and dangerous role on the fringe of the European struggle, they would simply choose to work around the government whenever they needed to. The fact that regency Spain, as Britain's ally in the European struggle, was potentially hostile to the United States, offered them some intriguing possibilities. Would the United States, they asked themselves, complain if the rebels used its territory as a staging ground for attacks on Spanish-held but poorly defended colonies?

The administration, for its part, was worried about a similar scenario, but rather a reverse one: that the Spanish regency, Britain's dependent partner in the European war, would not be able to stop British use of Spanish

4. Filibusters, American and Émigré

territory to attack the United States. Florida was the main area of concern. The border, delineated in 1795, was all but undefended by the resource-poor Spanish governors at Pensacola and St. Augustine. The Americans had a few forts along the border, with a mission however designed less to defend America from the Spanish than to keep American settlers and adventurers from creating difficulties over on the Spanish side. The border as a result was highly permeable along its entire length, with a miscellany of American settlers, fugitives, runaway slaves, smugglers and adventurers living on both sides. Completing this volatile mixture were Spanish settlers, a few French, British settlers and traders left over from the British occupation in the previous century, and a large and angry population of Creek and Seminole Indians whom the British had often in the past incited into raiding the American settlements.

The unstable and vulnerable nature of the Florida border was demonstrated repeatedly in the years before the 1812 war. To Madison, looking at the probability of war with Great Britain, Florida was a potential weak spot, from which the British could, ignoring or brushing aside their weak Spanish allies, attack either directly or by egging on their Indian allies.

The West Florida insurrection of 1810 had shed a glaring light on the weakness of Spanish Governor Vicente Foch's position. When the giddy inhabitants of the temporary republic of West Florida began to organize an expedition to capture Spanish Mobile, Folch sensed that he could no longer defend his province, threatened as it was by both the direct challenge of the rebels and the undermining tactics of French agents in New Orleans. Preferring negotiation with the United States to capitulation to the insurrectionists, he wrote to Secretary of State Robert Smith, through the ex–Indian agent Colonel John McKee, an old acquaintance. In his letter Folch offered that, if he did not receive reinforcements from Havana by the end of the year, he would be ready to negotiate a temporary handover of West Florida to the United States, its final disposition to be determined an eventual resumption of the negotiations that had begun back in 1803. Intrigued by this opportunity to obtain physical possession of the remainder of West Florida, Madison urged McKee to come to Washington to discuss the options. Also invited was the elderly ex-governor of Georgia, George Mathews, who was already advising the administration on the situation in the Pensacola region. At the same time, the president opened consultations on Florida with Congress, using an implied British threat to intervene as a goad to rapid action.

Mathews and McKee met with the president and secretary of state in mid-January 1811. The discussions moved rapidly beyond the question of West Florida, to include East Florida as well, even though Governor Folch had no authority there. At the same time, Congress was responding to Madison's request, and on January 15 passed what became known as the No Transfer Act. Stating that Congress "cannot without serious inquietude see any part of the said territory pass into the hands of any foreign Power; and that a due regard to their own safety compels them to provide under certain contingencies, for the temporary occupation of the said territory," it authorized the president to do exactly that. The act, presuming from the earlier presidential decree that the United States already had a valid claim to all of West Florida (even though Governor Folch and the Spanish still occupied the eastern section), specifically gave authority to act in East Florida as well. Although technically the act was to remain confidential, it soon became public knowledge (leaked by Federalist legislators) and served as the first explicit statement, and warning, by the United States that it would not countenance new European encroachments in the neighborhood.

Mathews and McKee were appointed commissioners to implement the act, with instructions that authorized them to negotiate with Folch for an "amicable surrender of possession." As for East Florida, they were to sound out the situation there, and "should [they] find an inclination in the Governor of East Florida," to negotiate a similar deal with him. In both areas, moreover, they were instructed to be on the alert for possible foreign designs to occupy the country and, "on the first undoubted manifestation of the approach of a force for that purpose," to "pre-occupy" the area.[1] As far as President Madison was concerned, this was good contingency planning—the British had been put on notice that any effort on their part to occupy Florida during the impending hostilities would be resisted, the Spanish had been reminded that the United States had a vital interest in the Floridas, and commissioners had been appointed to protect American interests in the area.

But there was more to it than that. Mathews, in spite of his age, was not a passive figure; he had good contacts with the settlers in southern Georgia, investments in the area, and a desire to see American influence expand. Madison knew this when he made him commissioner, they both were aware of the benefits that had accrued as a result of the West Florida events, and one can only guess at the winks and nods that were inherent in their conversations. Both men, it can be assumed, expected him to seize such opportunities as presented themselves. Madison, perhaps, did not expect Mathews to create his own opportunities. The line between acting as agent, or as agent provocateur, was thin and undefined.

Mathews and McKee, on returning to the area, found that Folch had been reined in by his superiors in Havana, instructed not to hand over the territory under any circumstances, and provided with funds (though not troops) to defend it. With Baton Rouge and its ex-republicans now subject to U.S. law, the threat to Mobile had dissipated, and the West Florida situation would remain unchanged for the time being. Mathews as a result turned his attention to East Florida, but he apparently made minimal if any efforts to initiate a negotiation with the Spanish authorities there. Instead, he decided, after a visit to the border at St. Marys River, that the presence of a number of British smugglers constituted a sufficient threat to justify taking action under the second part of his instructions. Unable however, to get support either from the American settlers in the area (who were happy enough with the lax Spanish rule), or the American military, he decided to follow the example of the settlers in the Baton Rouge area and launch his own patriotic liberation movement, but from southern Georgia, where he had friends.

The border between Georgia and Florida on the Atlantic coast is marked by the St. Marys River, which at the time provided easy access by its tributaries into United States territory. To the south, in Florida, lies Amelia, a Manhattan-sized sea island backed up on the land side by a maze of waterways ideal for laying-up or hiding small craft. The site was well suited for smuggling, and the growth of its one straggling town, Fernandina, stemmed directly from that activity—particularly in the years following 1808 when the United States both prohibited the slave trade, and then imposed a total embargo on American trade in a vain effort to gain leverage with the European powers. Virtually undefended and practically ungoverned, Amelia Island was an attractive target for anyone wishing to concoct a symbolic victory over Spain while at the same time taking over a profitable port and smuggling operation.

By March 1812, Mathews had raised his patriot army of several hundred men, and convinced the local U.S. Navy commander that his instructions as commissioner could be construed as to sanction the use of the commander's anti-smuggling gunboats. Across the river they went, and with a show of force which included the navy's gunboats, convinced the commander of the Spanish fort to surrender, along with his feeble garrison of ten men. A short-lived Republic of Florida was declared, and the patriot army moved south to invest St. Augustine, where it promptly bogged down in the face of more serious opposition.

The news, when it reached Washington in April, was a severe embarrassment to Madison, who wrote to Jefferson that "in E. Florida, Mathews has been playing a strange comedy, in the face of common sense, as well as of his instructions. His extravagances place us in the most distressing dilemma."[2] While the president and the new secretary of state James Monroe tried to defend themselves with publication of Mathew's instructions, which clearly did not countenance a self-initiated occupation of foreign territory, some degree of collusion was all too evident. Monroe rapidly removed Mathews from command for overstepping his instructions, while U.S. officials and troops were ordered to Amelia to restore order and seek a Spanish pardon for the American settlers who had taken part in the rebellion. However, considering the near probability of war with Great Britain, and faced with an obvious lack of Spanish ability to control the situation, Madison could not safely withdraw the troops. The occupation continued until spring 1813, long after the rapid rise and fall of the inglorious Republic of Florida.

But the damage was done. While the so-called patriot movements in West and East Florida had been largely instigated and driven by adventurers, it was clear that the Madison administration had put few barriers in their way, was implicated in more than tangential fashion, and was prepared to rake in the benefits. For Don Luis de Onís, staunch defender of Spanish sovereignty and diplomatic cynic, the events were clear proof that the American strategy was to whittle away at the vulnerable Spanish borderlands whenever and wherever possible. As he wrote a decade later in a memorial on his tenure in the United States, the Florida incursions were confirmation that "our weakness disclosed to the United States that they might, without risk, attempt to unite to their territory those possessions of the monarch that most suited their wishes." Moreover, he added, "the United States have formed their plan with wisdom and mature thought, they follow it fearlessly, regardless of who is governing."[3] This, then, was the mindset with which the envoy would enter the crucial years of his mission to Washington. Nor was Onís wrong; the Madison administration, like Jefferson's beforehand and Monroe's to follow, most decidedly had their eye on acquiring Florida from Spain, and diplomatic pressure as well as insurrections were equally useful tools to that end.

For the Spanish American patriots, the events in Florida were rather peripheral to their immediate concerns. On the other hand, as they were

4. Filibusters, American and Émigré

increasingly on the defensive in South America after the fall of the Venezuelan republic, they could not fail to note that Spain's grip on its colonial empire might be weaker in North America.

Events were conspiring to test that idea, this time in Mexico. Even though the initial impetus for events there came from a revolutionary movement that had already been crushed, the Madison administration would once again be implicated in a filibuster into Spanish territory.

Miguel Hidalgo, the leader of the first Mexican revolt, had been captured and executed in July 1811, and the royalist forces were for the moment victorious. But, two months after Hidalgo's death, a prosperous creole rancher named José Bernardo Gutiérrez de Lara turned up at the American border town of Natchitoches claiming that he had been appointed as an agent of the Hidalgo forces to travel to the United States in search of arms and, if possible, official help. His credentials, he told his questioners, had unfortunately been lost, along with his money, during an ambush by royalist forces, but he claimed to have no diplomatic status, only the rank of lieutenant colonel in the revolutionary forces (as indeed he was). His story was plausible enough to convince the local Indian agent John Sibley, who became his prime contact, that Gutiérrez's presence and purported mission might be useful to the United States. Uncertain however how to handle this quasi-diplomatic agent, Sibley—who had already informed Washington of the Spaniard's presence and objectives—encouraged Gutiérrez to make his case to the national authorities. Gutiérrez eventually wrote to both Secretary of State Monroe and Secretary of War William Eustis describing his mission, exaggerating the potential revolutionary forces back in Mexico, and requesting an opportunity to plead the revolutionary case in the capital city. When he got a favorable reply from Washington, Gutiérrez set off for the capital overland, his expenses footed by Sibley. He arrived in Washington in December, having been well received along the way, particularly in Tennessee, where anti–Spanish sentiment continued to be strong.

In Washington, Gutiérrez found that he had been passed into the care of the State Department, where John Graham, Secretary Monroe's Spanish speaking expert, acted as his escort. He met several times with Eustis and Monroe, and once with President Madison, and while those conversations were positive in tone and potential assistance was discussed, no commitments were made. Gutiérrez in fact bridled at the suggestion, made by both Eustis and Monroe, that America's claim to Texas up to the Rio Grande might justify an invasion and American occupation. (They presumably had the West Florida situation, which was unfolding at the time, in mind as a precedent.) Gutiérrez, who came from the Rio Grande area, may have been a bit of a country hick but all the same was alert and shrewd: "Maria Santisima, help me and rescue me from these men!"[4] he wrote in his diary upon hearing the suggestion that these gringos might ignore Mexican rights to his own land.

Although no promises were made by the American officials, there had been enough talk about contingencies that might arise if the United States were to go to war against Spain's ally, Great Britain, to give Gutiérrez hope that a renewed Mexican uprising would eventually get support. Monroe and Madison were likewise intrigued enough over the possibilities offered by Gutiérrez to keep him friendly and available. They offered him travel money to return to New Orleans, and Graham wrote him a letter of introduction to Governor William Claiborne. With the situation in Mexico clearly in a state of flux in spite of the defeat of Hidalgo's army, Washington's view was that keeping an insurgent agent at hand might be useful.

While in Washington, Bernardo Gutiérrez met with a number of other dissidents, including the Venezuelan Telésforo de Orea, whom he considered a fine gentleman but too haughty for his taste, and whom he clearly did not trust enough to accept as his translator. But his most fateful encounter was with another recent arrival, José Álvarez de Toledo, a prominent dissident who had also been invited to Washington. Favorably impressed by the more worldly and charismatic Toledo, whom he described as "a man of great talents, and passionately devoted to the cause of Mexican liberty,"[5] Gutiérrez decided to travel to Philadelphia to further their discussions before leaving for New Orleans.

Toledo was, at about 32, some years younger than Gutiérrez, but a great deal more experienced in politics and dissent. Born in Cuba to peninsular parents, he had been educated in Spain, served as an officer in the Spanish navy, fought the French invaders, and was then selected to represent Santo Domingo at the Cádiz Cortes. During the Cortes, he fell in with the more liberal members, joined the semi-masonic secret society the Caballeros Racionales, and became a prominent spokesman for a group of dissident deputies from the American colonies. His open complaints about the leadership eventually made him fear arrest, he claimed, and so he fled with his wife to Philadelphia. He had arrived in September, and rapidly connected with William Duane, Manuel Torres and others, who helped him publish a substantial work that he must have written on shipboard. The

"*Manifesto*," as he grandly called it, was at one and the same time an effort to justify his political behavior and exile, and a propaganda screed calling for independence of the Spanish American colonies. It succeeded in both aims, and also in a third, unspoken one: to make him a recognized and respected actor in the struggle for the future of Spanish America.

The ambitious Toledo made clear that he wished to be invited to Washington to talk with administration officials. President Madison, somewhat leery about contact with a man so prominently at odds with the regency government, asked Alexander Dallas, the district attorney in Philadelphia, to give his recommendation. Dallas had a talk with Toledo and found him to be a talented propagandist in spite of a tendency to indiscretion, and proposed that he be received. Political Philadelphia being a small town, the Spanish minister Luis de Onís of course missed little of this commotion surrounding the new arrival; he had already spotted Toledo as potential trouble, put him under surveillance, and was attempting to recruit a talented liberal editor and writer, Miguel Cabral de Noroña, to write articles to counter the effect made by Toledo's *Manifesto*.[6] Onís and Toledo would eventually get to understand each other better, but for the moment watchful waiting was appropriate.

Toledo's trip to Washington took placed in mid to late December, shortly after Gutiérrez had met with the president. But when Toledo met with Monroe and the president, it was his discourse on alleged schemes of the British to establish bases in, or actually seize, a number of Caribbean islands—maybe even Cuba—that caught their attention, along with his views on a possible confederation of American republics. It was in the context of the Antilles, then, that Monroe offered Toledo money for his return to Cuba, and an introduction to the American commercial agent William Shaler (who in fact was in the process of transferring to New Orleans). For the two Virginians, whose party had always coveted Cuba, the prospect of having a Shaler-Toledo team on the island to inform them of Caribbean developments, maybe even encourage them, had its obvious attractions.

But Álvarez de Toledo did not go to Cuba. He and Guttiérez met, walked around the Capitol building to admire its architecture, and agreed to meet again in Philadelphia. In that subsequent meeting, it appears, Toledo began to see New Spain, or Mexico, as a potentially more fruitful field of action than Cuba, which was a tougher target as it remained faithful to the regency. He and Gutiérrez may have considered possible courses of action, but it was not to be joint action. Toledo remained in Philadelphia rather than raising sedition in the Caribbean, while Gutiérrez left for New

Orleans in early February 1812 to try his hand at assisting the patriots in Mexico.

New Orleans and its region made a fine place for this kind of intrigue. Its racially and nationally mixed population had correspondingly mixed loyalties and resentments, its borders were porous, a fleet of smugglers and pirates operated openly in Barataria Bay, speculation and sharp business were prevalent, public officers were often venal, and even the U.S. military commander of the region, James Wilkinson, was known to have been in the pay of the Spanish. All that made it a major center of expansionist schemes and piratical ventures, most of them directed at Spanish shipping or possessions in Texas and Florida. Over the years, Blount, Burr, and others had plotted to replace the Spanish in Texas, and there was no shortage of adventurers, drifters, horse traders, and would-be plunderers to man potential and actual cross-border raids. Even the Neutral Ground between the Calcasieu and Sabine Rivers, set up in 1806 to keep apart would-be troublemakers in Louisiana and the Mexican province of Texas, had instead turned into a no-man's land, a place where anything was permitted.

In the midst of all these activities and threats, which included revolutionary activity and widespread Indian raids in Mexico proper, the Spanish authorities remained highly distrustful of American intentions, and on high alert. The undermanned Spanish consulate in New Orleans tried to keep Onís, the Texas governor, and the governor general in Havana informed of hostile events, both real and suspected. But in the local political climate, and because it was not fully accredited as a diplomatic mission, the consulate's protests to the local authorities about suspicious activities were seldom acted on with sympathy.

In this atmosphere, Governor William Claiborne preferred to have the newly-arrived Gutiérrez out of town, away from suspected and known French, English or Spanish spies, and closely escorted by William Shaler, who had arrived only shortly beforehand from Cuba. After a few weeks in the city, during which Gutiérrez lodged with Shaler (presumably the better to keep an eye on him), the two took the twenty-day barge trip upriver to Natchitoches, where they arrived by late April and lodged with the Indian agent John Sibley. Keeping in mind the neutrality restrictions, they began modestly with propaganda, which they could easily get into Texas across the neighboring neutral zone. Maintaining a plausible semblance of neutrality was important to Washington, where Monroe was preoccupied with preparations for war with Britain and concerned not to inflame relations with Spain in a way that could give the British an excuse to intervene on behalf of their ally. The cautious secretary of state gave no written instructions to the American officials in Louisiana; nothing was on the record.

But Washington was quite aware that some sort of filibuster was contemplated—Shaler kept them informed of Gutiérrez's efforts to raise a body of armed men to assemble in the neutral zone, and had even recommended arming the Mexican rebels. His advice to Gutiérrez, on the other hand (at least as he reported it to Washington), was not to move without a U.S. government go-ahead signal. Somewhat impatient and frustrated at this weak and ambivalent support from the American officials, Gutiérrez moved forward to discuss participation in an expedition with local military figures, among whom was an army lieutenant, Augustus Magee. Things moved forward rapidly after Magee, sensing a better opportunity than his flagging army career, resigned his commission in late June to openly gather the core of a filibustering group. He signed up over a hundred men, assuming that if the operation went forward, more men could be recruited among Tejano rebels and the rootless fellows in the neutral zone.

Gutiérrez leaned increasingly on Magee. He needed the military officer to recruit and lead the armed men, while Magee for his part needed the sponsorship of Gutiérrez to give a filibuster some legitimacy in Mexican eyes. It was an alliance of convenience, and not unfortunately of fully shared objectives. Shaler, increasingly an observer, began to sense that his admonitions of caution were not being followed, and lost his trust in Gutiérrez, whom he now saw as imprudent. But he did little to stop the actual process.

By early August, Magee was ready, and—taking advantage of a short illness of Shaler's—launched the operation into Spanish territory. Gutiérrez left a week later, but not, Shaler reported, without first apologizing for having deceived him.[7] (One can only conjecture as to the sincerity of any apology, or the veracity of the report.)

The expedition started auspiciously. Magee crossed the neutral ground with a hundred and thirty men, and bloodlessly captured Nacogdoches in Texas. Bernardo (as Gutiérrez was generally known) joined the force at the middle of the month and began issuing republican manifestoes, while keeping Shaler informed of the progress by letter. The victory ensured a flow of new recruits, and the army paused for most of a month to reorganize and reach out to local rebels. By mid–September, it had grown to a motley but impressive force of some 800 American adventurers, Mexican-Tejano rebels, and disaffected Indians, grandly calling themselves the Republican Army of the North.

The confident expedition left Nacagdoches in September. A November setback found them besieged at La Bahia, however, and began to expose differences between the Mexican and American groups. Another setback was Magee's illness and death in February. Nonetheless, the army rallied, broke the siege of the surrounding royalist army in February, and by April 1, 1813, it had defeated the royalist defenders and captured San Antonio, the capital of Texas.

Meanwhile, back in Washington, Secretary Monroe, forced by this runaway development to pay attention to what had been only winked at months earlier, sought to counter any accusations of American complicity in the raid by instructing Shaler to stay in Natchitoches without contacting the rebel army. Other efforts, Monroe reported, were also underway in an effort to calm Spanish indignation over the evident breach of neutrality.

Following the capture of San Antonio, the Army of the North began to suffer from its internal divisions. Gutiérrez's complicity in the brutal execution of fifteen royalist officers marked a turning point, after which the Americans began to separate themselves from him, and even the expedition itself. The American contingent in particular was alienated by Bernardo's insistence that, in spite of the Americans' leading contribution to the defeat to the royalist forces, the victory was for the Mexican cause alone. The republican government of Texas which Bernardo had set up was also dismissed by the Americans as filled with incompetents and crooks, and his leadership was increasingly damned as headstrong and erratic. The army's successes were beginning to look hollow, and indeed the height of the expedition's achievements had been reached.

Back east, Álvarez de Toledo had been watching these developments with considerable interest, and perhaps not a little jealousy. He had not been in touch with official Washington since his trip there in early 1812, but while considering his next steps he had become a key figure in Philadelphia's dissident community. Toledo and his wife had been joined in their boarding house by the old revolutionary Juan Picornell, recently fled from the fall of Caracas and hoping to practice medicine in the city. Also lodging at the boarding house was the Vermont patriot agitator Ira Allen (Revolutionary War hero Ethan's younger brother), who had developed an active interest in the South American revolutionary movement

4. Filibusters, American and Émigré

both from family tradition and a calculation that it might help restore his fortune. With this nucleus of prominent champions of liberty, the boarding house naturally became a minor center of South American dissident activity, or at least revolutionary scheming. Equally naturally, its tenants attracted the close attention of the Spanish mission's agents, one of whom, Onís bragged, had actually infiltrated the Toledo circle.[8] But as news of the growing successes of the Revolutionary Army of the North reached Philadelphia, members of the group began to think that it was time to escape the intrigues of the city and join the actual struggle for liberation of Mexico. Toledo, left out of what was beginning to look like a successful operation, nonetheless saw opportunity for himself.

Before departing for the frontier, however, Álvarez de Toledo made an extraordinary move. Calling on Luis de Onís in early October of 1812, he offered to betray the expedition. Admitting that he had been in contact with the U.S. government with the aim of fomenting rebellion, he claimed to have realized that his basic loyalty was to Spain and wished to be treated (as Onís reported their conversation) "with the benevolence with which a father treats a wayward son, [but] he would not be satisfied with the pardon unless, before obtaining it, he gave proofs of a repentance consecrated by some essential service."[9] Arranging the neutralization of the rebel force would have a price, however: Toledo asked for five thousand pesos. Onís, perhaps caught by surprise but certainly suspicious of this sudden approach, did not reject the audacious proposal, but claimed he did not have such a large sum at hand and could not at the moment satisfy the request. No commitments were made and no follow-up taken by either man, but a card had been played, and both would remember that it was on the table.

Two months later, in December, Toledo left for Pittsburgh and the long trip down the rivers to Natchez and then up to Natchitoches. His party of a dozen men included Picornell, who had decided to join the expedition as its propagandist, and was armed with a portable printing press. In the party was also one of their Philadelphia group, a Colonel Nathaniel Cogswell, whose growing suspicions led him to desert the party (or perhaps he was expelled: the versions vary). Cogswell then wrote letters to Shaler and Gutiérrez from Pittsburgh, warning that Toledo was in fact a Spanish plant, a kind of mole in the patriot movement. Cogswell's suspicions, however, were largely circumstantial in nature, and Shaler chose to ignore them.[10] To the contrary: when Toledo and his group finally arrived at Natchitoches in April 1813, they found Shaler ready to cooperate.

In fact, Shaler had become disturbed enough by repeated reports of Gutiérrez's mismanagement of the campaign to see in the newly-arrived Toledo a man of distinction, a man who could consolidate the advances made by seizing leadership of the expedition. Soon the two were plotting together, establishing an anti-Gutiérrez propaganda machine through Picornell's specialty newssheets the *Gaceta de Texas* and *El Mexicano*, and building support for Toledo across the border—including obtaining Toledo's nomination as a delegate from Nacogdoches to the new revolutionary government in San Antonio. Waiting their time, they used the dissatisfaction in San Antonio to undermine Gutiérrez. The situation was ripe by mid-July, at which point Toledo travelled to San Antonio to try his hand at seizing command. (Shaler, who left with him, had to turn back on the command of Washington.) In the new republic's capital, Toledo was quickly able to exploit the general dissatisfaction with Gutiérrez, and strong support from the American faction, to maneuver himself into command of the army. Several days later, cornered politically, without adequate support from the Mexicans, and faced with the threat of an approaching royalist army, Gutiérrez resigned his posts in disgust and left Texas.

Wise or not, the change of command was too late. The royalist army soon arrived at San Antonio, offering battle at the Medina River. On August 18, 1813, Toledo led the Republican Army into what turned out to be an ambush and a crushing defeat. Toledo, Picornell, and those who could escape the rout fell back to Louisiana, where Gutiérrez had preceded them. There, the would-be Texas republicans would continue to plot new incursions into Texas with the other adventurers and patriots who frequented the place.

Surprisingly, there were few recriminations. Monroe, perhaps with a premonition of the upcoming disaster, had tried to cover his tracks in June by a letter rebuking Shaler for having exceeded his instructions.[11] But Onís, who had complained earlier about the recruitment of the force, uncharacteristically did not vociferously denounce the administration's evident connivance in the actual expedition until much later, in 1816. He had not, it seems, taken very seriously the group's chances of success, and had other issues more important than a complaint about another failed invasion of Spanish territory. Even more surprisingly, Toledo somehow escaped blame for his abject failure at the battle of the Medina, and continued to be respected and trusted by the other Spanish American patriots lurking in New Orleans. The Madison administration, however, did keep a closer eye on the volatile border area following the failed filibuster, actively—and largely successfully—discouraging any further filibusters across the Texas border.

The story of the Republican Army of the North, as well as that of the Republic of Florida, were of course small and unimportant incidents leading up to and during the War of 1812, or for that matter the titanic European struggle going on at the same time. America's attention, briefly attracted to South America before the war by the initial anti-colonial developments there, was now strongly focused on the war, with only the *Aurora* still regularly championing independence for the Spanish colonies. Moreover, American grain exporters and shippers were doing a very good business selling to the Spanish regency and to the British armies fighting against Napoleon, thanks to a special exemption from the British blockade of American ports that Onís had helped arrange. Trade with Spanish America on the other hand had dropped severely, with only a few brave entrepreneurs willing to run the British blockade with arms for the rebels.

All the same, the struggle between the Spanish government and its rebel South American colonies had continued its uneven and often bloody course. The United Provinces of the Rio de la Plata remained self-governing and free of Spanish royalists, but engaged in a series of coups and inter-provincial conflicts, as well as with the Portuguese empire in neighboring Brazil. Chile was also self-governing but rent with internal, factional feuds, while neighboring Peru on the other hand remained strongly loyal to Ferdinand and the regency council. Along the Caribbean coast, the patriots had found a refuge and base, after the fall of Caracas, in the interior of Venezuela or in the neighboring United Provinces of New Granada. Simón Bolívar had even succeeded in establishing a second Venezuelan republic for a short time in 1813 and 1814, before being obliged to retreat once again to New Granada. In short, nothing was decided, but the reestablishment of the monarchy in Madrid meant that the royalists could be expected to take the offensive before long.

Of the American envoys who had been sent to Spanish America in 1810, only Joel Poinsett managed to weather the difficulties of the wartime years. In Venezuela, Robert Lowry had been asked by the victorious royalist forces to leave Guaira in early 1813. And William Shaler, as noted above, had left Cuba for the United States and his ambitious but ultimately frustrating Mexican adventure. Poinsett, on the other hand, had managed to operate in areas that had effectively broken away from royalist rule, and where his activist nature and lack of close supervision from Washington allowed him to play a dramatic and controversial role.

Poinsett had left the Rio de la Plata area in 1811, leaving the consulate in the hands of William Miller. Arriving in Chile, he found the province to be free of royalists but divided between rival aristocratic factions. Poinsett fell in with the faction of General José Miguel Carrera, a charismatic and wealthy leader who would overthrow the first junta in 1812 and become dictator. The two became close personal friends, and Poinsett became so identified with the Carrera faction that he even took a general's commission and an active and controversial part in one of the general's campaigns against the royalists in Peru. He was joined in support and sympathy for the Carrera faction by Captain David Porter, captain of the U.S.S. *Essex*, which was engaged in its famous campaign against British shipping in the Pacific, and using Valparaiso as a base. Poinsett was also instrumental in assisting American merchants who sold arms, and some even their ships, to the Chilean patriots for use against the Spanish. As in peacetime Buenos Aires earlier, Poinsett's activities and freely voiced opinions infuriated the resident British.

Unfortunately, Carrera was an ineffective leader in spite of his personal charm and magnetism; he was sacked after a disastrous military campaign and replaced by the rival general, Bernardo O'Higgins. But Carrera was no quitter; he seized power again, only to be finally driven out of office when the key Argentine general José de San Martin threw his influence behind O'Higgins. Carrera had to flee. So when the *Essex* was finally forced to surrender to a superior British force in March 1814, Poinsett found himself without friends or support in Santiago, and was obliged to sneak out of Chile on a Portuguese merchant ship bound for Buenos Aires. It was just as good. By the end of the year, the royalists were back in control in Santiago, while the patriots were in temporary exile.

In Buenos Aires, Miller, finding the consular fees badly reduced in wartime conditions and wanting to concentrate on his business, had given up the consular function in 1813. Poinsett, who much wanted to get back to the United States but could not get a ship in the wartime conditions, occupied himself in negotiating a commercial agreement with the junta. He appointed Thomas Lloyd Halsey, another local businessman, to take his place when he finally found transport home. Poinsett arrived back in South Carolina only in May 1815, well after the war was over.[12]

Both wars, in North America and in Europe, had been winding down since mid-1814. Ferdinand had been restored to the Spanish throne in early 1813 and actually returned to his capital in 1814. In April 1814, Napoleon abdicated and was imprisoned on Elba. With the French threat thus seemingly eliminated, Britain had no reason to continue the war with the United States, and peace talks began in September. The last half of the year nonetheless saw important battles in America: the British burned Washington but were repulsed at Baltimore; a British invasion from Canada was stopped at Plattsburgh, and Andrew Jackson drove a British expedition out of Pensacola in November, briefly occupying the town over Onís' strong objections. None of those events however significantly changed the course of the negotiations, and the Treaty of Ghent ended the war with minimal changes to the pre-war situation. Jackson's subsequent early 1815 victory at New Orleans was a bonus for the Americans, entitling them to believe they had actually won the war.

Peace in Europe and North America however by no means meant peace in South America or Mexico. Bourbon regimes were back on the thrones of Spain and France, and King Ferdinand was determined to stamp out the rebellions that had broken out in the colonies while he was a prisoner of Napoleon.

Chapter 5

Bringing American Privateers into the Fight

The end of the war in Europe and the restoration of the Bourbon monarchies would change the nature of the struggle for South American independence, bring the United States more directly into that struggle, and complicate the efforts of the government to maintain a neutral stance.

Ferdinand VII had been released from his French captivity in early 1814. His victory was not however of his own making; it had been earned by the sacrifices of the Spanish people during the bloody peninsular campaign, and thanks as well to Napoleon's disastrous Russian adventure. On his triumphant return to Madrid, Ferdinand failed to sense how much had changed during his seven-year absence. Acclaimed by his conservative supporters as "The Desired One," and an absolutist by temperament, he was flattered into a conviction that Spain's problems could be resolved by a return to the old ways, and was determined to reestablish Spain's imperial grandeur by rolling back the clock. He annulled the liberal constitution of 1812 that had given the colonies a voice in government. He caused many of its drafters and supporters to be arrested, reconstituted the Inquisition, and declared invalid all the colonial juntas and laws passed since 1808. In place of the constitutional government, he reestablished the Bourbon principle of royal sovereignty and recentralized—at least on paper—colonial administration. Those policies, plus his erratic rule—heavily influenced as it was by an obscurantist *camarilla* of archconservative palace favorites— assured that his reign would be a troubled one.

In the provinces of Spanish America, where the various juntas had been fighting against the remaining imperial officers for local control, Ferdinand's intent to return to a centralized autocracy only sharpened the struggle. The general population, finally relieved from the Bonapartist threat, was divided between loyalty to Spain and a desire for greater self-rule. But the juntas, even those proclaiming full loyalty to the regency council, had no desire for a return to rule by arrogant peninsular courtiers, a mercantilist trade policy, or the Inquisition. Ferdinand's retrograde policies simply sharpened their desire for autonomy and nudged the undecided among them toward independence. However, the king's determination to bend the juntas and their supporters to his will meant that it would be a long struggle.

King Ferdinand had ascended the throne of a country that had been bled dry by the long peninsular war and whose political demands were largely ignored by the major powers in the post–Napoleonic settlements. Spain's desires had been equally brushed aside by the British in their peace negotiations with the United States that culminated in the late–1814 Treaty of Ghent. The Bourbons had been returned to the thrones of Spain and France by the other European powers, but none of them provided Ferdinand with meaningful support for his ambitions to regain Louisiana or to reestablish effective Spanish rule in Florida or the rest of the at-risk American colonies. In spite of this initial rebuff, Ferdinand was determined to bring the separatist American colonies to heel. Formation of the arch-reactionary Holy Alliance in 1815 gave him hope that, even though Spain had not been invited, he could eventually bring the other European monarchies onto his side in crushing the rebellions.

Concern that King Ferdinand might succeed in this effort also became a significant factor in postwar American diplomacy toward Spain and its colonies. From the time of Jefferson's administration, sentiment had been solidifying in American political circles that the European powers should be denied opportunity to intervene in Western Hemisphere affairs whenever possible. As a result, in conducting relations with the breakaway regimes and their agents, great caution would be necessary to avoid any steps that would allow Spain a pretext to rally the Holy Alliance to its side. It would mean, to some extent, showing greater sensitivity to Onís's denunciations of alleged neutrality violations. It also suggested careful avoidance of any steps that would stir royal sensitivities, particularly by providing any meaningful form of recognition to the rebel regimes.

The determined King Ferdinand would not wait for the Holy Alliance. Already, in the summer of 1814, he had appointed General Pablo Morillo as expedition commander and captain general, with a mission to bring the rebel colonies back into obedience to the throne. By early 1815, Morillo had gathered a force of nearly ten thousand men and sixty ships and set sail for the north coast of South America. After regrouping on the island of Margarita in April, Morillo took his troops onto *terra firma* in nearby Venezuela, where they met up with remaining royalist forces in the province and occupied Caracas in May. Pushing rapidly westwards along the coast, they joined up with more royalist forces in Santa Marta and fell upon Cartagena, which surrendered in December of the same year after a five-month siege. The fall of that city-state involved the capture and harsh imprisonment of several dozen Americans who had resided there since its unilateral declaration of independence in 1811, a situation that became yet another irritant in U.S.-Spanish relations. General Morillo, unconcerned and probably not even aware of the murderous reputation that he was gaining in the American press, methodically continued his subjugation of rebellious New Granada. By May of 1816, assisted once again by royalist forces from the region, he had effectively defeated or driven off the rebel forces. The key areas of today's Venezuela, Colombia, Peru, Ecuador, and Chile were once again under royal control, as were the loyal Caribbean islands, including Cuba. Ferdinand's effort appeared to be ascendant.

But the rebel cause and its leaders had not been defeated. The provinces around the Rio de la Plata remained free of royalist control, although still riven by regional and factional rivalries and warfare. Simón Bolívar had left the mainland to plot a renewal of the fight for independence from a base on the island of Haiti, which had declared and defended its independence from France since 1804. José Carrera and Bernardo O'Higgins had fled from Chile to Argentina, the first to Buenos Aires, the second to Mendoza, each plotting rivaling schemes for the liberation of the west coast of the continent. As was also the case in Mexico, the South American fight against colonial rule had devolved into a guerrilla strategy, awaiting the opportunity to resume larger-scale campaigns against the royalist forces.

The fact that land campaigns against the royalist forces were for the moment out of the question, however, brought to the fore another option—namely, to attack Spain, and its hold on its colonies, from the sea. With the end of the European wars, Spanish merchant and naval vessels were once again making the voyage to and from America. Seizure of those merchant ships, or the royal treasure ships, would not only fray royalist lines of supply to and from the Americas, it would provide a useful source of

5. Bringing American Privateers into the Fight

loot to help finance the revolts. Both Argentine and Venezuelan patriots (the latter from their exile in the Caribbean) would establish navies of a sort, but not until 1814 and later, when their circumstances permitted. But neither region had much of a maritime tradition, and would always lack qualified ships and sailors. In the circumstances, the only recourse was to wage war by proxy, and to issue commissions to entrepreneurs willing to fit out privateers that would harass Spanish trade by seizing prize ships, under the flag of one or another of the rebel juntas.

It was not, of course, a new idea. The Caribbean had been a field of buccaneer or politically-sanctioned privateer activity for centuries, and treasure ships carrying the imperial specie to Spain had always been choice targets. The Spanish themselves had resorted on occasion to the practice, as when Spanish-flagged privateers operating from Cuba and Puerto Rico plagued neutral-flagged shipping to rebel-held territories in 1812 and 1813. Britain and America, at war with each other but each determined to maintain its neutral status between Spain and its breakaway provinces, had a common interest in this case. Britain, the Spanish regency's chief ally but at the same time the main neutral-flag trader with the rebels, soon persuaded the Spanish government to cease issuing the troublesome privateer commissions.[1]

The first rebel regime to offer privateer commissions to enterprising sailors who would seek their fortune by attacking Spanish ships was the city-state of Cartagena in New Granada, which had declared itself independent in 1811. Louis-Michel Aury, an ex–French sailor who had joined the ranks of Caribbean privateers, was one of the first takers. Although he had received an earlier commission from the Venezuelan envoy Pedro Gual, he switched to the new flag and in 1813 was appointed as commander of Cartagena's growing squadron of privateers. Cartagena's privateer commissions also found a ready market in New Orleans, where the Spanish were detested and a nest of pirate-smugglers already operated out of secluded but nearby Barataria Bay. Tolerated because of the merchandise, slaves and money they smuggled into the city, Barataria buccaneers such as Jean and Pierre Lafitte, Dominique You, and Renato Beluche (all of them French-born) began in 1813 to operate on occasion under the Cartagena flag. As privateers commissioned by a de facto if not actually recognized rebel regime, the pirates could now add a veneer of legality to their seizures of Spanish vessels.

The Barataria base, however, was closed down by the Madison administration in 1814, after the illegal smuggling and slave trade became too egregious to ignore. The pirates-turned-privateers needed another base of operations. The New Orleans merchants were of course pleased to help, in order to keep up the profitable business of supplying the privateer ships and receiving their confiscated cargo. Once the 1812 war was over, they helped set up a new base down the coast (on Spanish, not American, land) at Galveston Bay, with Louis Aury as their partner.

What brought the privateer campaign up to a scale that constituted true and damaging proxy warfare against Spain, however, was Argentine cooperation with American venture capitalists. The United Provinces of Rio de la Plata, as the region was then called, were not at all united; a number of the provinces had gone their own way or were still in royalist hands, and wars and changes of government were regular occurrences. But the area around Buenos Aires had remained self-governing since 1810, providing a temporary refuge for other rebel leaders, and its leaders were interested in expanding contacts with the United States. Recollections of the 1810 Aguirre-Saavedra mission to Washington and Joel Poinsett's mission in South America were all favorable, and a small but active American business community in the city encouraged further connections. The juntas had even, in 1813 and 1814, sent messages to President Madison suggesting closer ties, but in the press of wartime it appears that Washington had never bothered to answer.

By 1815, the newly organized Argentine navy had had some local successes in the struggle against separatists in the Banda Oriental (roughly modern Uruguay), but for lack of local maritime resources was not capable of far-flung operations. With the encouragement of members of the resident American business community, the regime decided also to issue privateer commissions. Not surprisingly, most of the commissions were at first issued to resident Americans who had assumed local citizenship. Scraping up vessels and crews, a number of those investors had initial successes that well justified their risk. Among them was Delaware captain Thomas Taylor, whose privateer *Zephir* had sunk following a highly profitable privateering cruise. David Curtis DeForest, a Connecticut merchant who resided in Buenos Aires as a merchant and auctioneer, was also involved as consignee of much prize merchandise. Other local Americans interested in expansion of the privateer business were the ex-consul William Miller, the new consul William Halsey, and John C. Zimmerman, who had been selling American arms to the junta.

Stimulated by these initial successes and the encouragement of the resident Americans, the Argentine government promulgated a set of regulations for privateering in 1816. The regulations permitted issuance of commissions (or letters of marque) to non-citizens, but required that the owners post bond for good behavior, have their prizes adjudicated and confiscated property sold at admiralty courts in Buenos Aires, and generally followed the requirements of international law. (Two exceptions, however, would cause problems for U.S. interests: one that allowed the issuing of commissions to foreigners even if they had never set foot in the territory, and a second one that allowed captains to send their prizes to admiralty courts other than the one in Buenos Aires.) With the international legal proprieties thus largely satisfied, the Argentines gave six blank commissions to Taylor and supported his proposal that he return to the Chesapeake Bay area to see if he could find American investors and sea captains willing to help the young regime harass imperial Spain by attacking its shipping. By involving Americans in the liberation struggle, however, this step would create new legal complications, both for them and for the administration's effort to remain neutral.

Thomas Taylor arrived in Baltimore in January of 1816, and found a ready audience for his business proposals. He had arrived at a propitious time because the city, and particularly the maritime business, was in a deep recession. The normally bustling and brawling town had led the nation during the War of 1812 in fitting out sleek and speedy privateers that had been able to run the blockade and play havoc on British commerce. But with the end of the war and the resumption of normal shipping, the city's fleet had become noncompetitive. Ships were laid up, sailors unemployed, and trade slow; capability was looking for an outlet. Baltimore merchants, struggling for business, were interested in Spanish America for new business but needed market connections. Moreover, Baltimore was a town with a nonconformist streak, and with its many Catholic residents it was also closely attuned and sympathetic to the Spanish Americans' grievances against their imperial masters. In short, Taylor had picked a promising market.

Taylor first approached Darcy and Didier, a local merchant house that owned a number of laid-up ex-privateer vessels that it was eager to put to use.[2] He offered a proposition to them and other potential investors that would create a close nexus of American and Argentine interests. The Baltimore investors would take the risk of arming and manning the ships and get fifty percent of any profits in return, while DeForest, as *armador* in Buenos Aires, would obtain the Argentine commissions, post the bonds, represent the owners in Argentine admiralty cases, and dispose of their prizes through his auction house for a ten percent fee.³ It was a tempting offer, as the ships and men were readily available and the potential earnings enough to justify the risks.

There was, however, a problem: for an American citizen to fit out a ship in an American port, in order to prey on the commerce of a friendly state such as Spain was, on the face of it, illegal under the neutrality legislation. But the Miranda expedition from New York had proven that a loophole in the 1794 law could be used: if a ship was not actually armed in a U.S. port, and captained by an American citizen, it could not be seized or detained by the customs officers. Suspicion that the law might be violated was not a punishable offense. The loophole had even been used by the Spanish, for example by Francisco Sarmiento who in 1810 had sent an armed ship the *Ramona* to the royalist forces in South America, but did not actually load the arms onto the ship until it was well out of port so as to avoid a possible violation.⁴ Moreover, the United States government had made the situation a bit easier when in July 1815 it had declared that its ports would be open to all ships, even if flying flags of states not recognized by the U.S. administration. That meant that privateers under the flags of the breakaway juntas could not be barred from using American ports, as long as they limited their visits to peaceful activities such as repairs, resupply, and so forth. So, it seemed, the letter of the law could be followed even as its intent was being circumvented. Provided, of course, that the government did not actively prosecute suspected cases.

A key issue, then, as to the viability of launching privateer operations against Spain from the United States would be the attitude of the Madison administration. The closure of the Barataria Bay operation had given little indication of the administration's thinking on the subject. It was violation of customs and slave traffic laws that had led to the intervention by the U.S. Navy, not the privateering operations there, and besides only one of the seven vessels seized at that time had been a privateer flying the flag of the rebel Cartagena junta.

But it was clear that the end of the European wars and the return of the Bourbons to the Spanish throne meant that Madison and Monroe had to tread more cautiously in dealing with Spain and the reactionary mood of Europe. Ministers had been exchanged with the Spanish court. Luis de Onís was finally fully accredited in Washington, in spite of the administration's distaste for his hectoring, not to mention his suspicious contacts with Federalist pro-secessionists during the war. He now had full authority and license to vent his government's anger at those American policies and behaviors that harmed Spain's interests. And even though Florida's future remained the major issue that perturbed the relations between Madison and Onís, the merchants had to take into account that it might not be politically wise for them to create yet another irritant to Spanish-American relations, by engaging in arguably hostile acts in U.S. ports.

Even so, that consideration was not enough to dissuade the ambitious Baltimoreans. Specific ventures began to take shape very rapidly. Henry Didier and John Darcy and their firm were in the project from the start. An informal group of major investors also formed, calling itself the "American Concern," and including the merchants Joseph Karrick, John Gooding, and Joseph Patterson, the ship captains Samuel Brown and John G. Johnston, and Matthew Murray, the sheriff. Supporting the main group, there developed a wider circle of privateer captains, suppliers, agents, and smaller investors who were ready to take shares in the individual ventures, sell goods and services to the ships, and provide a broader market presence and political base.

Public opinion in Baltimore, influenced by William Duane's *Aurora*, Hezekiah Nile's *Register*, and the *Baltimore Patriot*, was already generally favorable to the South American patriots. It was scarcely surprising then that many in the city warmly welcomed the prospects for greater employment, sales, and profits that a revival of privateering would bring, and were able to justify it under a humanitarian and patriotic label. There was of course opposition, or at least criticism, from other merchants and businessmen, and it is interesting to note that the town's leading merchants such as William Patterson,[5] Alexander Brown, Samuel Smith, or Robert Oliver (who did substantial business with royalist Mexico) refused any cooperation with the privateering crowd. But the general sentiment in the city, at least in the early years of this business, was probably well summed up by the *Patriot*, which commented on June 29, 1816—even as the first ships were being sent out—"We do not consider the sale of American vessels to the Spanish patriots, with a view to convert them into privateers, as an act of the least criminality; nor will the subsequent irregularities of their officers and crew at all change the nature of the original transaction."

In the prevailing atmosphere of civic boosterism combined with sympathy for the patriots, the gentlemen of the American Concern were able to find valuable sympathizers among the town's political figures. Chief among them was John Stuart Skinner, the postmaster—who, as prisoner of war exchange officer, had accompanied Francis Scott Key on the "star spangled banner" night two years earlier, when the British bombarded Baltimore. Skinner, an enthusiast for the patriot cause, was in fact more than a sympathizer; he had helped set up the Concern and would later become an investor. James McCulloch, the customs collector, was also a sympathizer, as was the renowned statesman and lawyer William Pinkney. Another potential sympathizer was Theodorick Bland, the local district court judge, who not incidentally was also Skinner's father-in-law. The fact that these government officials raised no objections to the privateer effort—indeed sympathized with it—helped create a permissive atmosphere in which it was assumed that there were no obstacles, legal or political, to proceeding. At the beginning, that was probably correct.

By summer, a number of Baltimore privateers were already at sea under the Argentine flag. Among the first were the *Romp* and the *Orb*, both of them Darcy and Didier-owned ships: speedy, clipper-type schooners built as privateers during the late war and mounting ten guns each. Taylor reserved one of the commissions for himself; he had a larger, more powerful ship built that he called the *Fourth of July*, which he took to sea in December. Further commissions arrived from Buenos Aires, some of them carried by a new Argentine envoy, Martín Thompson. By 1818, some twelve privateers had been fitted out in Baltimore, almost all of them under Argentine commissions. Baltimore's connection with Buenos Aires was solid, thanks to the American Concern and its members at both ends. During the height of the privateer campaigns, some 35 Argentine privateers would come to American ports for refitting, very often to Baltimore, where they could expect a safe welcome and friendly facilities for resupply. New Orleans was the second most active privateering port, fitting out some eight vessels by 1818 to sail under the Mexican or Venezuelan flags, while New York, Philadelphia, and Charleston followed with two ships each.

The owners and captains of the vessels were able to evade the neutrality laws by a simple procedure: they would depart port under their American registration, with a false destination and no armament on deck, thereby giving the customs collector no cause to stop them as armed vessels. The collector, of course, might have seen the vessel loading warlike supplies for weeks, but could take refuge behind the fact that he had no legal grounds to interfere, and could not stop the departure on suspicion alone. Then, often somewhere in American coastal waters, the putatively innocent merchant vessel would heave to, bring up the guns from below decks (or meet up with a supply ship carrying the cannon), paint a new

5. Bringing American Privateers into the Fight

name on the stern, and run up a new flag under the authority of its (previously hidden) foreign state commission. On occasion, the extra crewmembers needed to man a privateer were also added at that time, or even the nominal American captain replaced by the commission holder. The transformation complete, the privateer would head to a new destination, one where it could prey on Spanish shipping.

An occasional skipper or owner took a different path. One of the most conspicuous was James Chaytor, a Baltimore businessman and fervent supporter of the South American patriots, who had fought with the Venezuelan navy in 1814. In May 1816, before Taylor had come to town with his blank commissions, Chaytor bought the large, 16-gun schooner *Mammoth* in Baltimore with the intent to support the patriots in Buenos Aires. Taking the ship to Buenos Aires, he completed its transformation into a warship, his own self into an Argentine citizen, and then reflagged the ship as an Argentine navy vessel (but still under his ownership). With the renamed *Independencia del Sud*, he conducted four highly successful cruises, always following the correct procedures and returning his prizes to Buenos Aires as required by his commission. But the cash-strapped junta took most of his prize court winnings, and replaced them with worthless IOU's, so that when Chaytor returned to his family in Baltimore in 1821, he had no fortune to show for his successes.

Chaytor and the other privateers did not limit their activities to the Western Hemisphere. They also hunted for prizes off the coasts of Spain itself, and with such efficiency that by 1819 Spanish shipping was once again almost driven off the seas.

Their very successes, however, created problems for the privateers. According to international law, only a properly recognized admiralty court could award ownership of prize ships or seized cargo. The Argentines had indeed set up an appropriate system in Buenos Aires, and during the next five or so years some 37 prizes were adjudicated there. But Buenos Aires was far away from the normal hunting grounds, and a number of Argentine-flagged ships chose to take their prizes to more convenient and somewhat less rigorous court locations. After 1816, rebel capture of the Venezuelan island of Margarita made it available both for the licensing of Venezuelan privateers and as a self-proclaimed admiralty court for all comers. Deeper into the Caribbean, the Mexican port of Galveston was also taken over in 1816 by Louis Aury and his fleet of privateers, under the Mexican rebel flag. That port and its court were open to all, and particularly useful to those operators who had been driven out of Barataria. Its admiralty court, as well as one in Port au Prince, Haiti, were farcical clearing houses for plunder, openly serving the interests of the Caribbean privateers flying the flags of the current rebel Mexican junta, the defunct Cartagena one, or the new flag of Venezuela.

There were also many cases in which the captures were never taken to any prize court. Some ships, with low-value cargo, were simply stripped of such valuables as they had and then burned, or allowed to sail home with the privateer's prisoners. The confiscated goods could be disposed of informally in many Caribbean ports, or they could be broken down, repackaged, relabeled, and given false documentation in order to sell in the best market. Goods were even sold offshore to fishing vessels. But each of these informal methods involved selling the undocumented plunder at a deep discount.

Even when the privateers were able to obtain legal title to the seized property (questionable as it may have been) from the self-proclaimed admiralty courts, they still had a problem of disposing of the goods. The local markets (except for Buenos Aires) had very limited capacity, and consequently low prices. From Galveston, conveniently, the goods could still be smuggled into the New Orleans market, where not many questions were asked. Otherwise, the main markets were on the east coast of the United States, which meant that the privateers—particularly the American ones, who also had families to visit and moneys to deposit in the bank—had strong incentives to return to home waters. They could do so legally as the administration, over Onís's objections, allowed vessels of all flags free entry as long as they did not engage in warlike preparation while in port. The problem for the privateers was that a return to American ports might leave them open to prosecution, by exposing their irregular departures and subsequent questionable privateering activities.

The strongest, indeed perhaps the only, voice for legal action against the privateers was that of Don Luis de Onís. The Spanish minister had complained (without much success) of privateer activity from New Orleans since 1813; but since the beginning of 1816 his voice had assumed greater resonance in Washington, since he had been accepted as the fully accredited representative of a restored, bitter, and important European power that America needed to handle delicately. Onís had been prescient in seeing that the end of the War of 1812 would create a pool of unemployed American soldiers and sailors ready to cause mischief for Spain's American colonies, and he and his colleagues stationed in Spain's consulates were poised to root out and expose any such activities. In one of his first official

5. Bringing American Privateers into the Fight

communications to Secretary of State Monroe, he had complained about the administration's decision to open its ports to ships of all flags. "You cannot but know that this measure puts these factionists, not only on a footing of equality with the Spanish nation, but gives them advantages over all independent Powers, since, according to the laws of neutrality, the United States would not permit any independent nation to arm its vessels in their ports, or to sell prizes in them, as is permitted to these revolutionists."[6] Now, in the summer of 1816, his objection in principle having been ignored, he moved to specific complaints of alleged wrongdoing by American privateers under rebel flags.

As information began to stream in from Spanish consulates in New Orleans, Baltimore, Norfolk, and New York, Onís bombarded the Department of State with a series of diplomatic notes describing the ships being armed in American ports, their owners and captains, and demanded that the government take action to stop the ships from going to sea, or arrest the captains for violating the neutrality law. Secretary Monroe, and, after he left in March of 1817, Richard Rush, replied with temporizing, non-specific answers, and eventually with periodic diplomatic silences. They tried to explain that applicable United States law did not allow for arrests on the basis of suspicion—a fact that the Spanish minister, either deliberately or out of honest inability to understand such a lax and decentralized system of justice, chose to ignore. Gather the facts and take a case to court, was the basic advice of the secretaries of state gave to Onís. But the truth was that they were disinclined to recommend preemptive law enforcement action, both for the cited legal reasons and because American public opinion, as well as their own inclinations, were sympathetic to letting the privateers sail. Onís all the same continued to apply pressure to correct what he called a notorious and disavowed "speculative system of fitting out privateers and putting them under foreign flag … for the purpose of destroying Spanish commerce."[7]

By early 1817, Onís began to have information that he hoped might lead to arrests or even prosecution. Reports of the privateers' captures had begun to arrive, and some of the ships had even returned to American ports, giving the Spanish consuls specific information that could be presented to American officials. A case in point was the open arrival in Baltimore of the privateer *Mangoré*, previously the *Swift* of the same town, with merchandise allegedly confiscated from seized Spanish vessels and which the captain James Barnes had brought ashore without being questioned. Onís wrote several diplomatic notes, arguing not that there was a violation of the neutrality act but that, because the ship's seizures were already under litigation in New York, the *Mangoré* and its captain be detained in port while an investigation was conducted as to the nature of its seizures at sea and the ownership of the cargo. The ship however was allowed to sail, then brought back under an order from the U.S. Marshall, but finally released again, under bond. Fuming at both the permissive climate in Baltimore and the passivity of the administration, Onís wrote to Monroe about the way "in which the orders of the President are eluded in Baltimore, in order to heap injury upon injury on a friendly nation, and promote the revolution of its provinces. In vain will it be alleged, in order to cover this proceeding, that the laws are not sufficient to pursue, without a positive evidence, those citizens who commit hostilities against Spain."[8] He got neither apology nor corrective action.

It would get worse. Two months later, in March, the *Orb*, now reflagged as the Argentine privateer *Congreso*, showed up in its old port of Baltimore under the captaincy of José Almeida, a Baltimorean of Portuguese birth—who was a particular bête noir of Onís as he had also delivered guns to the rebels in Cartagena. Almeida had conducted two successful cruises off Spain and in the West Indies, during which his ship captured several dozen Spanish ships, all properly sent to Buenos Aires for confiscation. Back visiting his family and refitting the ship, as was permitted by the regulations, Almeida was also suspected by Onís of having landed some of the seized cargo. The Spanish minister did not go after the cargo, however, preferring to accuse Almeida of piracy in his demarches to Acting Secretary of State Rush, and demanding Almeida's arrest under the neutrality legislation. In this case, Rush acted on the information, ordering the district attorney in Baltimore, Elias Glenn, to open an investigation. In a promising manner, Glenn did investigate and bring the case to court. But there, in the Federal district court headed by Judge John Houston, the case fell apart.

Even though it was common knowledge in Baltimore that the *Orb/Congreso* was a Baltimore ship, fitted out in Baltimore with a largely American crew and captained by the Baltimore resident Almeida under a blank commission filled out on the spot by Taylor, that information was not decisive. Almeida's defense, led by William Winder, a Mason and open friend of the patriots, presented evidence that the ship was in fact owned in Buenos Aires by Pedro Aguirre (the 1810 envoy to the U.S.), that Almeida had taken Argentine citizenship and was operating under a valid Argentine commission, and that the ship had stopped in Baltimore only

5. Bringing American Privateers into the Fight

because of bad weather. When Judge Houston asked the prosecutor to rebut the evidence thus presented, Glenn (whom John Q. Adams later called a "weak, incompetent man")[9] could produce none, and the case was dismissed. Onís, furious, succeeded in having Almeida arrested again (in fact, twice). But in one case the Maryland court ruled that it had no jurisdiction over infractions of Federal law, and in the other case the jury was directed to acquit by circuit court judge Gabriel Duvall, whose decision was never published.

Onís was not deterred. He continued to gather information on the privateer activities and pass it on in complaints to Acting Secretary Rush. Onís seems to have learned, however, a basic fact that most Americans had absorbed during the 1807–09 efforts to enforce the hated trade embargo: that the Washington administration was often unable to enforce its law in the local jurisdictions, where public officials were often inattentive or swayed by local popular opinion, and jury trials could result in convictions only when the evidence was watertight. Both he and Rush had been let down by the Almeida decisions, and Onís subsequently restrained himself from demanding action for each perceived injury. More often, he simply asked that his information be passed on to the president, "who, I ought to expect, will take such measures as he may think best adapted to the correction of this disorder."[10]

Onís was not as passive however as this might imply. He was, in the background, pushing the Madison administration to strengthen the neutrality legislation. In this, he had a useful ally in the Portuguese minister in Washington, the Abbé José Correa de Serra, a celebrated liberal intellectual who had become one of the ornaments of Philadelphia and Washington society. Correa was involved because the ships of the Portuguese monarchy, which was still headquartered in Rio de Janeiro, were being attacked by privateers commissioned by the breakaway regime of José Gervasio Artigas, the ruler of the Banda Oriental (more or less modern Uruguay). As Artigas was at war at the same time with Portugal, Spain, and the Buenos Aires regime, privateers operating under its flag could prey on a wide variety of targets. Its commissions were consequently of some value to the less scrupulous privateers; and as its system for issuing and enforcing the commissions was haphazard at best, the situation had become scandalous. Correa's many and forceful interventions, added to those of Onís, and the administration's own realization that the situation needed remedy, led President Madison to propose to Congress in December 1816 that the 1794 and 1797 Neutrality Acts be strengthened.

Congress acted rapidly and decisively. Monroe, in presenting the administration's case, admitted that few prosecutions of alleged infractions had been instituted "from the difficulty of obtaining the necessary evidence to establish facts on which the law would operate."[11] There was virtually no opposition to the administration's basic premise that a tightening up was needed. A few congressmen voiced resentment over Onís's role in inspiring the legislation, or, as the wags had it, that this was a case of "the kingdom of Spain against the city of Baltimore." William Duane's *Aurora*, predictably, attacked the bill as a surrender to monarchy and an abandonment of the patriot cause, and a few congressmen, including Henry Clay, took advantage of the occasion to put on the record their support for the patriots.

What specific opposition did emerge in Congress centered on weakening the proposed new authority for customs collectors to detain suspected vessels. An amendment to that effect having been defeated, however, the bill was easily approved by the pro-administration majority in both houses and signed into force on March 3, 1817. In addition to increased fines and the increased powers given to the customs collectors, its main provision was to require that any American-owned armed ship leaving port be required to post an expensive bond to ensure that it did not engage in "cruising or committing hostilities, or in aiding, or cooperating in any warlike measure, against the subjects, citizens, or property of any prince or state, or any colony, district, or people with whom the United States are at peace."[12]

The intent of the Act was clear, the penalties substantial, and the language seemed to cover all the bases. Yet it did not stop Americans from continuing to take up, and use, the privateering commissions offered by the Spanish American patriot regimes. The administration for its part had made the letter of the law a bit more explicit, but had neither the legal tools to prohibit the practice nor in fact the will to do so in the face of public opinion or its own basic sympathy for the independence of the colonies.

Chapter 6

More Rebel Schemes for Armed Intervention

The Spanish American patriots in the United States had helped launch a proxy war—the privateering campaign that was fueled by *norteamericano* capital and manpower. Ever enthusiastic to help their colleagues in the homeland, the patriots then began to look for more direct means to attack the Spanish imperium. They aimed to channel some of America's restless energy, and readily available arms, into efforts to assist the rebellions in neighboring colonies. In 1816, a number of these plots took shape, and once again the neutrality laws were not triggered, or were circumvented. In the end, the various plots and expeditions had little effect either on the course of the wars of independence or the U.S.-Spanish relationship, but they did demonstrate the lengths to which the patriots were prepared to go in using the North American platform to achieve their aims.

In Philadelphia and Baltimore, the patriot groups met secretly to plot their next moves. They were being watched, of course—by the Spanish even more closely than by the Americans. Minister Onís and his consuls in Boston, New York, Norfolk, Baltimore, Charleston, and New Orleans were the Spanish monarchy's first line of defense against the patriots' schemes. Digging out local news as well as rumor, Onís and his colleagues kept Madrid as well as Mexico City, Havana, and other key royalist posts informed of the rebels' activities, signaled imminent threats, and supported royalist forces through arms and other supplies shipped from the ample American market.

Onís also kept up a steady stream of demarches to the department of state. Convinced that American professions of neutrality were scarcely more a screen to hide expansionist aims, he assiduously complained about any activities that seemed to him to be in violation of American neutrality legislation or bilateral treaty obligations. While his accusations were on occasion overblown or even wholly inaccurate, his purpose was as much tactical as informational: he wanted to create a record of alleged misdeeds that could put pressure on Washington's policymakers. Correcting the neutrality abuses was one goal, but another and perhaps equally important one was to influence the atmosphere of the upcoming negotiations.

Even before presenting his credentials as Spain's minister, Onís had repeatedly raised the issue of patriot activity in Louisiana. Pointing out that they had already violated Spanish territory in 1813 by the capture of San Antonio, he demanded the arrest of Bernardo Gutiérrez and José Alvarez de Toledo, as well as other members of what he called a factious band of insurgents and incendiaries. Among the other objects of his ire were a recently arrived Mexican emissary, José Manuel de Herrera, and the ex-French general Jean Joseph Amable Humbert. The two were plotting, Onís correctly charged, with Toledo and others to launch new incursions into Spanish territory. In response to these demands, secretaries Monroe and Rush (who was acting secretary at the beginning of the new Monroe administration) retreated into denials and evasions. If any armed bodies were gathering, they responded, it was off in the Neutral Ground, and the persons allegedly involved were French or Spanish anyway. And if any armed force chanced to be gathered on American territory, Rush claimed, it would be dispersed, but there could be no arrests unless a crime had actually been committed.

The administration of course had no wish to act as Spain's policeman; it was already under attack for tightening the neutrality laws in Spain's favor, and it had absolutely no problem in seeing the Spaniards under pressure in the neighboring colonies. Onís was right when he commented to the Spanish viceroy in New Spain (Mexico) that "the laws of this country lend the government plentiful support in excusing itself from correcting evils that it is not to its advantage to obstruct."[1] It was clearly not to Washington's advantage to help Spain maintain its grip on the colonies.

New Orleans and the Louisiana Territory were a hotbed of anti-Spanish plots, and events there were the objects of many of Onís's complaints. Indeed there was a considerable amount of truth in the Spanish accusations, even if most of the threats, in hindsight, appear relatively inconsequential. Onís was well informed by his consul in New Orleans, Diego Morphy, the somewhat inexperienced son of the previous consul of the same name, but who benefitted from the intelligence network his father had established. And what Onís did not mention in his diplomatic protests, obviously, was that Morphy and his group were not simply complaining; they were working hard to penetrate and undermine the plots.

In fact, Morphy and his colleagues had already recruited a mole within the patriot community. Juan Picornell, the old revolutionary and propagandist who had been at Toledo's side when the Republican Army of the North was routed, had turned up in New Orleans, working in the public health sector. In 1813, he got involved with the French émigré General Humbert, a man with an interesting past who had fallen out of favor with Napoleon for republican sympathies and, reportedly, having taken to bed the emperor's favorite sister Pauline. Having fled Napoleon's wrath to the United States and New Orleans, Humbert in late 1813 was trying to put together an expedition into Mexico—ostensibly to form a colony that would be a haven for French exiles from Europe and Haiti. Picornell was somehow attracted to his scheme, which turned out however to be a farce: the two and their few supporters, without any apparent means to do so, went to the border and boldly but emptily proclaimed a Republic of the Internal Provinces of Mexico (Texas), of which Picornell was to be president. On their return to New Orleans, however, they found very little support for the idea, which soon died on the vine. Picornell publicly abandoned his non-existent presidency in mid–February 1814. And while Humbert would continue to scheme on behalf of his fellow French émigrés, Picornell went back to his medical work. At least on the face of it.

Picornell had been recruited by the Spanish royalists, sometime between the braggadocio of his announcement as president of Texas, and his renunciation of the empty title. Back at his low-paying job in New Orleans, "wrinkled with age," as he had been described during the Gutiérrez-Toledo misadventure, and now without prospects, he presumably had lost much of the zeal that had characterized his rebel activity a year before. It was at that point that Spain's spy chief, the widely respected Fray Antonio (or Père Antoine) Sedella, who had kept his eye on Picornell since his arrival in town, sensed his new vulnerability. Sedella sent one of his agents, a businessman called Ángel Benito de Ariza, to try to recruit him. It worked. Picornell decided to rally to the crown; he quit his revolutionary work, wrote out a long confession to the Spanish government, and stepped away—publicly and apologetically—from the Humbert scheme. But he also published an article in the journal *L'Ami des Lois*, calling for independence for the Spanish colonies—thereby presumably providing himself with enough credibility to maintain his credentials with the revolutionaries. From then on, he would continue to live his life as a medical official, keep up his contacts with the resident Spaniard activists and remain their ostensible friend, yet also report assiduously on their activities and, on occasion, steer them in ways useful to the royalist cause.[2]

The Capuchin monk Sedella, priest of St. Louis cathedral, commissar of the hated Inquisition, and all the same widely beloved for his modest behavior and humane devotion to the poor and the slaves, had been a significant figure in the city since his arrival over forty years earlier—and also a controversial one, due to his periodic conflicts with both civil and church authorities. But he was also a Spanish patriot and a political conservative who had been urged by the departing governor in 1803, when Louisiana had been returned to the French and then sold to the Americans, to stay on and help protect Spanish interests in the city. It was a smart choice. Uniquely situated as a reporter and recruiter, Sedella became a mainstay of Spain's intelligence service in the city, reporting directly to Onís and the captain general in Havana, and only coordinating lightly with the local consul (particularly so in the case of Morphy Jr., whom Onís did not particularly trust). Now, with Picornell inserted as a sort of mole in the rebel circle, he could keep an even closer eye on the other potential troublemakers such as Gutiérrez and Toledo.

Neither of the two, however, was as yet engaged in serious revolutionary activity. Toledo was arrested in the fall of 1814, and charged to answer, at the next sitting of the circuit court, to an accusation of having raised a force in violation of the neutrality law. However, with "no testimony whatever having appeared against him"[3] during the ensuing six months, the charges were dropped. (The district attorney who reported this had of course not conducted an active investigation, and could scarcely have expected prosecution witnesses to walk in the door.) In any case, by 1814 the attention of everyone in wartime New Orleans was centered on the much more troublesome American-British rivalry in nearby West Florida, where British incitement of the Creek Indians had led to General Andrew Jackson's punitive invasion into Spanish territory, a British occupation of Spanish Pensacola, and Jackson's subsequent capture of that city. And then, when faced with the dire threat of a major British force coming up the Mississippi to capture New Orleans, almost all elements of the trilingual city—Americans and French warmly, Spanish selectively, pirates self-servingly—joined in Andrew Jackson's triumphal defense. After the victory, the war was over. The border with turbulent,

6. More Rebel Schemes for Armed Intervention

revolutionary Mexico also fell quiet in 1815, following crushing Spanish royalist victories over the rebels.

When patriot activity in the Gulf did spring up again, in 1816, it was largely initiated by a miscellaneous group of rebel agents, adventurers, and revolutionaries who had gathered on America's east coast, and specifically in the key cities of Philadelphia and Baltimore. Among the most active of these was Pedro Gual, who had returned to Baltimore in 1815 as representative of the government of rebel New Granada (he had served as governor of Cartagena until it fell to Spanish General Morillo's troops). As a result of New Granada's fall in the summer of 1816, Gual once more found himself in the United States without an official sponsor. But he was not without energy, or a sense of purpose. Looking at the condition of the Spanish American revolutionaries, he saw the royalist army in firm hold of the northern regions of South America, the Argentines still preoccupied with their own internal divisions, the Caribbean islands firmly in royalist hands, and only Mexico still in a state of smoldering rebellion. Bolívar on Haiti, and San Martín and O'Higgins in Argentina, were plotting their returns, but lacked the means for any early success. Gual was a man of action, unready to wait for events. He began to envisage a plan to reverse the recent tide of royalist victories, using United States territory as a base.

Gual began to believe that the key to the situation might be Mexico, or New Spain, the source of much of the empire's silver and where, in spite of bloody victories by royalist governors, the rebellion kept springing up again and again under new local leaders. If émigré rebels like himself could somehow gain control of a seaport along the long Mexican coast, Gual concluded, it could be used to stockpile arms, supply reinforcements to the rebels in the interior, and also develop a base from which they could attack Spanish shipping, or even mount attacks on royalist-held areas of South America. He began to promote his vision among the other patriots in America, and soon was in correspondence with Toledo with that aim.

In New Orleans, Toledo was already working with a man who purported to be an emissary of the Mexican Congress. That was José Manuel de Herrera, who indeed had been appointed by the leader of the latest revolt, José Maria Morelos, to represent republican Mexico in the United States. At the height of his success, in 1813, Morelos had established the Congress of Anáhuac, which had drafted a constitution for an independent Mexico and agreed to send one of its delegates, Herrera, as emissary. Unfortunately, a string of royalist military victories over the rebels had put an end to the insurgent government as well as Morelos' life by the end of 1815. Herrera as a result found himself, like Gual, an emissary without a government to represent. But in the permissive atmosphere of New Orleans, where the business community was deeply involved in selling arms, and U.S. district attorney John Dick (who was sympathetic to the rebel cause) held the position that any and all commercial arms sales were none of his official business, Herrera could find ways to ship arms to the remaining rebels back in Mexico. He was soon in contact with Toledo with that purpose. The two arranged several shipments of arms for the Mexican insurgents, with the active collaboration of the U.S. Navy commander in New Orleans, Daniel T. Patterson.[4] One of the shipments, in early 1816 on the *Petit Milan*, was reportedly lost at sea—much to the pleasure of Consul Morphy and Onís.

The project to seize a port on Mexico's Gulf coast began to take shape in the summer of 1816. Although Gual was sick much of the time, he drew in other Spanish American dissidents resident in the United States such as Manuel Torres, and fellow Venezuelans Telésforo Orea, José Raphael Ravenga and Juan Germán Roscio, to help with the planning and by contacting American businessmen for the necessary financial support. The scheme was centered in New Orleans, where Toledo, Herrera and Henry Perry, an ex–U.S. Army officer who had been on the Gutiérrez-Toledo expedition, had gathered support and even a volunteer army poised at Point Bolívar. The scheme also included a number of Bolívar's lieutenants on Haiti, the privateer commodore Louis Aury who would supply the ships, and on the Mexican side, Manuel Mier y Terán, one of the leading insurgents, who would provide the ground troops. Veracruz or Tampico was the proposed target. The whole scheme collapsed, however, when Terán backed out, Aury's ships were damaged by a storm, arms for the expedition were lost at sea, Perry's force at Point Bolívar dwindled for lack of pay and action, and Bolívar's plans for a return to the mainland drew away any help from that quarter. The collapse of this particular scenario, however, by no means damaged Gual's determination to proceed. Another chance would soon present itself.

It is not clear to what degree Gual and Toledo's plotting became known, either to the ever-alert Onís or the United States authorities. Onís's complaints to the state department at the time centered on privateering violations and the activities of Bonapartist refugees in the United States, who he thought were hatching a plot to invade Mexico. He also seemed to believe that his consular colleagues in New Orleans had penetrated rebel circles there and were effectively spreading dissension among the

6. More Rebel Schemes for Armed Intervention

conspirators. As for the American administration, it certainly placed no priority at the time on efforts to unearth patriot conspiracies against Spain, and would have been incapable of stopping such plotting in any event unless there had already been a clear breach of the neutrality legislation. Real or pretended ignorance, for the administration, had its advantages.

If Gual and the other conspirators were working on their plan to invade Mexico in relative obscurity, part of the reason may have been the simultaneous presence in the United States of a South American patriot who attracted, indeed welcomed, a good deal of attention. He had in fact arrived back in January 1816, on the same ship from Buenos Aires that had brought Thomas Taylor. The visitor was the Chilean aristocrat and former ruler of a separatist regime, José Miguel Carrera. Since losing a power struggle in his native country to Bernardo O'Higgins, he had been in exile in Argentina. But, when yet another change of government took place in Buenos Aires and supporters of his political rivals O'Higgins and José de San Martín took power, he was forced to flee once again. He had decided to come to the United States to buy the arms, ships, and material that would allow him to free his country of Chile from the royalists.

Carrera represented no existing regime or junta; the country he had once ruled was occupied by the troops of King Ferdinand, and he had little money. But he had influential friends, a magnetic personality, and a politically correct agenda: to liberate his homeland from the grip of the retrograde Spanish monarchy. His initial supporters in America were Joel Poinsett and Captain David Porter, the representatives respectively of the departments of state and the navy, who had worked with and admired him in Chile. With the help of their influence, Carrera soon was introduced to many famous and influential men, from Baltimore to New Haven: President Madison, Secretary of State Monroe, John Jacob Astor, Aaron Burr, Eli Whitney, DeWitt Clinton, even Joseph Bonaparte, the ex-king of Spain who had taken refuge in the United States after the fall of his brother. All listened attentively, found Carrera an attractive and plausible spokesman for his cause, and wished him well. But none offered him the material help he wanted: arms, ships and money.

Support would come, instead, from different sources: journalists and politicians who carried a torch for South American liberation, and businessmen who supported the cause because they wanted long-term free access to that growing market or, even more simply, short-term profits from arms sales or loans. At this level, Carrera found Poinsett to be disappointingly standoffish, but Captain Porter, using his influential position as chairman of the naval commissioners in Washington, was ready to help by providing propaganda and access. It was he who introduced Carrera to some of the group that would eventually allow him to reach his goal.

The key members of Carrera's support group were, unfortunately, also controversial figures. John Stuart Skinner, the Baltimore postmaster and privateer supporter, was one; he in turn reinforced Carrera's contacts with Darcy and Didier, the merchant ship owners. Skinner was a wealthy man at the time, a warm supporter of South American independence who wrote pro–Carrera articles for the newspapers under the pen name "Lautaro." He was also a man of other talents; he would eventually become publisher of one of the country's leading agricultural magazines, the *American Farmer*. But Skinner was the kind of operator who created enemies: John Quincy Adams would in time have this to say of him: "He is a man of mingled character, of daring and pernicious principles, of restless and rash temper, and yet of useful and honorable enterprise. Ruffian, patriot and philanthropist are so blended in him that I cannot appreciate him without a mingled sentiment of detestation and esteem. I consider him the originator and cause of all the Baltimore piracies which have injured and still dishonor this nation. He has infected not only that city, but the moral feelings of the whole community."[5] The other key member of the group was the journalist and polemicist Baptis Irivine, an Irish-origin radical whose anti–British, anti-colonial stance had led him into warm support of the patriot cause, and who gave Carrera frequent access to the columns of his paper the *New York Columbian*. Carrera also kept in contact with other resident patriots, largely through Pedro Gual.

Carrera's favorable reception, however, began to lose its gloss when news reached the United States of the degree to which Carrera was out of favor with the new regime in Buenos Aires. The new leader, the autocratic Supreme Director Juan Martín de Pueyrredón, was allied with Carrera's political enemies. In spite of the favorable image evoked by Carrera, his visit to the United States was exposing an uncomfortable fact: that Spanish Americans were by no means united in their fight for liberty, and that the liberal constitutionalists like Telésforo Orea were losing ground to other factions of a much more nationalistic and authoritarian bent.

American politicians and opinion shapers now had more complicated choices: they could not be in favor of liberty for Spanish America without some sort of involvement with one faction or another. At the end of the war with Great Britain, the issue of support for South American independence movements had regained some attention, with Henry Clay leading the pro-patriot group in Congress. Clay had spoken out as early as January 1816 for American intervention on the side of the patriots. Others, such as the influential representative John Randolph, held that republicanism inevitably would fail: "This struggle for liberty in South America," he argued, "would turn out in the end something like French liberty: a detestable despotism. You cannot make liberty out of Spanish matter."[6] The debate had now become narrower; factionalism in South America was now producing factions in American public opinion as well. Sides were being taken, and particularly with regard to Buenos Aires, the only territory that had kept itself consistently out of the hands of the royalists since 1810. Henry Clay and others eager to promote the South American cause would soon push for recognition of the Pueyrredón regime. This of course affected Carrera's efforts negatively, and his supporters would fight back.

Carrera nonetheless persevered. With his limited funds and large ambitions, he had a weak bargaining position and as a result attracted a number of unscrupulous offers. He was aware of Onís's spies on his tail, disappointed in one way or another by Thomas Taylor, John Jacob Astor, Joel Poinsett, and even by his facilitator, the American turned Argentine privateer David Jewett, who tried to rake off some of the scarce funds for bribes and commissions. Carrera bargained in New York to buy and arm a ship, the *General Scott*, only to have Luis de Onís outbid him and put it to royalist service instead. As he wrote to Poinsett, "I am getting nowhere with my objectives; many promises but no fulfillment, many desires to get rich, but none of activity."[7]

In the end, he took the only deal he could get: a four million dollar loan from John Skinner that allowed him to buy and fit out two Darcy and Didier brigantines, the *Clifton* and the *Savage*, as well as a small schooner. Skinner and Darcy and Didier were taking a risk, but not without potential profit: the money was to be repaid in a year, at one hundred percent interest. Carrera's diary reeks with his impatience and frustration, but he had few choices: "it is better to sacrifice money than liberty," he had commented earlier.[8] In the end, he sacrificed both.

In late December 1816, Carrera finally set sail with his three ships and a band of some seventy adventurers recruited in the United States. His mission, however, turned out to be a complete failure. On arrival in Buenos Aires, he found that he had arrived too late and his opponents were firmly in power. His ships were confiscated, his supporters melted away, and he was thrown in prison. His struggle, and the arguments over his debts, would last several more years, and continue to color the North

American reaction to South America's fight for independence and recognition.

In the midst of Carrera's stay in the United States, there arrived in New York a hotheaded young Spanish patriot, with a ship full of fellow adventurers, arms, and a declared intent to undermine King Ferdinand through an attack on his colonial empire. For Pedro Gual and his associates in the failed plot to capture a Mexican port city, it was the second chance they had hoped for.

The newcomer was Francisco Javier Mina, a hero of Spain's war of liberation who had courageously led bands of guerrillas and then whole military units against the French. His hopes for his country however had been crushed when King Ferdinand cancelled the liberal constitution and persecuted its supporters. Before long, Mina had become an enemy of the monarchy he had fought to preserve. Following a failed coup in which he was implicated, he had fled to London. There, he met fell in with the resident Spanish American patriots, who included Palacio Fajardo, the Granadan envoy to the United States in 1812, and in particular the Mexican Servando Teresa de Mier. Mier, an ex–Dominican priest whose liberal views on Church doctrine, the monarchy, and Mexican nationalism had made him a figure of controversy for twenty years and led to a half dozen arrests, believed that the Spanish empire could be successfully attacked through its colonies, specifically his native Mexico. In time, he convinced the restless young patriot Mina to undertake that mission. They let it be known around London that they were planning an expedition to invade Mexico, and gathered enough volunteers, plus money from British bankers, to make the first step possible. As that step was to be a visit to the United States to put together a full expeditionary force, they consulted with the influential and respected American general Winfield Scott, who was visiting Europe to study European tactics. He led them to understand that, as foreigners, they might not be subject to any prohibitions and could avoid prosecution. It seemed to them that they had a green, or at least a yellow light.

Mina, Mier and their supporters arrived at Norfolk in June 1816 on their ship, the *Caledonia*, with the nucleus of an expedition. But they needed to double their force, which meant more men and money. Pedro Gual rapidly mobilized the Baltimore and Philadelphia patriots to help, which now also included the Mexican Miguel Santamaria and the Venezuelan Mariano Montilla. Servando Mier for his part employed his London banking contacts to raise additional funds (which unfortunately

6. More Rebel Schemes for Armed Intervention

hampered Carrera's simultaneous search for money.) The Baltimore moneymen, not surprisingly, were attracted by Mina's prospects. Dennis and Alexander Smith, local financiers and speculators, put in substantial funds. The Mexican Company of Baltimore was also set up, bringing in some key members of the privateering circle. By late summer, with the additional contributions of New York merchants and other sources—including open recruitment in New York and other cities—enough men, arms, and money had been raised to bring in two more ships: the *Dolphin* and the *Calypso*. It was time to start actual operational planning.

All this coming and going was no more secret than had been the preparations of Francisco Miranda over a decade earlier. Luis Onís and the Spanish consuls of course marked each step of the preparations, and devised countermeasures as the opportunity arose. Shortly after the ship arrived, Onís was in possession of a list of the Spaniards on board and pursued them selectively. A few deserted, another few became informants. Onís got one of his henchmen, Segundo Correa, enrolled as a volunteer (and spy, although Mina later claimed he was an assassin).[9] Onís also alerted the department of state to developments, but got the usual noncommittal response that, if violations of the neutrality laws were suspected to be taking place, the Spanish would have to provide strong evidence and sworn statements to the district attorney to initiate an investigation. Onís's most useful weapon against Mina's plans, however, suddenly came from an unexpected source.

Specifically, it came from New Orleans, where Juan Picornell's undercover work with Fray Antonio Sedella was paying off. Picornell had, some months earlier, succeeded in recruiting the Lafitte brothers to work for Spain. The Lafittes' actions (and, as necessary, lack of them) had in turn played a role in derailing the proposed Herrera-Toledo-Gual plot to seize a port in Mexico. With the failure of that plot, the demise of the Mexican Congress, and the absence of a viable rebel partner with whom to deal, Álvarez de Toledo now found himself at a sort of dead end. He decided to backtrack—first to his unfinished conversation with Luis Onís of almost three years earlier, and then on the road back to royal Spain. At the end of June, he arranged a private interview with Sedella. By early July, he had recanted, confessed, asked for a pardon, and agreed to work for the King's interests. The apple had finally fallen,[10] but to take advantage of the occasion the Spanish had to keep the secret in order to put Toledo into action against his former colleagues. Fortunately for Onís, information moved slowly in 1816. But unfortunately, the mail was never entirely secure.

Following his defection, Toledo returned rapidly to the East Coast, meeting discreetly with Onís to receive his instructions at the diplomat's summer home in Bristol, Pennsylvania in late July. With his reputation and past work assuring him access to all the major players, Toledo strove to sabotage the Mina expedition. First, he visited the financial backers. He told them that the recent fall of the Mexican Congress had prejudiced the chances for the expedition, and also that he believed the Washington administration might question their financial involvement. He was persuasive enough to give some of the potential investors cold feet, with the result that a few members of the Mexican Company of Baltimore withdrew. (Dennis Smith, a speculator accustomed to long odds, nonetheless stuck with Mina. He and his brother talked a handful of other investors to stay in the game by effectively underwriting their risks.)[11] Toledo also tried to convince Mina that the expedition should be directed instead at Pensacola, thereby attempting to divert it from the much richer prize of Mexico. Although Toledo had no success with this subterfuge, he nonetheless created some confusion among the planners—in addition to passing on their confidences and plans to Onís and the royalists.

The conspirators, having developed at least a broad outline of their project, realized that it would be politic to provide the Madison administration with at least some indication of their intentions. Pedro Gual, diplomatically astute and fluent in English, was chosen to go to Washington for the purpose, accompanied by Toledo, whom everybody still believed to be loyal to the cause. Arriving in Washington in early September and not finding Secretary Monroe in town, they met with his assistant John Graham. Graham's memorandum to his boss on the subject makes clear that, in addition to assuring him that they intended to operate in conformity with the neutrality laws, they might also move to seize Pensacola. But they harbored no intent to keep it, they insisted, as the region should rightly become American. Graham tried to caution them on the idea, suggesting that it might be provocative both to Britain and the United States.[12] As the administration cautiously and wisely never gave a written response to this feeler, each of the participants apparently drew the conclusion he wanted: Gual that the Pensacola idea was not viable; Toledo (and Onís) that the administration was all but complicit in the patriots' schemes.

As he made his rounds in Philadelphia and elsewhere, Toledo seems also to have tried to undermine young Mina with discreet criticism, both to encourage new defections and to sow doubt. Mina's qualifications were, in the eyes of some observers, already suspect. Onís had reported his opinion, shortly after Mina's arrival, that "This expedition would be something to fear, if the said Mina were not a reckless young man, incapable of carrying out the vast plan that he has been given." Carrera seems to have felt much the same. He noted in his diary, after a conversation with Toledo—who undoubtedly led him on—"Poor Mina! His ambition will condemn him." (Carrera had little good to say of Mier, either; after a two-hour conversation, he concluded that the radical friar was self-important and full of bluster.) But even Mier may have had his doubts about Mina's leadership, calling him—some years later, admittedly, and with the wisdom of hindsight and desire for self-justification—"gullible and naïve."[13]

Neither Toledo's sabotage efforts, however, nor doubts about the young leader, could stop the expedition's forward movement. Onís was a bit more successful, at least creating a short delay when his appeals to the New York authorities against allowing the fully armed *Caledonia* to sail were heeded. The captain was obliged to unload all the cannon and other arms before he could leave port, or be considered in violation of the neutrality legislation. The success, however, was ephemeral: the armaments were put on another vessel as cargo, and reloaded onto the *Caledonia* off Annapolis. The ship, along with the *Dolphin*, sailed off, with Mina himself following from Baltimore on the *Calypso* at the end of September. After regrouping on Haiti, Mina, his ships, and about 150 men sailed on to Spanish territory at Galveston. Arriving there November 22, they set up camp next to Louis Aury's privateer base.

Mina was finally in Mexico, but only marginally, as Galveston had already been pried from Spanish control by Aury. What's more, the next step was still under discussion. Mier, who had been sent ahead to New Orleans in order to make contact with the Mexican insurgents, arrived in Galveston urging Mina to travel to that city to get supplies and discuss possible help from the American business community there. Mina went, and with a contingent of his men stayed in New Orleans several weeks, increasing supplies, recruits and buying two more ships. And getting into trouble: there were several incidents with the Spanish consulate, including one involving the theft of official correspondence, in which consul Diego Morphy was badly beaten.

It turned out that what the American businessmen—an informal but powerful group calling itself the New Orleans Association—had in mind was a scheme they had proposed earlier to Bernardo Gutiérrez,[14] specifically to seize Pensacola and its armory from the Spanish. While the Pensacola alternative had some support among the rebels due to the weakness of the revolutionary forces in Mexico, Mina had the sense to realize that the Association's proposal was a commercial and not a patriotic maneuver. He turned them down. He may also have come to understand that the intended plan was considerably more than a raid, and that the backers hoped to seize the Pensacola region and then sell it to the United States—something no Spaniard could support. In any event, Sedella had already unearthed the scheme and warned the Spanish garrison—and moreover, the armory was not full of weapons, as the businessmen had supposed.

Mina and his group returned to Galveston in early April, 1817. There, they joined up with Louis Aury and his ships, plus the perpetual filibuster Henry Perry, who now brought a hundred adventurers to reinforce Mina. The entire contingent, now almost 250 soldiers and officers strong, sailed down the Mexican coast to Soto la Marina, where they launched the actual invasion. From there, amidst internal disagreements, misunderstandings with the Mexican insurgents, and bad management, they fought their way inland until they met a major royalist force at Venadito, somewhat southeast of San Luis Potosí. There, at the end of October, they were soundly defeated. Perry committed suicide, while Mina and two dozen of his colleagues were executed. Mina was twenty-seven years old.

In spite of this second disappointment, the vision of making North America a springboard of the independence movement still was alive for Pedro Gual.

Chapter 7

The Rise and Fall of the Republic of the Floridas

At the beginning of 1817, the South American patriots resident in the United States finally had positive news—something that helped to balance the grave disappointments of the failed Mina expedition and Toledo's betrayal. Simón Bolívar had left his exile base of operations in Haiti and was in the process of establishing a foothold on the Venezuelan mainland, on the great Orinoco River, where the royalist forces would have great difficulty if they tried to root him out. Although it was not yet clear, from that base Bolívar would in time succeed in regaining Venezuela and New Granada from the royalist forces.

While the patriots did not know it at the time, the year would also bring a new opportunity, and their first, if short-lived, victory. They would succeed for a moment in liberating a piece of colonial Spain, but also provoke a strong reaction from the United States, and trigger the first major debate in Congress concerning future relations with South America.

While the good news from South America held promise for the future, at the moment the problem for the expatriates was limiting the damage from Toledo's defection. The patriots had learned of his betrayal only in mid–November, when a privateer arrived in port with incriminating royal correspondence that it had intercepted. The exposure of Toledo's turn of coat was a serious shock for the patriots, who suddenly realized that much of their planning, even their correspondence, was probably in the hands of Onís and the royalist forces. Pedro Gual wrote to his Washington friend William Thornton as soon as he learned. "I have the mortification of communicating to you that Mr. Toledo has proved to be a traitor to the cause," he lamented, adding that Toledo had promised in his letters to the Spanish officials that he would work to "quell the insurrection of Mexico."[1] Had he disclosed Mina's plans? They had trusted him with their major secrets; he had been a key participant in the schemes being discussed in New Orleans and, more recently, on the east coast. Now it had to be assumed that everything that had been shared with him over the past four or five months had been compromised.

Onís, too, had reason to worry, since the details of Toledo's recruitment to the royalist cause had also been exposed. Fray Sedella's messages to and from the captain general in Havana were part of the intercepted packet—Toledo's father in Cuba had written promising his son $2,000 if he returned to loyalty to the crown. Onís worried most that Sedella and his network had been compromised, as well as his own agent Segundo Correa, who had infiltrated the Mina expedition. (Correa indeed was exposed and kicked out, but the Sedella operation amazingly continued to operate.) Onís also was concerned that Toledo's very life was at risk; he reported having received threats of assassination.

Toledo, even with his double-dealing role so openly exposed, characteristically did not slink away. Much as he had done when he arrived in Philadelphia five years earlier and published his *Manifesto*, he resorted again to a pamphlet in an effort to uphold his honor and defend his change of allegiance. In his *Justification of Don José Álvarez de Toledo*, he described why he had become disillusioned with the rebel movement, which he argued was disorderly, excessively influenced by foreigners, and sadly corrupted by "converting the war for liberty into a war for speculation."[2] Although he and Onís (who helped get the pamphlet published) hoped it would get wide circulation, the Spanish authorities were uneasy about propaganda from so controversial a figure, with the result that its circulation and impact were limited. It was Toledo's last American performance. He had sold out his colleagues in order to reconcile with his father, his wife (who, according at least to journalist William Duane, had been an important factor in his defection), his king, and perhaps even his conscience. José Álvarez de Toledo left the Americas at the end of December to return to Spain, where he served his government as an advisor on American affairs until his death in 1858.

Surprisingly, the Mina expedition—openly recruited and launched as it had been from the United States—did not markedly raise the temperature of U.S.-Spanish relations. Minister Onís treated it as just another issue to bring up in his series of diplomatic notes of protest, another example of American support for the patriot cause. His complaints look like having been largely for the record, and for good reason: Onís now needed to focus on a broader field of action. In early January, he had received full authority from Madrid to take over the bilateral negotiations aimed at resolving all outstanding issues between Spain and the United States. He and Secretary of State John Quincy Adams (who took office toward the end of September 1817), would have much bigger issues to face: American demands for reparations from past Spanish attacks on shipping, the fate of Florida, the western borders of the Louisiana territory, and others. The Mina expedition was over; Onís had predicted that the fellow would fail, and he had. There was no need to make a major issue of it, as doing so could in no way improve his leverage in the upcoming talks.

For the dissidents, it was time to regroup. The Venezuelans among them began to look aspiringly at Bolívar's progress in establishing himself on the Orinoco, wondering when it would be timely to go home and assist in the liberation of their country. They had been joined at the turn of the year by a new representative from Bolívar, General Lino de Clemente, who came with a primary mission to buy arms for the Venezuelan patriots. Coordinating with Manuel Torres and Pedro Gual (whom Bolívar had also designated as a purchasing agent), they were able to procure and ship some eleven thousand muskets plus bayonets, flints and other supplies to the Orinoco.

A new envoy, Martín Thompson, had also arrived from Buenos Aires back in the summer of 1816. His mission, however, was not primarily a diplomatic one: he came with a handful of privateer commissions to distribute, as well as instructions to procure arms, including two ships for the Argentine navy. Thompson started badly, however, launching himself into the increasingly controversial privateer business without any effort to clarify his status with the administration.

It is worth emphasizing at this point that the United States was serving as a military supplier to both sides in the struggle for Spanish America, having taken the position from the start that American commercial markets were open to all belligerents. Many enterprising merchants had taken advantage of the opportunity, and had loaded cargoes of munitions on their ships to be sold by whichever buyer in South America was prepared to give a good price. The patriot agents had also done well, considering their unfamiliarity with the market and, usually, lack of good credit—they often were able to offer only barter terms. The royalist diplomats, with their established connections to American merchants and superior credit, undoubtedly did better yet. (General Morillo's army of repression, patriot supporters often complained, had been generously supplied from the United States while the patriots were faced with commercial and legal challenges.) Onís and his colleagues were particularly successful between 1816 and 1818 in procuring American ships for the Spanish navy squadron that was trying to police the Caribbean. Not only had Onís outbid Carrera for the 32-gun *General Scott*, he also bought the famous War of 1812 18-gun privateer *Chasseur*, another privateer, *Young Wasp*, a brig, *Reindeer*, and the 28-gun *Regulus*.

This short period of business as usual was interrupted in late February by the unexpected arrival at Baltimore of yet another catalytic figure: Sir Gregor MacGregor. He was a man well known by the patriots; he had been fighting in one capacity or another with Miranda and then Bolívar since 1811. A Scot, he had previously served in the British army before deciding to throw in his lot with the Spanish American patriots. He had risen to the rank of brigadier general in Bolívar's army (though with a spotty record on the battlefield), and had married a Venezuelan woman, a cousin of Bolívar, who came to the United States with him. But MacGregor was also a fabricator; he had invented his British knighthood, had alienated many of his fellow officers with his bragging, and was totally unclear as to his current connection, if any, to Bolívar. And yet he was plausible, energetic, and a vocal supporter of the patriot cause. Pedro Gual and the other patriots, even the very measured Manuel Torres, were swayed by his enthusiasm, and perhaps by their own desire to finally mark up a major score against Spain.

MacGegor's plan was simple, and had the advantage of meshing neatly with that of Pedro Gual. It also fit well with the schemes for seizing territory in Florida (either Amelia, Pensacola, or both) that the patriots had discussed with Mina and Toledo. MacGregor planned to establish a patriot base on Spanish soil in North America, but this time not in Mexico, which had proved to be beyond the patriots' reach. He proposed instead to seize Amelia Island and perhaps much of East Florida from Spanish rule, and create a base from which the insurgents could conduct raids and supply their colleagues in the Spanish provinces. Pedro Gual, Lino Clemente, and Martín Thompson all saw this as a chance to set up a sort of "Florida Libre" in the Empire's front yard, and bought into the plan from the beginning. An additional motive for their support was fear that the upcoming negotiations over the fate of Florida would result in the cession of the territory to the United States. If they could seize Florida first, they would have a voice in its future.

7. The Rise and Fall of the Republic of the Floridas

Finding the patriots supportive, MacGregor then began to look for American backing. He recruited openly, and found a number of men immediately available. He also recruited two men who promised to add their own corps of volunteers, plus money and supplies, to the effort. They were Ruggles Hubbard, an ex-sheriff from New York, and Jared Irwin, an ex-congressman from Pennsylvania. In trying to raise money, MacGregor found John Skinner a helpful ally both in Baltimore and Philadelphia. MacGregor somehow managed to get together enough support, but he often did so by altering the message to suit his audience of the moment. When talking to Americans, he suggested that his long-term intent was to offer the territory to the United States—the involvement of the Spanish American patriots, he suggested, was simply a temporary facade to allow the expedition to circumvent the neutrality legislation. His sales pitch ignored the patriots' desire that the territory remain in their, Spanish American, hands. MacGregor, it seems, was engaged once again in selling two different versions of the truth at the same time.

With the nucleus of his expedition thus in hand, MacGregor sought political cover. He first got the patriot representatives to give him a formal commission. Signed the 31st of March by Pedro Gual for New Granada and Mexico, Lino de Clemente for Venezuela, and Martín Thompson for Rio del la Plata, the commission stated that his objective was "that possession should be taken, without waste of time, of East and West Florida," and that he should proceed on his own authority as well as that of the signatories to take such measures as he saw fit to achieve that aim (including the arming of privateers), while at the same time observing the American neutrality restrictions.[3] He then went to Washington, where he called on William Thornton, an enthusiastic if politically naïve supporter, and more importantly, Richard Rush, the acting secretary of state. Rush, it appears, raised no objections to MacGregor's presentation. For MacGregor, such absence of a formal rejection of his plan amounted to—or at least could be portrayed as—acquiescence.[4]

MacGregor and his recruits moved on to Charleston, and then Savannah. In those cities, he raised yet more money—some of it through selling to his backers rights to buy Florida land at a dollar an acre after the takeover. In order to prepare the way for an easy conquest, he also sent agents south of the border to spread rumors that a large force was organizing to seize the territory. As he recruited still more adventurers of various nationalities and skills to join in the expedition, he had to admit to one of his backers that "some of my materials are not of the best description; but this I must expect, when I consider that they are taken, at random, from a populous sea port town; they appear to be much fonder of money than military fame and glory."[5]

The expedition, now approximately 150 strong, arrived in northeast Florida in July. The American and British residents of the area, numbering about two hundred, had organized themselves with Spanish permission into a local self-government called the Northern Division of East Florida. Things had settled down since the events of 1812; they were happy with their relationship to the Spanish, and most decidedly did not welcome the potentially troublesome intrusion of the adventurers. They would give the expedition no support. MacGregor may have been disappointed, but he did not really need their help. Fernandina town, on Amelia Island, remained under direct Spanish control, as it was a garrison town boasting a small fort, San Carlos, that dominated the St. Mary's River. But it was weak—indifferently governed, owing its daily bread to the smugglers who profited from the back-door access to the United States, and garrisoned by only fifty or so regular troops. Nobody wanted a fight, and MacGregor's agents had already spread concern among the townspeople, weakening the garrison's will.

Fernandina town was captured with no difficulty at the end of July.

The Republic of the Floridas was launched, with its own flags and commemorative medals. Its title spoke to MacGregor's ambitions; he intended to march on St. Augustine, drive off the Spanish garrison, then take over all of East Florida, and even, perhaps later, West Florida. A rudimentary government was set up, patriotic proclamations issued, privateer commissions issued, but then things stalled. His progress to date, and keeping his undisciplined men together, had cost much money, and before long MacGregor was running short. When, at the end of August, Ruggles Hubbard showed up with none of the promised supplies or money, MacGregor realized he could not succeed. He did not have the capacity to attack the Spaniards at St. Augustine; rather it was they who were preparing to march north to crush the presumptuous new republic. In the first week of September, he pulled out. Without arranging for any formal transfer of authority, MacGregor, his wife and a few officers simply boarded a ship whose captain they knew and sailed off to New Providence. His connection with the liberation of Florida was over.[6]

Hubbard and Irvine were left in control of the enterprise, which soon began to unravel due to internal disagreements, lack of money, and the impending Spanish counteroffensive. It might have collapsed at that point,

7. The Rise and Fall of the Republic of the Floridas

had it not been for the fortuitous (or, seen in another light, disastrous) arrival of the privateer commander Louis Aury and his Mexican-flagged, Haitian-crewed ships.

Aury's arrival needs an explanation, for which it will be necessary to back up a few months, to April to be specific. Aury had continued his privateering operations after the failure of the Mina expedition, but became increasingly unhappy with the Galveston Bay site. In spring, he decided to move down the coast to Matagorda, and did so in April—but then found that site not much better. In the meantime, he had heard from Gual and others about MacGregor's initial success at Amelia. He decided, with Gual's encouragement, that Amelia would suit his purposes admirably, and moreover he knew MacGregor—they had fought together at Cartagena. He would move his base to the Atlantic coast.

There had also been another new development while MacGregor was in Savannah, and that was the arrival in Baltimore of a new group of determined and energetic patriots—these ones from Buenos Aires. They had come, not as emissaries from their government, but in fact the opposite. They had been expelled as a result of their opposition to the latest change in rulers of that unstable province. The new supreme director, Juan Martín de Pueyrredón, had been put in his position by the Congress of Tucumán, which had also declared the province's independence in July of 1816. Pueyrredón, a member along with José San Martín of the patriotic Lautaro Lodge,[7] supported the latter in his efforts to retake Chile for the revolution. But he at the same time had no problem repressing those patriots who opposed his policies. He expelled many opponents who favored a more decentralized, federal form of government, and among those were the men who had shown up in the United States. The leader of their political party, Manuel Dorrego, had already fled the year before, and now, in June of 1817, another seven expellees joined him in Baltimore, of which the two most active in our story were Manuel Moreno and Vicente Pazos Kanki. The group soon realized that they could take advantage of American freedom of speech to launch a press and pamphlet campaign against the Pueyrredón regime back home. It was Pazos, however, a lively journalist with Indian blood, who also became involved with the Philadelphia group of Venezuelans: Torres, Gual, Ravenga, and Roscio, and their friend and supporter William Duane. Through them, he saw a still more immediate opportunity to serve his fellow patriots by involving himself in the MacGregor scheme.

Gual and Pazos entertained great expectations for MacGregor's newly liberated Republic of the Floridas, and intended to go to Amelia to help establish what Gual optimistically envisaged as a "rising state."[8] They took passage, along with other patriots and adventurers, on a Venezuelan-flagged privateer, the *America Libre*, which had been recruiting and buying supplies openly in New York (acts which were the subject of yet another fruitless complaint from Onís). The ship left port in early September, so it was not until it stopped at Charleston that they all learned that MacGregor was no longer in Amelia. And when they arrived at Amelia in early October, they found Louis Aury there, but locked in disputes with Hubbard and Irvine. What's more, the Republic of the Floridas had ceased to exist.

Aury had arrived in mid-September with his five ship flotilla of armed, French-speaking Haitians. His arrival at least had the advantage of thwarting the Spaniards' attack, so that the expedition was no longer threatened from without. But it was still divided within. Aury, on arrival, had sized up the situation quickly: with the departure of MacGregor and his formal if dubious written commission from the patriot representatives, the so-called republic had no plausible legitimacy, and Hubbard and Irvine's management had only led to desertions and disorder. He offered them an ultimatum. If they wanted to continue as a free port and privateer base, with his men and ships for protection, they would have to accept his leadership and legal protection, as a commissioned officer of the Mexican government. (Of course, Herrera's commission was also dubious at best, but that did not matter in the revolutionary situation that prevailed.) The Mexican flag would fly over Amelia, Aury insisted. Hubbard and Irvine, having no worthwhile option, accepted grudgingly, but that did not stop the growth of a simmering animosity between the "American" and "French" groups on the island.

This was the situation that Gual and Pazos found on their arrival: something quite a bit more unsavory than their hopeful expectation of a new, Spanish American, free state. It was, to put it bluntly, a pirate-smuggler base with tension among its renegade components, under a spurious Mexican flag, alienated from the local American settlers, and threatened by the Spanish forces in St. Augustine down the coast. To their credit, the two patriots jumped into action in an effort to help the illiterate Aury put a more plausible external façade on the subtly renamed Republic of Florida. A government of sorts was organized, regulations and proclamations issued, elections held, and the first draft of a liberal constitution prepared. In their enthusiasm to create (or, at least, to present the appearance of) a legitimate polity, however, they chose to ignore or gloss over the uncomfortable facts that the state had no defensible legal basis, and depended for its survival on a process of stealing from the Spanish, and then smuggling the goods, including many slaves, into the United States. Their actions were aggravating both governments.

The Spanish consul was watching developments from distant Charleston, but the U.S. Navy was just across the St. Mary River. The brig *Saranac* had been ordered there in August, with instructions to detain and search vessels in the river or offshore, paying particular attention to ships attempting to smuggle slaves. Although few arrests were made, it was a useful point from which to monitor the activities in Fernandina, and Washington was thus kept informed of activities on the Spanish side of the river. The departure of MacGregor and the non-participation of the American settlers had ruled out the possibility that what was occurring was a friendly takeover. By mid–October, the information reaching the president was troubling enough for him to put the question to his cabinet: should the United States intervene to stop the growth of this renegade state and its smuggling activities? The cabinet's answer was affirmative, but it was also decided to wait until December in order to sound out not only the Spanish American sponsor governments, but also to see if the British would pose objections. In mid–November, a frigate as well as army units from Charleston were sent to reinforce the naval force on the river. By December, the political and diplomatic soundings were completed, satisfactorily. But the go-ahead orders had in fact already been given.

President Monroe's annual message, delivered to Congress on December 2, 1817 announced the impending takeover. The United States, he emphasized, had tried to keep an "impartial neutrality" in the civil war between Spain and her colonies, with American ports and goods "equally free" to both parties. But The Amelia expedition, he asserted, could not have been countenanced by the governments of the breakaway colonies, with whom the United States enjoyed friendly relations; it was apparently no more than a "private, unauthorized adventure ... the island being made a channel for the illicit introduction of slaves from Africa into the United States, an asylum for fugitive slaves from the neighboring states, and a port for smuggling of every kind."[9] Both it and the privateer base at Galveston would, the president announced, be suppressed.

On December 22, Louis Aury was told, by the American military force across the river, to surrender Fernandina. In his answer, he acknowledged there would be no armed resistance, but protested that the Americans had no right to expel his group from Spanish territory seized by them in the process of a legitimate independence struggle. This answer, undoubtedly drafted by Gual and Pazos, foreshadowed a tactic of trying to take their case to the public, appealing to the pro-independence movement in the United States. But it nonetheless acknowledged that their hope of establishing a liberated state within Spanish territory had, once more, been frustrated. The Mexican flag came down, Aury's ships and the various groups of adventurers soon departed, and Amelia was occupied by the American military.

To Luis de Onís, the American takeover of Amelia was as grave an outrage as the MacGregor expedition had been. He had reported since MacGregor's arrival that the aim of the general's scheme was Florida, and as it became clear that the target would be Amelia, not Pensacola, he had sent one of his consuls to Charleston to keep close track of developments. He was convinced that American policymakers aimed to whittle away at Spanish control over Florida so as to prejudge the result of the bilateral negotiations. Onís saw the occupation of Amelia as further proof of his fears, which were compounded by the situation in West Florida, where Seminole raids across the porous border had inflamed the settlers, and American forces under General Jackson were mobilizing in response. Onís complained to the secretary of state in early January that, regardless of motive, the Amelia takeover amounted to a violent invasion of a peaceful country. Adam's reply, though, was a stiff one: if Spain was unable to control activities in its own territory, he said, it could not blame its neighbor for taking action. Onís could not have failed to notice that the argument applied equally to the growing crisis in troubled West Florida.

The controversy, however, soon grew beyond the realm of diplomatic exchanges, and into a battle for public and Congressional opinion. The patriots, as soon as they were faced with the probability of eviction, had been preparing their case. Vicente Pazos, the experienced journalist and propagandist who had been the principal drafter of the island government's declarations and constitution, was appointed as Aury's spokesman. At the beginning of 1818, Pazos traveled to New York, where he inspired newspaper stories questioning the government's right to invade what he termed a peaceful foreign state. He then proceeded to Philadelphia to consult with Manuel Torres and Lino Clemente as well as to plant more news stories, and finally went to Washington, where he looked up Pedro Gual's friend and patriot enthusiast William Thornton. With a press campaign supporting the patriot side already underway, Pazos and Thornton

7. The Rise and Fall of the Republic of the Floridas

collaborated over the next few weeks to prepare the key piece of the patriot argument: a memorial to the president, on behalf of the erstwhile leader of the ex–Republic of Florida, Louis Aury.

The memorial was sent to President Monroe in early February 1818. In it, Pazos laid out the patriots' basic contention, that is, that "the establishment at Amelia is to be viewed as one formed by the new republics of the South, at the hazard of the perils of war, and authorized by the regular proceedings of their ministers."[10] MacGregor's commission, Pazos asserted, was issued by fully accredited ministers (whom the American government had unfortunately ignored), and therefore his capture of Spanish territory was a legal act of war. The United States moreover had no right to intervene. As for the alleged misgovernment and smuggling on Amelia, Pazos either dismissed the charges or blamed them on Hubbard and the American faction for having diverted the expedition into "disorder and confusion." Finally, he demanded return of the island to the patriots, and the establishment of a commission to assess the compensation due to the patriots from loss of property resulting from the U.S. government's illegal takeover.

Adams and Monroe were in no hurry to answer. For one, Adams was incensed at the presumption of Martín Thompson and Lino de Clemente, neither one of whom had been acknowledged as official representatives of their governments, but nonetheless had authorized MacGregor's adventure. Nor could he be bothered to argue the legal points with Pazos, the spokesman for a man (Aury) whom Adams considered to be no more than a pirate. By March, Adams had secured statements from the rebel governments concerned that they had not authorized issuance of the commission to MacGregor. The president also had the support of General Jackson, which was useful in deflecting criticism from pro-patriot American politicians. Adams's early March response to Pazos as a result was coldly dismissive: the president "sees no reason for revoking any of the measures which have been taken by his directions in respect to that place, and nothing that requires any other answer to your representations."[11]

The issue would not go away that easily, however. Thornton, William Duane, David Porter, and other friends of the patriots had kept the controversy alive through articles in the press, which by this time was showing a lively interest in Spanish America's struggle for independence. Duane's *Aurora* hammered the administration repeatedly with charges of duplicity, alleging that they had known about the patriots' plans for Florida through the state department's interview with Gual and Toledo, and had not objected; they had only turned against the plan after Toledo's defection and under pressure from de Onís. Other journals took a more balanced view. The pro-administration *City of Washington Gazette*, for example, suggested that the well-meaning patriots should not have been "unjustly stigmatized as pirates and freebooters"[12] simply in order to justify the government's real motive, which was to emphasize that Florida was off limits to any outside powers. In general, though, the administration had weighted the argument about Amelia successfully against the patriots by stressing exactly those lurid details of piracy, smuggling and slave trading on the island. Most of the press (even the usually pro-patriot *Niles' Register*) wound up emphasizing and deploring those aspects of the short-lived patriot republic.

Pazos[13] and his supporters decided to try another avenue. Knowing that the patriot cause had friends in Congress, the main one being the powerful speaker of the House Henry Clay of Kentucky, they petitioned Congress to accept the memorandum. Clay was amenable, and a motion to accept the memorandum for study was submitted to the House. The debate on that motion, nominally simply a procedural one, would bring to a head the political tensions in shaping policy toward the Spanish patriots and the Spanish government.

While the political debate broadened to cover the range of American relations with the South American patriots, the situation in Amelia was governed by tactical considerations. American troops would remain on the island, the administration insisted, on a temporary basis, pending the outcome of negotiations with the Spanish. But on this point, indeed, the negotiations were already largely prejudged. It was common knowledge that the Spaniards had hinted earlier that they might be willing to exchange Florida in return for settlement of past American claims for damage to shipping; thus the prospect was strong that Florida would end up in American hands. The patriots had wanted to use Amelia as a pawn in their war with Spain, but had been brushed aside by their hosts—ostensibly in defense of American trade and neutrality. In reality, the American government wanted that pawn in its own possession, to strengthen its hand in any impending deal with Spain.

Chapter 8

Hindering the Privateers

While the South American expatriates had been involved in their Mexican and Floridian schemes, the privateer campaign launched from American ports reached its peak, began to change in nature, and then to decline in significance. The attitude of the U.S. government had also evolved against the privateers, while the Spanish had learned how to fight them in the courts.

Nonetheless, a number of years would pass before the practice died out. And though the Amelia Island base had been closed, that act had by no means closed down rebel privateer activity from Caribbean ports. Louis Aury, for example, continued to prey on Spanish shipping, as both pirate and privateer, after his eviction from Amelia. But except for a short visit to Charleston, where he was recognized and arrested on a complaint from the Spanish consul, but then released, he never again came to the United States or had any operations connected with the patriot representatives. His old base of Galveston, however, was soon put back to use, but under new management.

The new proprietors of Galveston were the Lafitte brothers, but they had come with mixed motives. One of Juan Picornell's successes back in late 1815, as an informer and recruiter for the Spanish, had been to help recruit the two brothers to the royal cause. The Lafittes, with their wide knowledge of the privateer and smuggling business in the Caribbean and their close acquaintance with the schemes of the New Orleans Association, had since then performed as valuable informants for the Spanish. In 1817, the new Spanish consul and intelligence operative in New Orleans, Felipe Fatio, was presented by the Lafittes with an ambitious idea. Their scheme was to infiltrate and undercut the privateer network. The Lafittes would reoccupy the Galveston base, setting up a prize court and the appearance of a base where seized merchandise could be sold at good prices. But the catch would be that those privateers who came to Galveston would be seized by the Spanish, lying in wait behind the screen of the Lafitte operation. The privateers would be picked off one by one; Galveston would masquerade as a privateer base, but would actually be a Spanish asset.

Fatio was intrigued, and recommended the idea to his boss, the Spanish captain general in Havana, José Cienfuegos. A trusted Spanish agent, Arsène Lacarrière Latour (another ex–Bonapartist officer who had shown up in the United States and joined with Jackson and the Lafittes to defeat the British at the Battle of New Orleans), was assigned as the Lafittes' primary contact.

Cienfuegos however was less enthusiastic than Fatio. The web of Jean Lafitte's multiple contacts and ambiguous commitments to Onís left some doubt as to the depth of his commitment to the project. It was certainly to the brothers' short-term advantage: the Spanish would enable an operation by which the Lafittes could gradually eliminate their privateer competitors, while still conducting a profitable smuggling business. But the racket, after all, could not last long; sooner rather than later the other privateers would discover the ruse, and the Lafittes would be in trouble with their friends. The scheme as a result fell apart from a combination of its own implausibility, Cienfuegos's doubts, and because the Spanish navy could not spare enough ships to provide the necessary force to assure success. Cienfuegos simply could not trust the brothers, and dropped them from the rolls of Spain's intelligence agents. This of course did not stop them from their double game; in the summer of 1819 they were typically both cooperating with and informing to the Spanish about the latest filibuster into Texas, a feckless effort led by James Long.

Nor did the collapse of the Spanish gambit stop the Lafittes from occupying Galveston, where they resumed their old business of privateering and smuggling of stolen goods. They also hosted, for some months in 1818, another forlorn attempt by Bonapartist exiles (under General Charles Lallemand) to establish a refuge in Texas. They even obtained the grudging acquiescence of the Monroe administration to their continued occupation of Galveston, and their operation lasted until 1821, in spite of President Monroe's 1818 statement that he would have the Galveston base suppressed. One of the reasons for delaying that action, ironically, was an objection raised by Minister Onís, who did not want to see United States troops once again on Spanish sovereign soil. And the Americans, who still claimed that the Louisiana Purchase had given them the right to Texas down to the Rio Grande (putting Galveston in the United States), were entirely willing to see another bit of colonial Spain alienated from the mother country, even if only by a pirate base. The Lafittes could continue to engage in business as usual because the United States and Spain had not yet settled their differences.

In the United States, however, the initial success of the rebel-flagged privateers was slowly being blunted in the courts, as well as by a slow evolution in the government's position.

When Don Luis de Onís complained to Secretary of State Monroe in 1817 that the privateer *Mangoré* had been allowed to leave Baltimore's port without investigation, he had good reason to be disappointed and angry at the permissiveness (indeed license) shown by local American officials toward the privateers. His anger stemmed from the fact that the ship's crew and captain were wanted for questioning concerning a case before the district court in Boston—something that was known by the Baltimore authorities, but not heeded. What Onís had wanted was that the *Mangoré* be detained so that its captain, James Barnes (who, the Spaniard insisted, was lounging in his Baltimore home while enjoying some $80,000 worth of luxury goods that he had plundered from Spanish prizes), could be interrogated concerning one of his captures.

At issue was the Spanish schooner *Divina Pastora*, which in December 1816 had shown up unexpectedly in New Bedford as a prize of the *Mangoré*. But John Stoughton, the alert Spanish consul in Boston, had quickly identified it as a Spanish ship, and had it impounded by the admiralty court, pending investigation into its status as a possible illegal prize. (The ship had in fact not yet been made a "good prize" and was, according to its prize captain, headed toward Buenos Aires for adjudication at the prize court there.) Stoughton needed information to prove the case that the *Mangoré* was in fact a vessel fitted out and manned in America, acting illegally under both international law and the 1795 treaty with Spain, which prohibited citizens of either country from taking out privateer commissions against the shipping interests of the other.

Although they did not know it at the time, Onís and Stoughton had chosen the right venue to try the case. Spanish and Portuguese officials had both been trying, for over a year, to find privateer captains or owners guilty of crimes under provisions of the neutrality legislation. But those were criminal charges, and necessarily heard in the circuit courts where trials were conducted before a local jury, and strong public opinion could be brought to bear. That fact, plus the reality that local officials were often lax in seeking information that could lead to prosecution, meant that no convictions at all had been obtained. Stoughton and his lawyers had in fact begun their arguments in the *Pastora* case on similar grounds, stressing the allegedly criminal act of the *Mangoré's* captain. The outcome at first looked predictable; the case would probably get hung up on quite familiar rocks, with the defendants countering successfully that the ship and captain Barnes were in fact operating legally under the law of the United Provinces of la Plata, a recognized belligerent if not a state.

The judge in fact never ruled on those issues of sovereignty. And that was the crucial difference: he did not need to rule on them because the case had been taken up as a case in admiralty law, not as a criminal offense. Admiralty cases were tried in district courts and without a jury, hence somewhat less susceptible to public opinion than a criminal proceeding. The judge decided on questions that were both simpler and more routine: was the property landed in the United States the property of citizens of Spain (a country with which the United States was at peace), and if so, had it been legally confiscated as a good prize, by a legitimate foreign privateer? The judge in the *Divina Pastora* case ruled on both of those issues in favor of the Spanish claimants. The case did not close there, however; it would be appealed to the circuit and then to the Supreme Court (with Daniel Webster appearing as attorney for the Spanish), and from there returned to the circuit court for a second judgment. Two years would pass before the initial decision was confirmed, and the owners of the *Divina Pastora* were able to reclaim much of their property. But the case was nonetheless a significant victory for the Spaniards.

The decision charted a new course for Onís and his colleagues. Seeking criminal convictions in the circuit courts, with all the attendant uncertainties of public opinion and weak government prosecution, was no longer the only legal recourse for fighting the privateering movement. Onís by no means abandoned his fight to toughen the laws, and to some degree he succeeded. But with this decision and others like it that followed, civil action in the district courts proved to be almost as powerful a disincentive to the privateers as the threat of imprisonment, as it threatened to take away the profits of their operations—as long, that is, as their prizes had not been made good by a properly constituted prize court, and that they were caught while landing their prizes or plunder in the United States. Moreover, the practice of allowing cooperating lawyers to take a percentage of the value of any recovered goods (usually ten percent) provided the Spaniards with a number of American allies ready to help sue the privateers. Although it was still necessary to prove a violation of the neutrality acts, the standard of proof was less rigorous in an admiralty hearing than in a criminal one.

The process unfortunately could be slow and expensive. Court costs, lawyers' fees, consular commissions, and other expenses and delays meant that the owners sometimes got only a very partial satisfaction, even when they won their case. Nonetheless, the new legal tactic raised the risks considerably for the privateers, and in time diminished their initial enthusiasm for waging war on behalf of the Spanish American rebels. Even James Barnes and the *Mangoré* had their comeuppance in 1818, when five sixths of the value of one of the ship's prizes, the *Providencia*, was returned to the Spanish claimants by order of a Norfolk court. By 1820, American involvement in the Spanish American privateer business had diminished greatly for a number of reasons, and among them the risk of confiscation of the booty was very significant. As David DeForest, the Buenos Aires businessman from Connecticut who had been one of the initiators of the business, confided to a business associate, "You do not know how much anxiety I have had on account of my fears of suits brought by Spanish claimants, though I have openly pretended to the contrary."[1]

As a result of the civil cases, privateering was clearly becoming a much less attractive investment. Although court records are incomplete, a study of applicable cases on the East Coast courts in Maryland, New York, Virginia, and Massachusetts, shows that the privateers lost 37 of 51 cases, either initially or on appeal. Even in Baltimore, where the great majority of cases were tried, the claimants won some 75 percent of the cases brought before the district court. And the New Orleans district attorney, John Dick, reported in 1816 that privateers had lost nine civil court cases over the past year in that city, returning almost $195,000 worth of restitutions to the Spanish owners.[2]

New Orleans remained an important base for privateer financing and operations, even though the Barataria Bay operation had been closed down since 1814 and, according to Mr. Dick's report, no privateers had been armed in the city or within a league of the shore during the preceding year. Mr. Dick, it should be pointed out, had told only a partial and very convenient truth, as any other answer could have raised the question as to why he had not prosecuted violations of the neutrality act. A more honest report was provided a little over a year later by Beverly Chew, the collector of customs at New Orleans. "I deem it my duty to state," he wrote, "that the most shameful violations of the slave act, as well as our revenue laws, continue to be practiced with impunity by a motley collection of freebooters and smugglers at Galveston, under the Mexican flag, it being in reality, little else than the reestablishment of the Barataria band, removed somewhat more out of the reach of justice." Chew went on to note that many of the vessels operating out of the unauthorized Galveston base had been financed by American businessmen in New Orleans, and captained by French and Italian mariners "who have been hanging loose upon society, in and about New Orleans" since the closedown of Barataria. "Fed and drawing all its resources from New Orleans," Chew emphasized, "an active system of plunder was commenced on the high seas, principally against Spanish commerce, but often without much concern as to national character, particularly where money was in question."[3]

Chew's report was bold. As customs collector, he was asking for more resources to limit the smuggling of seized Spanish goods and slaves into Louisiana, which had continued virtually unabated even if from further away, in Texas. But at the same time he was also taking on some of the pillars of the local business society in which he and his wife lived. The privateering-smuggling interests were both influential and popular. They could feed off the general disdain for Spain, and also wrap themselves in the colors of patriotism—pirates like the Lafitte brothers, Dominique You, and Renato Beluche were virtual heroes for their roles in the Battle of New Orleans—feats that had earned them a pardon from General Jackson. But behind the flamboyant pirates/privateers/smugglers lurked a business network that financed operations but was itself very tight-lipped—virtually secretive. Calling itself the New Orleans Association, it included the important New York-origin lawyer Edward Livingston, ex–Federal officials such as John Randolph Grymes and Abner L. Duncan, businessmen John K. West, Vincent Nolte, and Auguste Davezac, the banker Benjamin Morgan, Army captain Henry Perry, and Francois Dupuis, a planter and associate of Aury. It even included one of Chew's customs inspectors, the creole Pierre Duplessis, and the commander of the New Orleans navy unit, Captain Daniel Todd Patterson, as a de facto member.[4] These were the men who supplied the money for the ships, for Aury's base in Galveston, provided entry and a market for the smuggled goods in full cooperation with the brothers Lafitte, smuggled arms for the Mexican rebels, or serviced the privateers when they came into port.

Beverly Chew also noted that as of the end of August 1817, some six Mexican-flagged privateers under Aury's operational control were openly in port, as well as five under General Bolívar's Venezuelan flag. The Mex-

8. Hindering the Privateers

ican flag that flew over Louis Michel Aury's ships and ramshackle "government" at Galveston was that of the defunct Mexican Congress of Anáhuac, which had disappeared at the end of 1815 as a result of a string of royalist victories. But the Congress's representative, José Herrera, remained in New Orleans and still had (or was seen to have) the power of the pen, which he used to issue illegal but still usable Mexican privateer commissions, plot with other nationalists and adventurers, procure arms for the rebels still operating in the interior, and provide specious legal cover for Aury's occupation of Spanish Galveston.[5]

Four rebel flags now flew over the privateer vessels attacking Spanish or Portuguese trade: those of the Argentine, Venezuelan, Banda Oriental, and Mexican regimes. There were probably also some ships operating, quite illegally, under the flag of the old Cartagena junta. And as the Argentine, Venezuelan, and Chilean governments had established small navies that also preyed on Spanish vessels, it was clear by late 1818—the peak year for privateer activity, in which some 180 ships were seized[6]—that Spanish merchant shipping would soon be all but driven from the seas. It meant, for the privateers, fewer potential prizes; only those captains operating under the Banda Oriental flag of José Artigas had license to attack the rich Portuguese trade. Only naturally, a number of privateers—operating since the beginning in a climate of evasion of the law—found it easy to take the next step, which was to make questionable and even illegal seizures, regardless of the flag or pretext. Privateering was gradually turning, in fact and also in the public eye, into an occupation that bordered on, and sometimes was, virtual piracy.

The variety of legally questionable situations involved in the business of privateering under the rebel flags can be illustrated by a quick look at the career of José Almeida as a professed South American patriot. One of the first captains to leave Baltimore in the summer of 1816, he commanded the *Orb*, a Darcy and Didier vessel, which soon thereafter became the privateer *Congreso*. On Almeida's return to Baltimore in the spring of 1817, Onís and his colleagues had demanded his arrest, but (as noted earlier) he had escaped any punishment even though exposed to several legal actions and court trials. Onís was left to fume to Acting Secretary Rush that, though he "would not permit [him]self to indulge in any reflection upon the form of law which may be laid down for cases of this nature," he expected that Almeida "will profit by the first favorable wind to put to sea, and continue with greater fury his atrocities and piracies."[7] True, for on Almeida's third cruise, he reaped 24 Spanish prizes in the vicinity of the Azores. With his substantial share of the prize money, he then bought his own ship, in fact one of his prizes—a fast sailer that he renamed the *Louisa*. But the new ship would need a substantial refitting to be useful as a privateer, which meant that he would have to risk another trip to Baltimore.

Knowing that the laws and their enforcement had been tightened under the new administration of James Monroe, Almeida had the ship registered as a merchant vessel in the name of his first mate, and kept his own name off the anodyne manifest. It was a successful ruse, at least at first. His ship at the dock, his earnings deposited in the bank and his family reunion conducted quietly, Almeida attracted little attention until the summer of 1818, when the final steps of refitting the *Louisa* into an armed privateer inevitably drew attention—*Niles' Register* even joking that it seemed ill-fitted for the sealing trip that was its declared voyage. Once again though, public knowledge did not stimulate legal action, nor could suspicion be a cause for legal action, so the *Louisa* cleared the see-no-evil port authorities with no problem. Not far down the Chesapeake Bay, however, just off the mouth of the Patuxent River, the ship met with supply vessels that loaded its cannon, gunpowder, and the extra men necessary to man a vessel in search of more valuable victims than seals. Once at sea, Almeida raised the flag of Buenos Aires and the *Louisa* became the privateer he had intended.

Off the northwest coast of Spain, Almeida and his crew soon captured a remarkable prize—the fast-sailing Spanish brig *Arrogante Barcelones*, from royalist-held Caracas with a cargo of valuable cocoa, indigo, coffee, rum, and cotton, and a treasure of over $150,000 in specie. Almeida decided that he wanted the ship for himself, and that he would reverse the usual procedure and take her, with a prize crew, to Margarita Island where he would seek to have her confiscated. He left the first mate and many of the *Arrogante Barcelones* crew on the *Louisa*, to continue their privateering cruise.

In Margarita, where the Venezuelan patriots had a prize court that could confiscate Argentine prizes, Almeida arranged the sale of the new brig to himself, with the expectation to convert it, after returning once again to Baltimore, into a privateer.

This time, however, Almeida did not enter his home port unnoticed, even though he tried the same tactics as the year before. Spanish intelligence already knew of the capture of the *Arrogante Barcelones*, and shortly after his arrival Almeida found himself and his new ship attached by virtue of a libel filed against them by Juan Bautista Bernabeu, the Spanish consul in Baltimore, representing the owners of the ship and its cargo, and demanding restitution. Bernabeu and Onís, having already tasted Baltimore justice and found it lacking, decided to seek an influential lawyer. They hired John Henry Purviance, a State Department lawyer untainted by the Baltimore privateering crowd and yet still from Maryland and, more significantly, a personal friend of President Monroe.

Purviance did his homework, and came to court well prepared to counter effectively the usual arguments of the privateers' favorite lawyer, William Winder, who produced a blizzard of South American documentation to prove that Almeida was the legal owner of the ship, and that its Buenos Aires papers were entirely in order. The district attorney Elias Glenn, as he had not done in 1817, also took forceful action, in fact starting a war of memos with Customs Collector James McCulloch as to whether the ship could leave port under bond, as the collector (who was an old friend of the privateers) wished. Glenn prevailed; the ship was attached—at least for a sufficient time. The case, this time, did not look like going Almeida's way.

Almeida sensed that the politics of his profession had changed since 1817, and that he no longer could rely on the Baltimore network to protect his interest. A man of many talents and with a striking persona, he decided to try his luck in Washington with a little first-hand lobbying. Calling on Secretary of State John Quincy Adams in late May of 1819, he tried to convince that righteous New Englander and practiced negotiator that he was just an honest businessman who wanted the court order on his vessel lifted so he could return it to trading. Adams, who certainly had his own opinions on the matter, waited out his visitor with noncommittal comments. That evening, Adams noted in his diary, "He went off, without any appearance of ill humor, saying he must then go back as he came. He did not appear to be conscious in the slightest degree that he had been doing anything wrong. So it is also with the slave traders."[8]

While Adams linked Almeida's case with slavery, a more obvious link was with piracy. The case had taken on a particular lurid notoriety by virtue of the fact that Almeida's old ship, the *Louisa*, had been taken over, shortly after his departure in the fall of 1818, by a mutiny of its crew. The mutinous sailors locked up the ship's officers and began a truly horrifying piratical cruise, capturing ships left and right with no pretense of legality, and sacking several towns in the Cape Verde Islands to boot. Eventually tracked down by the U.S. Navy, with advice from Almeida, the mutineers were brought to justice in Georgia, and the two leaders, David Bowers and Henry Mathews, put on trial for piratical murder and found guilty. The decision was appealed up to the Supreme Court, William Winder once again appearing for the defense and assisted this time by the renowned Daniel Webster, but the initial verdict was upheld in 1820. Whether or not to carry out the death sentences, as well as those of others who were now being caught and convicted of piracy, would bother the administration for several more years.[9]

A third case before the courts in 1818 and 1819 was perhaps even more closely followed by the public, since it represented a determined effort by the Monroe administration to finally obtain a conspicuous criminal conviction for violations of the neutrality laws. Their chosen target was the faux Argentinian Thomas Taylor, the man who had first channeled the energy of American capitalism and organization into support of the patriot juntas.

The new administration headed by President Monroe and Secretary of State Adams was not entirely of one mind as to how to deal with the Spanish American patriots, or in particular those of their actions that undercut America's professed neutrality. Monroe was generally sympathetic to the patriots' desire for liberty,[10] and moreover had an unfavorable view of the royal Spanish regime based in part on his short diplomatic mission there some years earlier. He was the more ready to suffer the excesses of the rebels, hoping that statehood would eventually calm them down and make them more responsible. Adams, on the other hand, was more of a cynic about human nature and insisted on the observance of international law as the means to keep order. The Spanish Americans, he feared, had little preparation for responsible self-government. A diplomat since his adolescence, he had a clear goal as secretary of state: to convince Spain to cede Florida and as much other territory as possible, in the negotiations that had already begun in Madrid. He saw the activities of the patriots as useful on the one hand because they created pressure on the Spanish negotiators, but on the other hand troublesome because they could create unforeseen problems for the bilateral relationship with Spain, and the outcome of the negotiations.

In the immediate term, Monroe and Adams shared the goal of bringing the activities of the privateers under control. They pushed for a further strengthening of the neutrality laws, which resulted in a new act of April 18, 1818, that consolidated the existing laws, adjusted the penalties against infraction, and broadened the enforcement powers of the collectors and

8. Hindering the Privateers

the navy. The law was renewed and marginally strengthened in 1820. Those steps were taken both to appease the Portuguese and Spanish, and because the growing excesses of the rogue privateers demanded action.

Adams had in many ways equated the American privateer industry with organized piracy for some time, and the shift in the administration's emphasis, from looking aside to fighting piracy, was probably due as much to his moralistic view of the problem as to the evolution of events on the high seas and in American ports. He despaired at the corruption surrounding the business, and railed in particular at Baltimore. One of his diary entries of the time reads. "The misfortune is not only that this abomination has spread over a large portion of the merchants and of the population of Baltimore, but that it has infected almost every officer of the United States in the place."[11] Some twenty years later, his indignation was still vibrant: "In 1819," he declaimed at the famous Amistad trial, "at a time when piracy, from her sympathetic and favorite haunts of Chesapeake bay ... was habitually sallying forth against the commerce of the world, but chiefly under the many-colored banners of the newly-emancipated colonies of Spain transformed into a multitude of self-constituted sovereign and disunited States, capturing wherever they could be found the trading vessels of Portugal and of Spain."[12] A rhetorical flourish? Surely. But it was also the expression of a moral view, in which the Americans were the guilty parties because they permitted the transgressions, while the Spanish American patriots were almost incidental participants. Of course, as a good diplomat, Adams did at the time also ask the patriots to play their part in the solution to this vexing problem.

Public opinion seemed to be moving in the same direction. The piracy scandal surrounding Almeida's *Louisa* had brought to public attention the fragility of the lines that separated the activities of patriot-flagged privateers, from abusive seizures, or from downright piracy. The "piracy" word was now being used more often in public discourse on the privateers, and there had been calls in the press voicing indignation "that the ports and harbors of the United States should become the refuge of buccaneers." Or, as another paper put it, "if we want to make war on the Spanish and Portuguese, let us do so, but this disgraceful system of plunder ought not be countenanced by honorable men of any description."[13]

So it was with some sense of confidence that the administration decided in September 1818 to take out a case against Thomas Taylor and his Baltimore allies. District Attorney Elias Glenn prepared the indictment against Taylor and twenty-eight associates on criminal charges, specifically for certain acts alleged to have been piratical. Taylor was already on trial in a civil case in New York, initiated by Spanish Consul Stoughton to recover over $90,000 of booty seized by Taylor's ship, the original *Fourth of July* renamed the *Patriota* and now flying the Venezuelan flag. Taylor however managed to slip out of that charge on a technicality. The Baltimore charges, however, were more serious, as they could involve jail time.

In Baltimore, the case against Taylor, and indirectly the whole privateer industry, was to be heard in that city's circuit court, headed by Judge Gabriel Duval with his associate from the district court, Judge John Houston. Neither of these men inspired much confidence in Monroe or Adams, the latter grousing to his diary that "both [are] feeble, inefficient men, over whom William Pinckney, employed by all the pirates as their counsel, domineers like a slave-driver over his negroes."[14] Recognizing that the famously eloquent and successful Pinckney would hopelessly outclass Elias Glenn in the upcoming debate, Monroe asked the attorney general himself, William Wirt, a man with no small reputation as a litigator, to take the case. Wirt agreed but, perhaps sensing the strength of the opposition, asked and received a special retainer of $1,500—a year's salary for a mid-level official. In the run-up to the trial, an anonymous article appeared in the *National Intelligencer*, more or less threatening the life of any judge who condemned Taylor. As the article was widely recognized as the work of one of the indicted—the controversial John Skinner—the stage was set for an interesting confrontation.[15]

On that score, there was no disappointment. The initial arguments between the two distinguished orators became unusually heated ("something like a personal difference," as *Niles' Register* described it with tongue in cheek)[16]; indeed it took mediation to avoid a duel between Wirt and Pinckney. Defense lawyers Pinckney and Winder then produced a mass of documents and precedents to show that Taylor had acted in all matters as a legitimate commissioned officer of a recognized belligerent. The court, after deliberation, agreed. Then, in consideration of one of the charges of piracy, in which Taylor was accused of capturing an American vessel, it turned out that he had, in fact, only taken Spanish-owned, and therefore legitimate, cargo from the ship. Indeed, it appeared to the jury of quite friendly Baltimoreans that, aside from the apparently minor fact that he had had a Spanish passenger hung from the yard arm by his ankles until he confessed to ownership of the confiscated cargo, Taylor had acted entirely like a gentleman, not a pirate. Shortly before Christmas, the jury rapidly acquitted Taylor, and among the others convicted only Joseph Karrick, a major investor in the *Fourth of July/Patriota*—and the charge against him was later dropped by application of a simple fine. It was an embarrassing loss for the administration. Wirt however took the defeat calmly, along with the money—his daughter was coming into society next year and it would come in handy. Adams to the contrary was, to put it mildly, chagrined, grousing to his diary about the weakness of Glenn's indictment and the corrupted political condition of Baltimore.

Don Luis de Onís, who as can be expected had been following the trial closely, commented even more acidly. He was under considerable pressure from the royal court in Madrid to get the Monroe government to clamp down on the privateers, and was having a hard time convincing his superiors that he could not do much more. As for the Taylor acquittal, he reported, the citizens of Baltimore simply wanted the captain to go free, so that the Spanish specie that he had brought home would remain snugly in the city's banks.

During the Taylor trial, the case against Almeida had been delayed because of Judge Houston's participation at the circuit court, and afterwards by his serious illness. When it was finally seen as necessary to replace him, Monroe proposed Maryland associate judge Theodorick Bland. Adams opposed the appointment because of Bland's known and controversial closeness to privateer interests, particularly his son-in-law John Skinner. That dispute caused a further delay, only relieved after Adams personally interviewed Bland and dropped (or swallowed, to put it more accurately) his objections. The case was finally resumed. Judge Bland's decision, issued in 1820, was perhaps influenced by his recent exposure to the secretary of state's grilling, as for once he did not side with the privateers but rather upheld the owner's claim for restitution of the *Arrogante Barcelones*. Almeida's having purchased the ship in Margarita, Bland's decision said, could not wash away the fact that it had been acquired initially in an illegal manner. On appeal, the case went to the Supreme Court and was not decided until 1822, where Judge Bland's decision on behalf of the claimants was upheld.

Even as these legal battles worked their slow way through the courts, the patriot-flagged privateering industry—started by Cartagena in collaboration with the Gulf buccaneers and brought to scale in Baltimore by the pseudo–Argentinian Taylor and the American Concern—was withering from a variety of causes. The first factor was the simple fact that by 1820 Spanish shipping had been so decimated that new investment was no longer highly profitable. True, the availability of commissions from the Artigas regime in Banda Oriental had opened up a new supply of potential Portuguese victims for privateers willing to associate themselves with that dodgy enterprise. But the controversies surrounding the questionable activities of the Artigas privateers only increased the salience of another cause for decline—the loss of public support for the privateers because of the acceleration of illegal and piratical practices. Spanish and Portuguese efforts through the courts to reclaim stolen property created yet another disincentive which, slow and marginal as it may have been, nonetheless reduced the prospect of profitable cruises with immediate payoffs. Even some successful privateer captains, such as John Chase of Baltimore, lost money through a combination of these factors. The financial crash of 1819 also played an important role, by drying up capital for such enterprises just as their profitability was being challenged. A number of the merchant houses that had backed the privateers failed during the panic, including Darcy and Didier, John Gooding and Joseph Karrick. Those economic factors that had made investment in privateering attractive in 1816 no longer existed in 1820. Only enthusiasm for the patriot cause remained, which for most American investors was a marginal consideration.

Action by the U.S. government proved to be, in the light of these other causes, of minor importance. Criminal prosecutions had been ineffective in spite of the strengthening of the laws; the few convictions having been obtained against low-ranking mutineers, pirates, and murderers rather than the important merchant interests that supported the industry. The U.S. Navy's closure of one pirate/privateer base after another only served to drive the business to another place. In fact, the achievement of Mexican independence in 1821, and the cancellation of privateering licenses there, probably had a greater effect in reducing the number of rebel-flagged privateers/pirates. Piracy, of course, would persist in its historical habitat of the Caribbean, no matter who (if anybody) flagged the vessel. The U.S. Navy had conducted cruises against the practice starting in 1817, and Congress, on 3 March 1819, passed a law authorizing the navy to establish a permanent anti-piracy patrol in the Gulf and West Indies, which went into operation the following year. And even though Luis Onís was quick to point out that the new law never defined the term "piracy," the maritime powers had their own operational definitions. When a new front opened in 1822 as a result of a Spanish effort to rescind the permission it had tacitly allowed for neutral flagged vessels to trade with Spanish American ports, a flurry of Cuban and Puerto Rican flagged vessels, scarcely more than pirates, emerged to prey on the chief neutrals—American and

British—engaged in the trade. British and American diplomatic and naval measures—the U.S. squadron alone captured 29 pirate ships that year[17]—soon put an end to this pretension, however, and by the end of 1823 that particular menace had all but disappeared.

Privateering for the rebel regimes had lost its luster from a combination of the factors mentioned above. But the death knell of privateering as a sort of contracted-out or proxy warfare would only come (as will be discussed later) when the commissioning governments themselves abandoned the practice, or the United States convinced them to cease.

Chapter 9

Recognition or Neutrality?

Failure of the Amelia Island expedition and the short-lived Republic of the Floridas was a major blow to the ambitions of the Spanish American patriots in North America. For more than five years, they had been trying to accelerate the liberation of their home countries from their North American position. Gutiérrez, Toledo, Herrera, Gual, Mina, MacGregor—all had tried to free a piece of Spain's empire, and all had failed. But, nonetheless, the patriots were not discouraged. Things were looking much better in the south.

By late 1817, the independence movement was held in check only in Mexico. In South America, the royalist military ascendancy had peaked, and the rebels were gaining strength. Bolívar had a firm base at Angostura, in the interior of Venezuela, the Rio de la Plata area was all but liberated, and Paraguay too, while San Martín had crossed the Andes and won a major battle at Chacabuco—a turning point which allowed him to look past the impending liberation of Chile to plan an attack on the royalist stronghold of Peru. As a result of these developments, the Philadelphia circle had begun to break up; soon Roscio, Ravenga, Gual, and even the Baltimore exiles from Argentina would head home to where the action was. And yet, the United States was still a vital element in the patriots' plans—as a source of arms, supplies, and the sea power that the privateers contributed, and also as a potential source of legitimacy and political support.

Recognizing the import of the changes in South America, and concerned at the lack of impartial information concerning the situation there, the recently installed President Monroe conceived, early in 1817, a project to send an official fact finding commission to the region. The idea was not translated into fact, however, until toward the end of the year, after considerable delay, both inadvertent and deliberate, and a good deal of maneuver as to who should be on the commission. The commission left only in December, and did not complete their reports until November of the next year. Its composition, travels, and reports will be discussed a bit later.

All of these developments played out before an increasingly attentive and concerned American public opinion. Newspapers once again carried regular reporting from South America, much of it generally sympathetic to the patriots or critical of royalist excesses in the "pacification" campaigns. The *Richmond Enquirer* had joined the *Aurora*, the *Columbian*, and *Niles' Register* among the papers most favorable to the rebel cause, badgering the administration for what they criticized as a one-sided neutrality and reporting rebel successes (and royalist atrocities) whenever possible. Other papers, largely from up east where the merchants were doing good business with royal Spain as well as loyalist colonies such as Cuba, supported the administration's hands-off position and projected doubt about the patriots' capabilities or dedication to republicanism; among them were the *National Enquirer*, the *Columbia Centinel*, and the *New York Evening Post*. Public opinion, it seems, was also divided. Generally, it could be described as sympathetic toward Spanish American aspirations for republican independence, particularly in the Western states and territories where anti–Spanish sentiment continued to smolder. But there was also evident skepticism concerning the patriots' republican credentials, as well as a good deal of disgust over the brutalities and racial conflict stirred up by the "war to the death" campaigns being fought by both sides. For most observers, the government's policy of neutrality seemed appropriate, if open to question.

Propagandists for both sides, royalist and revolutionary, continued to use the American press to publicize their views. The more important works, appealing to American pride in republicanism while exploring the developing crisis, were sympathetic to the revolutionaries. Among the influential works published after 1815 was the informative "Outline of the Revolution in Spanish America," written in London but also published in New York by Manuel Palacio Fajardo, the erstwhile envoy to the United States in 1812. Another influential work appeared in 1817, "South America: a letter on the present state of that country, addressed to James Monroe," by the prolific author Henry M. Brackenridge, in which he attacked Spanish rule while supporting republicanism and urging American recognition of the Buenos Aires government. Manuel Torres, the dean of the Philadelphia circle of Spanish Americans, made a well-received contribution in 1816 with his "An Exposition of the Commerce of South America," a valuable reference for those businessmen eager to enter the new market. William Davis Robinson's "A Cursory View of Spanish America," published in 1815, was more political, serving as an indictment of royal rule in the colonies. And Juan Roscio, before leaving Philadelphia to serve at Bolívar's side in Angostura, published his republican appeal, "The Triumph of Liberty over Despotism," addressed however primarily to a Spanish speaking audience. Finally, on the royalist side, Miguel Noroña at the Spanish mission continued to offer articles and commentaries to the press, until his transfer to London in 1818.

Regrettably for the patriots, however, much of their propaganda output in America reflected a continuation of the political divisions that characterized their efforts in their home countries. José Carrera and his American supporters such as David Porter, John Skinner, and Baptis Irvine had been the first to draw American attention to the internecine struggles among the South American patriots, with their criticisms of Pueyrredón, San Martín, and O'Higgins. But after Carrera's departure—and even as his struggle against his opponents continued in South America—the debate was inflamed anew by the almost simultaneous arrival, in the summer of 1817, of the dissidents expelled by Pueyrredón, and the Argentinian ruler's new envoy to the United States, Manuel Hermenegildo de Aguirre.

Manuel de Aguirre had been sent by both Pueyrredón and San Martín, with a primary mission to buy up to six warships to support a plan to free Peru by a naval expedition from Chile. But Aguirre also carried with him the declaration of independence of the United Provinces of Rio de la Plata, decided at the Congress of Tucumán the summer before, and his secondary mission was to pave the road for American recognition of the new state. Aguirre was a wealthy merchant, the brother of the previous envoy Pedro de Aguirre, and also a cousin of Pueyrredón as well as his colleague in the patriots' secret society, the Lautaro Lodge. Proud, well connected, and determined, Aguirre was assisted by José Gregorio Gomez, a personal friend and lodge brother of San Martín. They would pursue both of their objectives doggedly.

But not without opposition. Pueyrredón critics—that is, both the Argentine dissidents and the supporters of Carrera—wasted no time to attack Aguirre's pretensions. The dissidents (principally Vicente Pazos and Manuel Moreno)[1] argued, through pamphlets and articles in the press, that the supreme director of Buenos Aires was in fact a despot not a republican, and moreover that large parts of the old viceroyalty were beyond his control—neither Paraguay nor Bolivia nor much of the Banda Oriental, with which Buenos Aires was actually at war. John Skinner, a prominent Carrera supporter, took a more indirect line in a series of articles under the pen name Lautaro. His articles contended that Buenos Aires was under excessive British influence and that Chile, rather than Buenos Aires, should be the focus of American interest in South America. Published in Monroe's favorite paper the *Richmond Enquirer*, and picked up by the Baltimore *Patriot* and other papers, these influential articles subtly undermined Buenos Aires' claim for early recognition.

As a result of this "artificial excitement stirred up in the newspapers" (as John Quincy Adams later characterized it),[2] Aguirre's late October proposal for recognition as the representative of an independent state was sure to be controversial. Monroe and his cabinet agreed that the time was not right for such a move. Secretary of State Adam's reply to the request consequently was a polite but firm rejection, in which he questioned whether the United Provinces regime indeed enjoyed full sovereignty over its territory, given the war with the Artigas forces in the Banda Oriental.

New on the job but a practiced negotiator, John Quincy Adams had dominated the cabinet decision on the matter. He was relying on precedent and prudence, but he was also buying time for tactical purposes: he was simultaneously engaged in taking control of the administration's foreign policy, resisting Congressional pressures for premature recognition, concerned over the rapidly unfolding situation on Amelia Island, unwilling to raise Spanish ire needlessly on the eve of major negotiations, and worried that the conservative European monarchies would back Spain in any dispute. Recognizing Aguirre, and indirectly his government, would undercut all those objectives. Fortunately, Aguirre's own letter of appointment from Pueyrredón did not give him diplomatic status; he was assigned as a purchasing agent without authority to request recognition. A technicality perhaps, but enough in itself to justify the rejection—although it did not stop Aguirre from repeated appeals.

Adams had taken over his job with a long-term view of the Spanish and Spanish American situation. His first goal was to negotiate a settlement with Spain, one that would settle the borders and gather in Florida, a goal of American administrations since the turn of the century. Essential to achieving that aim was maintaining a plausible neutrality in the struggle between Spain and her colonies, and that meant not recognizing the

United Provinces or any other revolutionary regime until relations with Spain were normalized. The press and Congress were clamoring for a change, which had to be resisted. With that objective in mind, Adams too got drawn into the propaganda "excitement," publishing a series of anonymous articles in the *National Intelligencer* in December 1817, under the pen name Phocion. In the articles, he heaped doubt on the republican credentials of South Americans, charging them with dissension and misconduct, raising fears of radicalism and racial conflict and often distorting the facts enough to paint a picture of conditions in South America that was sufficiently disturbing to slow down the building enthusiasm for recognition. The articles created a certain buzz in Washington, and while his authorship was guessed at, it was never confirmed. As he would do a month later when justifying the takeover of Amelia Island, Adams knew how to choose only such facts as were useful to support his argument.

Henry Clay, the leading spokesman in Congress for the Spanish American patriots, had already set in motion a process that would lead to Congressional debate on the administration's position. When Congress convened in early December, he proposed that the foreign affairs committee be given a broad mandate to look into the neutrality policy, which he claimed favored Spain at the expense of the patriots' interests. His motion passed, and though the committee would take several months to make its report, the administration knew it would have a fight on its hands. Moreover, for Monroe and Adams this was a political issue as much as a policy debate: Clay was a political rival whose presidential ambitions, as they saw it, were based on attention-getting opposition to administration policies and support for popular causes such as the South American patriots. He had to be checked, both for political and policy reasons.

The debate in the House of Representative finally took place in late March of 1818. The administration had prevailed in a preliminary test of strength, just a week or so earlier, by gaining acceptance of a bill that would expand the coverage of the 1817 neutrality act, in spite of Clay's efforts to water it down.[3] Also facing Congress and the administration at the time were other issues bearing on relations with Spain and the colonies: repercussions from the occupation of Amelia, and General Jackson's impending campaign against the Seminoles, which would take him into Florida. The March debate however was framed by Clay's proposed bill appropriating money to appoint a U.S. diplomatic representative to Buenos Aires, and the documentation submitted by Monroe and Adams on the subject. The documents included Aguirre's letters of credence and a series of communications from Aguirre, in which he requested accreditation, charged the government with "indifference" to the patriot cause, protested the application of the neutrality legislation, and proposed negotiating a treaty, even while admitting that he had no authority to negotiate.

Speaker Clay opened the debate with a talk that lasted three hours. He reviewed current events as well as history and urged that the resolution pass: the cause of the South Americans was just, he said, the government of Buenos Aires was legitimate, that sending a minister there would not compromise American neutrality, and that Spain would not go to war for such a reason. John Forsyth of Georgia, chairman of the foreign relations committee, was the first to respond, noting that Clay had minimized the risk of war with Spain, which would likely be backed by its fellow conservative monarchies in Europe.[4] He also questioned the qualifications of the Buenos Aires regime, criticized its persecution of Carrera, and praised the prospects of Chile—an indication of how far American policymakers had been drawn into this South American feud. The debate continued for four more days, with repeated themes: the justice of the patriot cause, the cruelty of the Spanish, a question as to whether the bill did not infringe on the executive's foreign policy responsibility, and the potential of South American trade. But when it came to the vote, Clay's proposal was badly defeated, gaining only 45 of the 160 votes cast.

As the debate that he had to some degree instigated went on in Washington, Manuel Aguirre was busy in New York trying to achieve his more immediate mission, or the purchase of warships. His instructions had been to purchase and fit out two frigates (or failing that, six smaller corvettes), to be used to liberate Peru. But Aguirre was faced with a multitude of frustrations. His first request, to the then acting secretary of state Richard Rush, had been for the U.S. government to sell him the two frigates. Rush told him that the government could not sell arms while remaining neutral, but that private firms could sell him unarmed ships.

In New York, Aguirre and Gomez found that their first frustration was financial. They had, as assets, 100,000 pesos (about $120,000 at the time) given them by San Martín, a credit of two million pesos from the Argentine government, and some twenty privateering commissions from each government. In addition, there was a promise of another 100,000 pesos from San Martín. The privateer commissions were, in 1818, no longer as valuable as they had been just two years earlier, and it appears that little money was raised from any sales that occurred. And, most importantly, the Argentine credit turned out to be a mirage.

The explanation for this state of affairs lies back in Buenos Aires, a year earlier. An American businessman and arms dealer who traded in South America, John Devereaux, had been appointed by President Madison in 1817 as a commercial agent, with the expectation that he would, in his travels in the region, report back to Washington on conditions and developments. He arrived in Buenos Aires while the Congress of Tucumán was meeting in that city and, sympathizing with the patriots' need for money to pay for arms, began to promote an American loan. He eventually put together a proposal that the Argentines found acceptable: a two million dollar line of credit from American banks, which would hold the money and disburse it for armaments purchases from American suppliers. Devereaux would get a substantial commission, and the U.S. government would guarantee the loan, so as to reduce the banks' risk and the interest rate. That is where Devereaux had seriously overstepped his authority: he was no longer arranging a commercial loan, but one that would commit the government to subsidize a form of aid to the United Provinces, and in effect recognize their legitimacy. When Secretary Rush learned of the proposal, he disowned the idea. The loan proposal quickly died, but in one respect it was too late. The United Provinces government had jumped to premature conclusions, and had sent Aguirre and Gomez to the United States thinking they could use the proposed loan to finance their purchases. When they arrived in New York, they discovered that the major part of their expected funds had evaporated.

Down to their cash holdings, they found no one willing to loan them money. Returning businessmen were reporting that the Buenos Aires government faced serious internal problems and was broke, while the New York banking community had been made wary by the earlier financial antics of Martín Thompson and José Miguel Carrera. Aguirre wrote to O'Higgins in March that Chilean as well as Argentine credit was not honored in New York because of the "irregularity of the promises and false deals (*compromentimiedos*) made by Carrera."[5] Adding to their financial problems, Aguirre and Gomez were faced with additional expenses because they had to conceal their activities from the constant surveillance of Spanish agents. And finally, they had to figure out how to circumvent the much more stringent terms of the new 1817 neutrality legislation, which prohibited persons of any nationality from fitting out armed ships in American harbors. On the advice of Secretary Adams, they consulted lawyers, who told them they could very likely be prosecuted if they purchased ships of war. Nonetheless, they decided to go ahead.

Aguirre and Gomez obtained a contract in March 1818 to build two new 30-gun sloops. These were somewhat smaller ships than the desired frigates, only what they could afford with their reduced means, but they were of good quality. Soon under construction at the Hudson River shipyards of renowned shipwrights Forman Cheeseman and Noah Brown, the two sloops would be among the largest armed ships yet built in New York, and were to be ready toward the middle of summer. Trying to avoid the neutrality legislation as well as the Spanish consulate's constant prying, Aguirre had arranged to have the contracts issued in the names of two Americans. One was Noah Brown, the owner of the shipyard; it was later transferred to John Skinner, that ubiquitous friend of the South American patriots—who apparently had hopes to be put in command of the flotilla to free Chile. The second contract was in the name of Paul Delano, a sea captain who also intended to join the Chilean navy. But as the construction progressed, Aguirre still had a major problem; he did not have enough money to pay the final installments. Hopefully, he sent Gomez back to South America to try to bring back the second tranche of Chilean money, and any other funds he could. Aguirre meanwhile stayed close, to keep an eye on the ships, cope with the harassing actions of the Spanish consulate, and continue his demarches to the state department about recognition and what he saw as the unfairness of the neutrality legislation.

The ships were ready at the end of July, facing Aguirre with two simultaneous crises. The first was legal: the Spanish consulate had gone to court to stop the ships from sailing. Aguirre, Delano, and Skinner were brought before the court, and Aguirre was actually imprisoned for four days and his house sealed by police order. By July 29, however, the legal impediment was resolved, to the undoubted annoyance of Luis de Onís who, as usual, had been pressing the government to take preemptive action. The judge ruled that merely building a ship of war was not an offense, only the actual arming and equipping. As Aguirre had been careful to keep the armament separate, but ready for subsequent transfer, he and the two ship captains were clear. But the second crisis was every bit as severe: Gomez had not returned with the needed money.

Despondent, frustrated, and angry, Aguirre wrote to Secretary Adams to lay out his predicament while at the same time complaining of mistreatment. Not only had he been thrown in jail and subjected to intimidation, he pleaded, but "For some time the natural enemies of [my] country" (that is, the Spaniards) "have brought up and carried out base means of intrigue and delay against the expedition, at time seducing and corrupting individuals from the crew of those vessels, at other times inventing or promoting direct or indirect questions designed to cause excess expenses, stoppages or delays."[6] His expenses climbing and out of cash, Aguirre was ready to abandon the exercise. He asked whether the U.S. government wanted to buy the two ships and take them off his hands.

It would be two weeks before Adams, who submitted the issue to Monroe, would reply. But in the meantime, John Skinner once again came to the rescue, as he had for José Carrera. He somehow arranged a credit from a New York commercial house of 69,500 pesos at 100 percent interest, the notes to be guaranteed by Aguirre. The ships could finally leave.

When it came, John Quincy Adams' reply to Aguirre's final diplomatic note was a firm if polite rejection of his claims. Monroe and Adams had had enough of Aguirre's regular and often bombastic demands; the usually forgiving president (when it came to South Americans, at least) confiding to the secretary of state that Aguirre's "whole proceeding here has manifested his utter incompetency for his trust."[7] Adams' letter as a result seems to be a sort of summation and justification, for the record, of the administration's conduct during the arms buying mission. Adams opened by stating that the executive did not have authorization to buy the ships. He then summarized the administration's position toward Aguirre's mission: its determination to keep to a strict neutrality, that it had advised him to seek legal advice before proceeding, that the court case was appropriate under the separate operation of the judicial system, and that his arrest was understandable as he had no diplomatic status. He concluded that "it is yet impossible for me to say that the execution of the orders of your government is impracticable; yet the Government of the United States can no more countenance or participate in any expedient to evade the intention of the laws, than it can dispense with their operation."[8] While recognizing that Aguirre had apparently found a way through the legal thicket, Adams wanted it understood, on the record, that the administration had not assisted in any way.

The *Horatio*, with Aguirre, Skinner, and a crew of 500, left at the end of August; the *Curiacio*, under Delano, sailed at the beginning of September, accompanied for the moment by the two chartered ships that carried the armament.[9] Aguirre, although bitter about his treatment, could be satisfied that he had at least accomplished, given the limit of his finances,

9. Recognition or Neutrality?

the first part of his mission. As for his government's demands that he push for recognition, he had done his best; he had found allies in the press and Congress, he had repeatedly pushed the administration, but he had not broken through. What he may not have realized was how unfortunately bad his timing had been. Pueyrredón's enemies in America had poisoned the atmosphere, while the claims of Buenos Aires to represent all of the old viceregal territory were shown to be patently empty. Moreover, Aguirre's tacit alliance with their political rival Henry Clay had simply stiffened the backs of Monroe and Adams against his demands, and Adams was insistent that recognition not be granted before the negotiations with Spain had run their course. With such a mixed result to report, though, Aguirre must have wondered how he would be received when he returned to Buenos Aires.

During Aguirre's absence, a number of events had taken place in southern South America that would bear on relations with the United States. Most important was the patriot victory over the royalist forces at Maipú in April 1818, a decisive battle in which San Martín and O'Higgins secured the full liberation of Chile. The patriot cause was looking still more hopeful.

O'Higgins' victory was a victory for the cause, but a severe setback for his rival, José Miguel Carrera. As mentioned earlier, Carrera and his two ships had returned to Buenos Aires in early 1817, to an unexpectedly hostile reception. Pueyrredón confiscated one of the ships, refused to honor Carrera's debts to Skinner and the other North American investors, and threw Carrera into prison. Carrera managed to escape and flee to Portuguese-occupied Montevideo, but while he was there his sister and two brothers undertook a madcap plot to infiltrate the Chilean army, arrest San Martín and O'Higgins, and take over the army. The brothers were soon arrested and executed, just days after the battle at Maipú. As a result of this personal tragedy, Carrera went into fully armed rebellion against the Pueyrredón government, on behalf of the dissident or Federalist provinces. His supporters in America followed his difficulties with anguish, and his debts remained unpaid.

The patriot victory at Maipú expedited the growth of American-Chilean trade, which had resumed following the liberation of Santiago in early 1817. Carrera's ship the *Savage* was an example. The ship, which actually belonged to Darcy and Didier in Baltimore, had evaded Argentine confiscation upon Carrera's return to Buenos Aires. Realizing that he could not recover Carrera's debt in Buenos Aires, the ship's captain determined to take the ship and its cargo of arms to Chile, where the arms could be—and were—sold to O'Higgins' army. Other American merchants also capitalized on the new trade opportunity, at fist largely in munitions and vessels that could be converted to warships for the growing Chilean navy. The *Columbus* of New York was an interesting example: originally fitted out as a privateer with one of the commissions issued by Aguirre in 1817, its owner-captain Charles W. Wooster (an old War of 1812 privateer) decided it was more profitable to bring weapons to Chile. Arriving in the summer of 1818, Wooster sold the ship, cargo and all, to the Chileans—who put it into their navy as the *Aracuano*, still under Captain Wooster.[10]

It should be noted on the other hand that the Americans were equal opportunity traders; they also did a brisk business with the royalists at Lima, Peru. Moreover, as the two sides in the war launched periodic paper blockades against each other, resulting in the capture of American merchantmen as well as the impressment of their seamen and the confiscation of their cargoes, it caused no end of headaches for the American consular officials in Chile as well as the U.S. Navy commanders who had been on patrol in the area since 1818. The underlying trade however, largely in munitions, was dependent on the war and peaked in 1818, when some fifteen American vessels arrived in Chilean ports with military cargo. It did set the stage for a substantial later trade between the two countries.

In Buenos Aires, the resident American businessmen continued to support the privateer business—Thomas Halsey, the consul, perhaps a little too enthusiastically. A vocal critic of Pueyrredón's rule, he would report to the State Department that the supreme director was "daring, arbitrary, [and] tramples down every thing that stands in the way of his avarice or his ambition."[11] Pueyrredón almost surely knew of Halsey's criticism, and when he learned that Halsey had also developed a side line of selling privateer commissions for the hostile Uruguayan leader Artigas (who at the time controlled no seaports), he demanded his immediate departure. Although the demand was subsequently withdrawn, Halsey was on the way out anyway, since Secretary Adams had cancelled his appointment when he learned the extent of his involvement in the privateer business.

There was a second American representative in the city at the time, as well: William G.D. Worthington, a Baltimore lawyer and patriot sympathizer who had been appointed a special agent to Argentina and Chile by Secretary of State Monroe back in January 1817; he had arrived in Buenos Aires just in time to inform the government that the Devereaux loan would not receive a government guarantee. Since then, he had been sending long, rather pompous reports on conditions in the United Provinces, and had unfortunately begun to take his situation with a bit too much seriousness. In late 1817, he drafted up a 45-clause treaty of friendship—in spite of the fact that he had no negotiating authority—and presented it to the foreign ministry. The Buenos Aires government, quite naturally, jumped at what it assumed was an official presentation, and after negotiating the draft down to 24 clauses, signed it. When the draft—which Worthington later would insist was conceived only as an interim, wartime measure designed to give American traders a competitive position with the British—arrived in Washington, Adams was aghast, commenting somewhat later in his diary that Worthington "has been swelling upon his agency until he has broken out into a self-accredited Plenipotentiary."[12] He took the problem to President Monroe, who ordered that Worthington be fired. Worthington by this time was in Chile, where he was also proposing not only a draft treaty but also a draft constitution, which fortunately the Chileans did not take as seriously as the Argentines had. Worthington was not recalled until early 1819, but his supposed treaty negotiation in Buenos Aires created a confusion that emerged later.

This then was the climate of American-Argentine relations in Buenos Aires when Manuel Aguirre returned from his long mission. Pueyrredón thought he had done a favor to the American administration by disowning Martín Thompson, and then recalling him after the Amelia Island affair.[13] He had gone through several awkward experiences with the North Americans, both in Buenos Aires where Devereaux, Halsey, and Worthington had misled him, and also in the United States where his enemies had been free to slander him, his envoy's mission had been made difficult, and his requests rebuffed. His response to these perceived setbacks would be to turn more and more to Europe for needed assistance. But at the moment, it was poor Aguirre who was made to feel this annoyance. His books and expenses were challenged, and the accounts referred to the Chileans, where it appears they were ignored. John Skinner, whose loan arrangements had made the ship purchases possible, was also given the run-around.

Skinner however was a stubborn man; he stayed in Buenos Aires on the *Horatio* almost six months, trying unsuccessfully to collect from either the Chileans or the Argentines. Frustrated and ill tempered, he eventually decided to pay himself back; in March 1819 he slipped out of harbor on the ship, sold it in neighboring Brazil to the Portuguese, and finally returned to the United States only in 1820. The other ship, the *Curiacio*, at least was put to the service it was intended for. It arrived in Valparaiso in June of 1819, and was taken into the Chilean navy, still under captain Paul Delano.[14] As for Manuel Aguirre, he eventually resumed his political career after the fall of Pueyrredón, holding several ministerial posts in succeeding governments, but losing most of his fortune in the process.

Pueyrredón, his current annoyance at Aguirre and the *norteamericanos* aside, had not given up his efforts to obtain recognition from the United States. When the businessman David DeForest, heavily involved in the local end of the American Concern's privateering, announced in 1818 that he was returning to the States to retire in his native Connecticut, he offered his services to the United Provinces government. Pueyrredón took him up, appointing him Consul General under the terms of the Worthington draft treaty, which he at the time did not realize was a stillborn initiative. That misperception would lead to still further misunderstandings.

Chapter 10

Agreement with Spain

Having just moved from the position of secretary of state to the presidency in the spring of 1817, James Monroe was nonetheless in need of good, impartial information on the rapidly evolving situation in South America. A fact finding mission to the area began to take shape in his mind. The project started small. In late April 1817, Monroe wrote to Joel Poinsett, whose previous reporting from Buenos Aires and Chile he evidently valued, and who shared Monroe's vision of eventual South American independence. The president proposed that Poinsett take on the task; he even offered a U.S. Navy frigate to take Poinsett to Venezuela, and then down the coast to Buenos Aires.[1] Poinsett however declined, being heavily engaged at the moment in South Carolina politics. But in declining, he offered the president a summary of the situation that, for its clarity and briefness, as well as its evocation of the concerns of a southern politician, is worth quoting.

"In Caracas there is no government," he wrote, "but the forces are united under the command of Bolívar. It would be important to know the connections between this Chief and the authorities of San Domingo [Haiti], and the number of negroes under arms. In Buenos Aires it will be well to ascertain the stability of the existing government, and the probable policy of their successors. It is rare that the same party remains in power more than two years. It will be necessary to enquire particularly into the extent of their Authority, as many of the provinces have established separate and independent governments."[2]

With Poinsett unavailable, Monroe's thinking turned toward a commission of several non-partisan observers. He invited Caesar Augustus Rodney of Delaware, an ex-congressman and attorney general with a good reputation for sound judgment, to take part.[3] As Rodney spoke no Spanish and was unfamiliar with the area, a second commissioner was selected who could fill those gaps: John Graham, the experienced diplomat who had been the department of state's Spanish expert for a number of years. Graham in turn encouraged the appointment of a secretary for the commission, namely Henry Brackenridge, the Spanish speaking writer of the pro-recognition open letter to President Monroe. The commissioners' instructions were drafted toward the end of July by Acting Secretary of State Richard Rush, who also was making arrangements for their departure. The instructions emphasized the fact finding nature of the commission, stressing the need for full and impartial information on the area's governments in view of the fact that some of the provinces might soon win their independence, and drawing on Poinsett's guidance in framing specific questions the commissioners should seek to answer.

The commission, however, did not depart. Caesar Rodney's son died, which caused a delay. But more significantly, the Amelia Island affair, and the arrival of the Argentine representative Aguirre, had stirred up controversy in Washington about relations with Spain and its rebellious colonies, with the result that the administration's opponents in Congress were pushing for moves that could prejudice its stance of neutrality. The administration needed to slow things down in order to keep control, and dragging out the commission's mission seemed appropriate for the purpose. Moreover, the supporters of Carrera had become alarmed over the proposed composition of the commission; they considered Rodney and especially Brackenridge to be entirely too friendly to the Pueyrredón regime, and wanted to block any movement toward early recognition of Buenos Aires. Their lobbying effort eventually paid off in November, when Theodorick Bland, the Baltimore judge and father in law of Carrera's financer, John Skinner, was added as a third commissioner.

It was not until December that the commissioners finally departed. They sailed with amended instructions, drafted by Secretary Adams. In those short but pointed instructions, they were armed with talking points that constituted a firm defense of the administration's actions with regard to Amelia Island, and instructed the commissioners to "remonstrate, in the most serious manner," against the indiscriminate issuance of privateer commissions to "the abandoned and desperate characters of all other nations."[4] Adams wanted them to be ready to go beyond mere fact finding, to defending the government's position as if they were virtual diplomats. They were also authorized, in a concession to the Carrera group, to visit Chile as well. In fact, as far as Adams and Monroe were concerned, the

10. Agreement with Spain

commissioners could take a very, very long time in South America. While they were away, congressional and other pressures for early recognition of the patriot regimes could be postponed, deflected, or ignored.

So when the congressional debate over Clay's motion to send a minister to Buenos Aires took place in March 1818, the administration and its friends in Congress had a convincing argument to deploy: that no action should be taken until the commission returned and turned in its reports. While tactically successful (as mentioned earlier, Clay's motion was soundly defeated), the administration had in effect put itself out on a limb by this tactic, because nobody knew what the commissioners would bring back. Periodic reports from or about the commissioners relieved only some of the following months' anxiety over the outcome.

Other developments however were more pressing. General Jackson's incursion into Spanish Florida in pursuit of the Seminoles, and his unauthorized capture of Pensacola in May, had aggravated the already strained relations with Spain. Onís naturally registered his government's strong objections to this new assault on its sovereign territory, causing the administration to scramble to define its own position. While there was some sentiment in the cabinet to censure Jackson for overreaching his instructions, Adams held out for holding the line and refusing to admit any wrongdoing by the popular general. Adams' motivation, however, was not political. It was diplomatic; he wanted to give no satisfaction to Spain that would weaken the U.S. position in his negotiations with Onís. Much as he had in defending the occupation of Amelia at the beginning of the year, Adams carved out a line of argument that attempted to place the blame for Jackson's incursion onto Spain itself, for its alleged inability to restrain the restless Indians in Florida from attacking American settlers across the border. While the argument may have been a bit of a logical stretch, it served the negotiating purpose of keeping some pressure on Spain to surrender its increasingly indefensible Florida colony.

The negotiations were Adam's first priority, although he kept his expectations low. At the height of the Amelia crisis, when Onís had suspended the negotiations, Adams had expressed his annoyance and disappointment to his father, writing: "Spain ... by the mode of her negotiation, provokes us to take a part against her." Even in March 1818, after Onís had agreed to resume the negotiations, Adams admitted to Richard Rush—after several exchanges with Onís that had broken no new ground—that he had slight expectations for a breakthrough: "Our new negotiation with Spain," he wrote, "like those that preceded it, is not likely to result in any agreement."[5]

The two countries were at loggerheads in many respects; on the major issues of borders and compensation there was no agreement. Jackson's raid, the alleged breaches of U.S. neutrality and aid to the patriots, the stalled negotiations: all these tensions added up so that there was even talk of war. The Spanish court entertained hopes that the major European powers, defenders of royal prerogatives since the formation of the Congress of Vienna and the even more reactionary Holy Alliance, would provide significant support for a new campaign to stamp out rebellion in the colonies. A Spanish military success in South America would in turn oblige the Americans to cease their tacit support to the rebels and ease the pressure on Florida and Texas. With Ferdinand and his court hanging on this hope, Onís was given little flexibility in his instructions, and the negotiations were making very little progress. The dialogue between Adams and Onís had in fact become so awkward and combustible that the French minister, Baron Jean-Guillaume Hyde de Neuville, interposed himself as a sort of informal facilitator between the two.

Slowly, though, the negotiations began to inch forward. A small turning point came in July 1818, when Onís's oral complaints about Jackson's capture of Pensacola turned out to be considerably milder than his for-the-record written demarche. As Adams confided to his diary after their conversation, "He [Onís] said he felt it had been his duty to write the note, but that it need not interrupt the progress of our negotiations." In the same meeting, moreover, Onís finally put formally on the table the proposition that had long been in the air: that Spain would surrender Florida to the United States, if Washington would take on responsibility to settle the substantial American claims against Spain for damages to American trade and shipping during the previous European wars.[6] It was hardly a serious concession; that part of the potential deal had already been considered as a given. But it was another signal that the negotiations still held promise. Shortly thereafter, the administration provided its own minor concession; it let it be known that it would soon withdraw the American troops from Pensacola.

Onís, some weeks later, fortuitously received authority to announce another small step: that the Spanish government had finally ratified a convention for the settlement of wartime claims that had been pending since 1802. These were small steps, but ones indicating that the king and his obstructionist court had begun to understand what Onís had held for some time: that the United States, self-confident and expansionist, already in occupation of West Florida and Amelia Island and posing a vague but continual threat on the undefined border of Texas, had the stronger hand, and to break off the negotiations would quite probably cause a war in which those colonies could be lost, without the hope of any balancing concessions from the Americans.[7]

Developments elsewhere were also helping to unblock the negotiations. European politics played a role, and particularly the decisive objections made by the British, during the November 1818 four-power conference at Aix la Chapelle, against the broad interventionist aspirations of the Holy Alliance partners of Russia, Prussia and Austria. The policy of non-intervention consequently adopted at that conference was a clear signal to Spain that it had to abandon hope of major power support for a major military campaign to subdue the South American rebels.

The British, while remaining neutral in the South American wars, understood that Spain's day in the region was coming to a close, and aimed to strengthen the strong commercial presence that their traders had already established in the rebel-held ports. Trying to keep a foot in both camps, the British had on several occasions offered to mediate between Spain and her colonies, and had even encouraged the Americans to join in a European effort. (President Monroe had declined, noting to Adams that mediation would only bring about a compromise, and that he felt that America's interest should be, instead, to "to promote the total independence of the colonies.")[8] British and American policies of neutrality toward the Spanish civil wars were in fact quite similar at the time, except for the reality of a commercial rivalry in which Great Britain was currently dominant. The British, all the same, were fearful that early American recognition of the rebel regimes could give American traders the upper hand in their turn. Britain and America were also in the process of resolving a number of outstanding issues, in a negotiation that resulted in November in the signing of the 1818 London Convention. In that agreement, the border between the United States and Canada was fixed on a line westward up to the Oregon Territory, which was to be jointly occupied.

These two developments would strengthen Secretary Adam's hand considerably in his negotiations with Onís. Not only had the Spanish lost their last hope of major power assistance in subduing the South American rebels, they now had to negotiate borders with an American side that already had a claim to a presence on the Pacific coast, bordering Spanish California.

Even as the negotiations with Onís were promising to become more intense, however, Adams was faced with a complication arising from the activity of a new Argentine envoy. The envoy was David DeForest, the American businessman and privateer sponsor from Buenos Aires, who had arrived with a commission from Pueyrredón, as an Argentine citizen with the title of consul general under the abortive "treaty" negotiated by William Worthington. DeForest had arrived in Washington in May 1818, and soon met informally with Secretary Adams. Adams informed him that the Worthington treaty was not authorized or accepted by the United States, and that he could not be accepted as consul general, as to do so would amount to recognition of the Buenos Aires government and compromise U.S. neutrality. Although DeForest acknowledged that his status was irregular, he also indicated that he would continue his work on behalf of the Argentines, and asked for and received a short meeting with President Monroe.

DeForest had already asked William Winder, the Baltimore lawyer and supporter of the patriot privateers, to become a spokesman for the Buenos Aires regime. (Winder cautiously sought Monroe's advice, and then declined the offer when Monroe's response was enthusiastic over the cause of South American independence but unsupportive on the question of taking the position.) Although DeForest soon went to his home in Connecticut for the summer, it was evident that such an active and determined agent (whose sponsorship of a number of the Buenos Aires-flagged privateers, moreover, must have rankled Adams) would not cease his efforts readily. When Congress reconvened in November, he was likely to be back in action.

Privateers and the war at sea were on John Quincy Adams' mind that summer for a number of reasons besides DeForest's sudden appearance in Washington. The administration had just convinced Congress to close some of the loopholes in the neutrality legislation, major legal cases against the privateers were underway or pending in Baltimore, piratical acts were multiplying, and even the South American navies had begun to seize American ships. One case in particular, in which Venezuelan authorities had summarily confiscated the ships and goods of two American merchants, had created enough of a commotion to have been a major reason for sending a special envoy to Simón Bolívar's headquarters in Angostura. The mission would have several aims: to protest and seek compensation for the merchants (who had been accused of violating a Bolívar-decreed blockade of the Venezuelan coast), to assure Bolívar that the United States viewed South American aspirations favorably in spite of its policy of neu-

10. Agreement with Spain

trality, and to seek a disavowal of Lino de Clemente's act in authorizing the MacGregor expedition to Amelia Island.

The envoy was Baptis Irvine, who arrived in Venezuela in July 1818. At first glance, the choice of Irvine as envoy seems to have been clever. The journalist was, after all, an outspoken champion of South American independence and supporter of the agents who had come to seek aid in the United States. Who better, to be the first semi-official U.S. envoy to that other champion of independence, Bolívar? And yet the mission misfired; the two men simply did not get along. Irvine, "a fanatic of liberty for the whole human race [who] sees everything through the medium of his prejudices," as Adams would describe him,[9] was sadly disappointed in Bolívar, whom he found to be too autocratic in his political intentions, overly ambitious, and an inadequate military leader. Bolívar, who for his part was already disappointed at the lack of material North American support for the Venezuelan cause and skeptical as to U.S. policy intentions, was unreceptive to Irvine's presentations. He remained adamant in defending the propriety of the Venezuelan blockade and seizure of the Americans' cargo (which was, in fact, arms destined for the royalists), and was also unresponsive to Irvine's declarations of U.S. friendship. In the end, Irvine's mission succeeded only in the last objective—obtaining a Venezuelan admission that Clemente had acted without official authority.

That statement at least gave the Monroe administration the evidence it needed to justify its claim that the MacGregor expedition could be dismissed as an unauthorized adventure. It was a bit irrelevant by late 1818, in any event, as the Jackson raid into West Florida had eclipsed the Amelia Island adventure as a subject of controversy. The signers of MacGregor's commission on the other hand were victims of the disavowals: Martín Thompson had already been dismissed by Pueyrredón for having exceeded his instructions, and Clemente was coldly informed by Adams toward the end of the year that no further communication from him would be received. Pedro Gual however escaped the censure, probably because there was no contact with the New Grenadan and Mexican governments which he had purported to represent. In spite of their lack of status, Thompson and Clemente stayed in the United States until 1819, trying to buy arms and complaining in reports home (Clemente at least) of American partiality to Spain.[10]

In late summer and fall, the members of the fact finding commission to South America returned and began to prepare their report. The result, awaited with some anticipation at their departure almost a year previously, had been foreshadowed by occasional progress reports and letters, and yet was a thorough anti-climax. The commissioners in the end disagreed on enough points to be unable to present a joint report. Instead, each commissioner submitted his own report, while Joel Poinsett submitted a separate set of observations as requested by Secretary Adams.[11] Henry Brackenridge, the commission secretary, also published his own, unofficial report, which came out in two volumes in 1819 as *Voyage to South America, Performed by Order of the American Government in the Years 1817 and 1818 in the Frigate Congress*, and may in the end have had more impact than the official documents.

The commissioners had been greeted amicably and with some expectations upon their arrival in Buenos Aires back in February 1818. They had met with Supreme Director Pueyrredón amidst mutual exchanges of friendship and cooperation, and soon began their investigations into the local situation. They were also hosted to a Washington's Birthday celebration by the resident American businessmen, among whom were a number of members of the privateering community and U.S. Consul Halsey, all of them enthusiastic backers of Argentine independence. The commissioners did not limit themselves to such set pieces, however; they were assiduous in collecting information even though they complained that unbiased information was hard to come by in a society so full of political conflicts. Their eventual reports are full of solid, factual information about the situation in the United Provinces, positive on the social changes taking place, and agree that reconquest by Spain would be highly unlikely, but differ in their evaluations of the Buenos Aires regime.

Caesar Rodney's report was the most positive toward the regime and the progress it had made, while Graham's report was more critical, exposing the limitations on civil liberty, the inadequate constitution, and separatist tendencies of the outlying provinces. Theodorick Bland's report, not surprisingly given his connections to the Carrera supporters, is the most negative on that score; pointing out that the government was not in control of large segments of the previous viceroyalty and that "the ruling party of Buenos Ayres has managed the affairs of the Union in such a strain of domineering monopoly as to retard reform, delay the progress of the revolution, and to render the most patriotic provinces extremely dissatisfied."[12]

The commissioners disagreed on procedural matters, as well, while in Buenos Aires. Bland had been pressing from the time of his appointment to the commission that it should also be authorized to visit Chile, and when he pressed his case in Buenos Aires it created a split between himself and Rodney and Brackenridge. As the amended instructions from Secretary Adams had authorized such a diversion, however, the commissioners eventually agreed that Bland could go. At the end of April, they wound up their business in Buenos Aires and, while Bland crossed the Andes to Chile, the others sailed for the United States, where they arrived in July.

Bland's report from Chile was generally positive but with no specific recommendations. It became clear subsequently that a major purpose of his trip there had been to try to find a way to settle the debts that Carrera owed to his son-in-law, John Skinner. That fact helped to explain his earlier difficulties with Rodney, which had been caused by the latter's anger over the fact that his colleague had an obvious private agenda as well as his public one. Bland, his Chilean mission completed with limited success, re-crossed the Andes and returned to the United Sates via Buenos Aires in September.

The divided opinion among the commissioners was a relief for Adams and Monroe. They had worried that any positive tilt by Rodney and Brackenridge toward the Buenos Aires government would play into the hands of Henry Clay and other supporters of diplomatic recognition, when Congress reconvened and once again picked up debate on South American policy. Indeed, the influential *Niles' Weekly Register* was already assuming that the recognition issue would be one of the great questions of the winter session, and that the report of the commissioners would favor recognition of the Buenos Aires government. Promoting recognition and minimizing the risk of provoking Spain and the Holy Alliance, the paper voiced the opinion that "we are very far from wishing war, even with contemptible Spain." Spain and the other Europeans, the paper argued, were unlikely to declare war simply because America had recognized the rebels. In fact, the paper continued, the British would welcome the step.[13]

In the end, the only member of the commission to recommend recognition was Brackenridge, the secretary, who did so unofficially in his book. As that did not get published until the following year, the administration was spared the need to fight off any controversial conclusions. The president's November 16 message to Congress consequently was able to dwell on the positive news: that the Amelia Island adventure had been disowned by the governments of the United Provinces and Venezuela, that the commissioners' reports would be distributed for the information of Congress, and that there was little likelihood of armed intervention by the European powers against the rebel regimes. The president concluded, rather hopefully, that "there is good cause to be satisfied with the course heretofore pursued by the United States in regard to this contest, and to conclude that it is proper to adhere to it, especially in the present state of affairs."[14]

Monroe and Adams had every reason to want the recognition issue to remain on a back burner during the coming months. The repercussions from American occupation of Amelia Island had not yet subsided, and moreover the crisis caused by Jackson's raid into Florida had further poisoned relations with Spain—as well as angering Britain (two British citizens had been summarily tried and executed under Jackson's orders, for alleged incitement of the Seminoles). And finally, the negotiations with Onís, though no longer frozen, were still making no progress on the major border issues. Adams, true to his tactic of applying pressure, even suggested at the end of the year that it was not worthwhile continuing unless the Spanish had something new to put on the table.

The talks were at a crisis point and so were relations with Spain. Keeping the Spanish minister and his government uneasy about American intentions with respect to recognizing the rebel regimes was useful leverage, but preemptive congressional action on the subject was to be avoided if at all possible, as it would undercut the administration's position and perhaps even tip the balance toward hostilities,

It was not welcome news, then, when Adams learned that both David DeForest and Lino de Clemente had arrived in Washington, ready to raise the issue of their credentials. Clemente's early December request for an official appointment was the easier one to deal with; his signature on the MacGregor commission was still held against him, and as that act of his had now been disowned by his own government, it was exemplary for Adams to refuse him any official status at all, even exchanges of correspondence. Clemente, low on funds like many of his patriot colleagues, had no recourse but to return to Philadelphia, where his lodging was presumably both more convivial and less expensive than Washington during the congressional season.

DeForest, however, presented a different situation for the secretary of state. The envoy was not tarred with the Amelia Island problem, and though he was suspect in Adams' eyes because of his Buenos Aires privateer connections, he was a man of consequence in U.S. circles and could not be brushed off as easily as Clemente. DeForest had been making calls in Congress and elsewhere since his arrival in Washington, where it could be assumed that he had been broadcasting the arguments that he made in his December 11 request for an official appointment—specifically, that the improved circumstances in Buenos Aires, and the need for consular protection for Argentine ships,[15] now justified acceptance of his credentials. Adams needed to respond, to make sure the record was put straight. He scheduled an appointment.

When DeForest called, Adams took a cordial but firm stance toward his request. Acknowledging that the president was willing in principle to establish relations with the United Provinces of Rio de la Plata, the secretary of state emphasized that the time nonetheless was not yet ripe, and in the meantime there could be no question of accepting DeForest's credentials as an accredited official of that government. At DeForest's request that he put his response in writing, Adams, realizing that it would at some time be requested by Congress, drafted a letter that made essentially the same points but somewhat more categorically. For the record, he also included an exposition of issues that had only been touched on in their conversation. In the same line, he addressed yet another letter to DeForest some ten days later, reverting to the shipping protection question that DeForest had raised in his first communication. He switched the subject slightly, however, to privateering—a problem much on his mind at the time as several sensitive legal cases against privateers worked their way through the Baltimore courts. He urged DeForest to inform his government of "the necessity of taking measures to repress the excesses and irregularities committed by many armed vessels sailing under their [Buenos Aires'] flag and bearing their commissions." Apparently unable to resist the temptation to prod at DeForest's own involvement, Adams went on to decry how those commissions "have been offered to the avidity of speculators, stimulated more by the thirst for plunder than any regard for the South American cause."[16]

DeForest's request nonetheless stimulated discussion within the administration as to whether the time had come to make some declaration of readiness to recognize the Rio de la Plata government, and whether or not to do so in coordination with others governments such as Great Britain's. The cabinet met at the start of the year to discuss the issue, and, as no decision was reached, it meant that the argument with Henry Clay's supporters would continue. It also served Adams' purpose, in that the continuing uncertainty could only feed Don Onís's anxiety.

For the moment, the attention of Congress was on a more pressing and politically sensitive issue—how to react to General Jackson's highhanded tactics in Florida over the summer. A motion of censure was being proposed, which was less motivated by public opinion (which generally favored the general's actions) than by jockeying for advantage in the competition to become the next presidential candidate. In his submission to Congress on what was called the Seminole War issue, President Monroe, in spite of some personal reservations, approved Adams's tough line. Blame was placed on the Spaniards for not controlling the Seminoles (and their British inciters), and Jackson's actions were rationalized away. It was a strong argument, if not necessarily a completely honest one. But the stakes were large: both to keep the Spaniards on the defensive, and to deny the administration's political opponents a victory. Debate began in mid-January.

By early January, however, Adams' attention was refocused on the negotiations with Spain. Or, to be explicit, with French minister de Neuville, who was busy trying to mediate between the two tough-minded principals. Neuville informed Adams that Onís had very recently received new, broader and more flexible instructions as a result of a government shakeup in Madrid. The rigid foreign minister, José García Pizzaro, had been replaced by Onís's predecessor as minister to the United States, Carlos Irujo. A new and more favorable Spanish proposal, Neuville suggested, would soon come forth. But Neuville also fished for Adams' reaction to a possible American concession: might the United States be ready to pledge that it would not recognize the new governments? Adams, though, could give the inquisitive Frenchman no satisfaction on that point. His refusal was not just a negotiating tactic, it was also a deeply held position—that true independence for those states was increasingly likely, and the United States could not have its hands tied as to when it would recognize them.

While waiting for a new proposal from Onís (or feelers from Neuville), Adams had two connected irritants to deal with: a congressional request for the documents involved in the Clemente and DeForest requests for accreditation, and another letter from DeForest that supported his case for recognition with arguments that Adams complained to his diary were "cunning and deceptive." Adams felt himself personally under fire: "In this affair everything is insidious and factious. The call is made for the purpose of baiting the Administration and especially of fastening upon the Secretary of State the odium of refusing to receive South American Ministers and Consuls General. I am walking on a rope, with a precipice on each side of me, and without human aid beyond myself upon whom to rely."[17] Attempting to close all avenues of criticism, he drafted a comprehensive covering letter in which he defended the administration's posi-

10. Agreement with Spain

tion toward the numerous arguments raised by Clemente, DeForest, and their defenders. The packet was submitted to Congress at the end of the month.

Shortly beforehand, DeForest himself had bowed out. He called on Adams to tell him that he was leaving for his Connecticut home, and to suggest that he had done nothing to instigate the congressional call for papers. Adams took the opportunity to remind DeForest that, while living in the United States, he would necessarily be considered as an American citizen in spite of his secondary Argentine citizenship. DeForest was struck by this, expressing concern that it could leave him unprotected if Spaniards sought compensation for damages from his privateer activities. Somewhat bothered at the prospect, he left Washington for a comfortable retirement in New Haven, where he would continue to commemorate La Plata independence day, and periodically but modestly renew his claim for official status.

The end of January also brought about new movement in the negotiations with Onís. (Adams had postured theatrically to his Spanish opponent less than a week earlier that the lack of progress was making him "nauseous.") Onís's new instructions now allowed him to table a proposal for a northern boundary to Spain's possessions in North America that would extend all the way to the Pacific. Where that line would be drawn would require more rounds of negotiation, as would the borders with Texas, but the negotiation had finally reached the decision stage. Baron de Neuville played a crucial role, shuttling back and forth between the two principals, allowing them to test each other's positions. By the first week of February, Onís had prepared draft treaty language which Adams felt he could take to the president and cabinet. A counterproposal was agreed to there, but only after some debate in which Adams—always sensing that Onís and Spain needed a treaty more than the American side—had to restrain President Monroe's readiness to accept the current offer. By the middle of the month, Adams could finally hope that an agreement might be reached; both sides were under pressure as they wanted to come to a conclusion if possible before the impending end of the congressional session. Adams and the cabinet yielded on a few points but stood firm on most; Onís had little choice but to yield ground, time and again. Final agreement was reached on the 20th, and on February 22 the treaty was signed.

The Adams-Onís Treaty of 1819, also called the Transcontinental Treaty, put to rest twenty years of sometimes ugly controversy between the two neighboring states. At the time, its most important provision for Americans was Spain's cession of the Floridas to the United States, removing forever the security threat to the southeastern settlers and any barrier to their seaborne trade. In return, the United State dropped its claim to a Rio Grande border, and Spain got the Texas border fixed at the Sabine river (the present western boundary of Louisiana), while the United States agreed to assume responsibility for settling the claims for damages against Spain—up to a limit of five million dollars. Looking into the future, however, the most important elements of the treaty were the fixing of the western boundary of Louisiana, and agreement on the 42nd parallel as the boundary between Spain and the U.S., all the way to the Pacific coast (the present northern boundaries of California, Nevada, and Utah). The United States was finally a trans-continental power, thanks to the persistence and hardheaded negotiating tactics of John Quincy Adams.

The treaty was rapidly ratified by the Senate, in spite of some vocal criticism by western politicians who were disgusted by the abandonment of claims to Texas. Monroe and Adams were also aware that there had been some maneuvers by Onís to set the cut-off date in the treaty so as to sneak in some last-minute royal land grants in Florida, and they insisted that any predated grants be annulled. Ratification by Spain would resolve that issue, the United States could then occupy the rest of Florida, and a commission would be set up to deal with the past claims. The treaty was generally acclaimed, with perhaps the most concise description of its benefit coming from the pro-administration *National Intelligencer*: "It terminates the only existing controversy with any of the European powers, it rounds off our southern possessions and forever precludes foreign emissaries from stirring up Indians to war and negroes to rebellion, whilst it gives to the southern country important outlets to the sea. It adjusts the vast western boundary."[18]

In the meantime, Monroe and Adams had other developments to celebrate. In early February, at the end of three weeks' debate in Congress over the Seminole War issue, the administration's defense of General Jackson's behavior was upheld by a substantial majority. And then, two days later, Henry Clay announced that it was too late in the session to raise the issue of recognition for the new Spanish American governments. The congressional session had ended, not only without damage, but with several useful victories.

The treaty was sent to Madrid, where it still needed to obtain ratification by the Spanish government, and where it would be subjected to the critique of the king's capricious and conservative clique, or *camarilla*, of advisors. Onís, exhausted by ten years of a difficult assignment, announced that he also would head home in the near future. When he eventually left in April, Adams almost admitted to nostalgia at losing such a competent adversary: "I part with Onís with regret, though he has more of diplomatic *trickery* than any of the other foreign Ministers here," he noted. An earlier Adams diary entry describing Onís's character is also interesting, in that the first four qualities he cites could easily be applied to John Quincy himself: "Cold, calculating, wily, always commanding his temper, proud because he is a Spaniard but supple and cunning ... bold and overbearing to the utmost extent to which it is tolerated, careless of what he asserts or how grossly it is proven to be unfounded.... He is laborious, vigilant, and ever attentive to his duties; a man of business and the world."[19]

The two diplomats had done their job; they had provided the opportunity for a new course in Spanish-American relations. But Spain was still at war with her breakaway colonies, and resentful and suspicious of the United States' role in that conflict. The new course was unlikely to be an easy one.

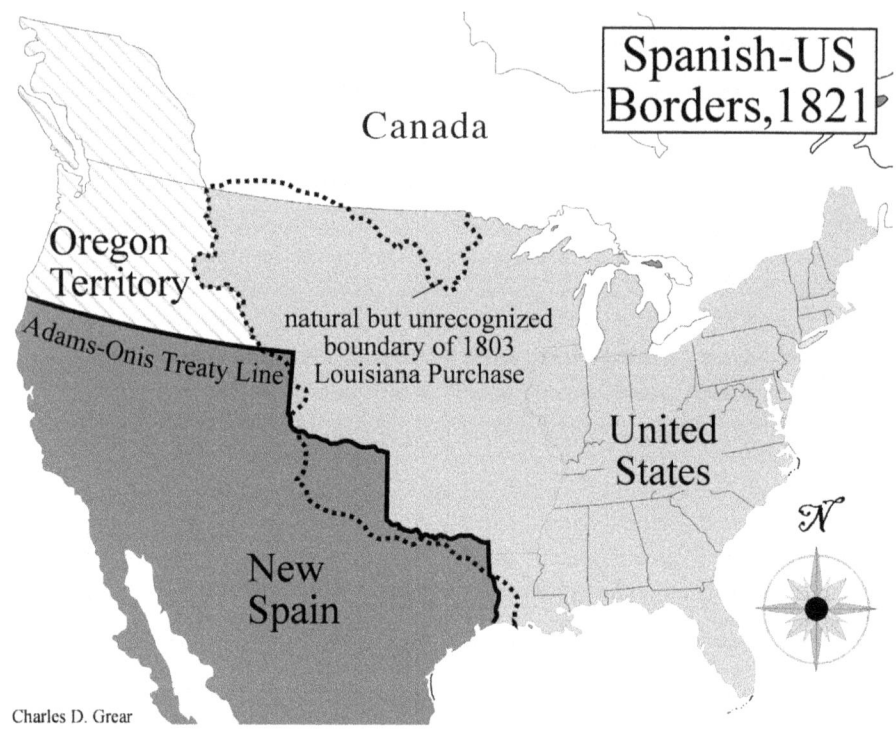

Charles D. Grear

By 1821, the U.S. borders to the north with Canada and to the south with Spain (soon to be replaced by an independent Mexico) were fixed, and the previously undefined boundaries of the Louisiana Purchase clarified. The instruments for this trans-continental division were the London Convention of 1818, which among other things provide for joint American-British occupation of the Oregon Territory, and the Adams-Onís Treaty of 1819 (ratified only in 1821). Note that a number of the subsequent state borders were effectively prefigured by these treaties.

Chapter 11

Success Is a Matter of Fact

Don Luis de Onís returned to Spain in August 1819 with limited expectations of a warm official welcome. He knew that some of the terms of the treaty (which had been sent ahead by a speedy ship) would open him to personal attack in the antagonistic atmosphere of Madrid's royal court. In the last stages of his negotiation with Secretary Adams, he had pleaded against linking the cession of Florida to a five million dollar limit on settlement of the outstanding claims. The conservatives who surrounded King Ferdinand, he had argued, would seize on that figure to attack the treaty, and him, for selling the king's patrimony for a song. Adams however had prevailed in the argument. He had on his side the pressures of both time and logic—Florida had always been a net drain on Spanish resources. Onís had been obliged to yield. He had also been obliged to agree that the last-minute Florida land grants made in Madrid to court favorites would be invalid under the treaty.

Onís had been right in fretting about his own vulnerability. The treaty had arrived at court in April; opposition to some of its terms (particularly those disallowing the suspicious last-minute land grants) had coalesced in the Council of State. Both he and Carlos Irujo (who had been maneuvered out of his short tenure as foreign minister in June) were quietly slandered by those who opposed the treaty. The agreement was attacked as a surrender of Spain's rights and a disgrace to the king's majesty; Onís, it was suggested, had been either cowed by the Americans or overly friendly to them—bribes were implied.

Militancy was in the Madrid air, and a large expedition of ten brigades was being assembled in Cádiz with the objective of putting an end to the South American insurrections. In the prevailing climate around the royal court, ratification of the treaty was unlikely to occur soon. Onís, proud and touchy, was glad to find out that at least he was still in royal favor. He was received courteously by the king, who awarded him with a medal and promised him the position of Spanish minister in St. Petersburg.[1] While awaiting his assignment and to clear his name, Onís sat down to draft a defense of his actions in America, which would be published as his *Memorial Concerning the Negotiations* in the following year. A self-serving document, the *Memorial* quickly crossed the Atlantic to Washington, where it was derided by Adams as not being truthful. It also prompted Adams to poke fun at his old adversary, alleging that "I have seen slippery diplomatists, more than one, but Onís is the first man I have met with who made it a point of honor to pass for more of a swindler than he was."[2]

The depth of the discord in Madrid was not immediately clear in Washington, however. The treaty provided for a six-month period to achieve ratification, and Congress had given the president authority to occupy Florida and set up government there whenever the treaty came into force. In the meantime, Congress was not in session, and the borders were more or less quiet. It was time to take care of other pending business.

High on Adams' list was the need to get the business of the patriot-flagged privateers under better control. It was hoped that the new Neutrality Act of 1819 would help control the situation in American ports, but the problem had become much broader. Abuses of innocent shipping and crimes of piracy had continued to multiply, with attendant claims for damages plus diplomatic complaints from friendly governments. American ships had been seized, too, by renegade privateers, and American citizens impressed into service on the South American-flagged privateers or naval ships. U.S. public opinion—as well as French, Spanish, and Portuguese diplomatic pressure—was calling for stronger action. Adams's concern and frustration over the issue was compounded by the administration's difficulty in getting convictions in the key Baltimore privateering trials. The privateer connections of Judge Theodorick Bland and other Maryland officials were another cause for irritation. Adams had been obliged to drop his opposition to Bland's promotion to the circuit court; that was an issue of domestic politics that he could not control. But as secretary of state he could at least push for diplomatic solutions in those places where the problem had in many ways originated—the young South American governments' loose administration of their privateering regimes.

The Baptis Irvine mission had achieved little in that respect in Venezuela,[3] and the U.S. commissioners seem never to have raised the issue effectively in Buenos Aires. So when Monroe raised the possibility, during a March 1819 cabinet discussion about the anti-piracy act, of sending a special representative to South America, the idea quickly took on form. Monroe assigned Captain Oliver Hazard Perry, a hero of the War of 1812 who could speak authoritatively both for the administration and on naval affairs, to lead the team.[4] Perry was given no diplomatic title, it being considered that he could speak more effectively as a sort of friendly spokesman for the administration. All the same, Adams armed the dashing commodore with a long letter giving him arguments to use in defending the United States' neutral stance.

Perry was to point out that Washington's policy was designed keep the European powers from interfering, while actually favoring the patriots by allowing them full belligerent rights.

The Perry mission sailed in June, arriving up the Orinoco River the following month. In Angostura—more a military headquarters than a seat of government—they were welcomed by the Venezuelan acting vice president Francisco Zea because Simón Bolivar was at the front with his army, just having completed a heroic crossing of the Andes to liberate New Granada. The discussions were friendly but inconclusive, with Juan Germán Roscio, now a secretary of state, serving as interpreter and spokesman for the Venezuelan side. The Venezuelans recognized some responsibility for illegal seizures by their ships, but made no promises to change their commissioning, prize court or confiscation procedures. The inconclusive nature of the talks resulted more definitively however from the sad fact that Perry, during his almost three weeks in the low-lying tropical town, had caught yellow fever. He died at sea, in a race to get him to a hospital in Jamaica. The mission to Buenos Aires was abandoned as a result, the Angostura talks were never written up officially, and the mission was, once again, a failure.

The disappointment at least stirred Adams into action on a point he had been concerned about: just as the independence struggle was nearing what seemed to be a turning point, the United States government lacked reliable eyes and ears in South America. John Graham, the reliable State Department diplomat, was headed to Rio de Janeiro, it's true. But American relations with the Portuguese government were already quite satisfactory, and Rio was not a good vantage point from which to evaluate events in the rest of South America, given Portuguese involvement in the war underway in the Rio de la Plata area. There was no official representation in Venezuela or New Granada due to the royalist dominance of the capital cities. (Halsey and Worthington, the last two envoys to Buenos Aires, had both departed and were discredited in any event.) Only in Chile was there an accredited American diplomat: John B. Prevost, a lawyer and friend of Monroe's who had arrived there in early 1818. His arrival however created an accidental surplus of American representatives, as Judge Bland and William Worthington were also in Valparaiso at the time—and the three disagreed on many points of policy and tactics. The confusion however was only temporary, as Prevost and Captain James Biddle of the USS *Ontario* soon left to proceed on their second mission—to assure the friendly handover to U.S. control of John Jacob Astor's base and trading post at the mouth of the Columbia River.

Bland and Worthington had departed Chile by the time Prevost and Biddle returned in the autumn, but Prevost's management of his responsibilities to protect the growing Pacific presence of American whalers and merchants failed to meet Secretary Adams' requirement for objectivity. Adams, indeed, was annoyed at far more than Prevost, as can be sensed from a later entry in his diary. "There is something disheartening in all our correspondence and transactions relating to South America," he groused. "We have done everything possible in their favor, and have received from them little less than injury in return. No satisfaction has been obtained from them upon any complaint, and they have been constantly endeavoring to entangle us with them and their cause. Prevost has been one of their dupes."[5]

New blood—new, more professional American envoys—Adams concluded, were needed.

A first order of business, however, had become the need to explain to a new session of Congress why the treaty's six-month term for ratification had passed without any action by the Spanish court. Monroe's December 1819 message to Congress was, by the nature of things, unclear on the point. It noted that the Spanish had mentioned the need for clarification on several points (one of them being the disputed land grants), and that they would not discuss the issue with the American minister in Madrid, but rather had indicated their intention to send a new envoy to Washington to seek clarifications—although so far no minister had been nominated. Monroe's message amounted to a spirited defense of America's interests, but all in all it was a temporizing message and unsatisfactory. The only proposal for congressional action, beside the implicit call for patience, was a suggestion that armed ships under foreign flag should be allowed entry to the United States only in certain designated ports.[6] But then, in mid-March of 1820, the president sent a second message to Congress urging patience to those who were arguing for a unilateral occupation of Florida. This time he specifically cited the "distress" of Spain as a reason for not pushing forward; any military pressure, Monroe argued, was more likely to delay ratification by Madrid than speed it up.

The cause of Spain's "distress" had gradually become known in Washington and was evident, but what it would bring about was anything but clear. In January, the army being marshaled in Cádiz had mutinied. Many of its officers were liberals opposed to Ferdinand's autocratic rule, whom the king had hoped to sideline by sending them off to fight in the provinces. Instead, they had turned the tables by taking advantage of the existing disgruntlement among the expedition's soldiers over bad pay and treatment; their mutiny expanded over the coming months into a broad revolt. By March the army had surrounded Madrid, and soon King Ferdinand was obliged to restore the liberal 1812 constitution. The restoration of liberalism however was not complete, and the mutiny had ushered in a period of internal division and civil unrest.

As the news of these startling developments reached the Americas, one thing at least was clear: there would be no major Spanish expedition to crush the insurgent governments. The royalist forces left in South America were henceforth on their own. But what effect the events in Spain would have on ratification of the treaty would only become clear with the arrival of a new Spanish minister to the United States.

When the new Spanish minister, General Francisco Dionisio Vives, finally arrived in April, he disappointed the American officials in that he brought neither a ratification nor the power to negotiate the handover of Florida; he only had authority to seek clarifications and report back to Madrid. Moreover, he claimed that American actions since the signing of the treaty allowed Spain to demand, as a condition of ratification, that the United States undertake not to recognize any of the rebel governments. Adams, speaking for an indignant president and cabinet, was rigid in his response. In a series of formal notes following his meetings with Vives, he refused to accept anything but the ratification that had been promised, in the kings' name and on his authority, at the time of signature. He dismissed the suggestions that America had countenanced violations of its neutrality or acquiesced in the land grants, and most emphatically insisted that any condition that the United States promise not to recognize was unacceptable, as it would violate both U.S. neutrality and honor. Vives was in no position to negotiate; he had presented Spain's case, clarifications had been given, but Spain's condition had been rejected. The general, whom Adams later flattered as having "the talent of a fair and candid mind, which for a Spanish negotiator was the first, because the rarest, of talents,"[7] explained a new feature of the Spanish dilemma: since Ferdinand had accepted to return to the 1812 constitution, he no longer had exclusive royal power to ratify treaties. Vives could only submit his report to Madrid, and Washington would have to wait for that troubled government's response.

Adams's effort to boost official contacts with the new South American governments also moved slowly. By the summer, Adams had recruited new agents to go to two key places in South America: John M. Forbes for Buenos Aires and Charles S. Todd for Colombia. (It was assumed that John Prevost, who was currently in Buenos Aires where he had recently reported the fall of Pueyrredón, would return to Chile.) The new representatives were assigned as special or confidential agents, with instructions to report on developments, pursue the claims of American ship-owners, promote American trade, and urge the governments to rein in their privateers. They were also instructed to defend the policy of neutrality, profess American friendship, but decline to discuss conditions for recognition.

Forbes arrived in Buenos Aires in October 1820 and found Prevost about to leave for Chile. In fact, Prevost had been asked to leave by the new authorities after some of his critical reporting about the recent change in government had become public. (Pueyrredón, he had reported, had been deposed in part because of his scheming to bring a Bourbon prince to rule as a constitutional monarch.) Forbes found the local officials to be unfriendly, decidedly pro-British, and disappointed that he had arrived with no diplomatic title. But he was an experienced diplomat; he settled in, reported frequently and well, and supported American interests in a way that won the respect of the Argentines. He would remain at post for eleven years.

Charles Todd, on the other hand, did not establish himself permanently in Colombia until the fall of 1822. The new state of Gran Colombia had been formed some two years earlier, following Bolívar's defeat of the royalist forces in New Granada and the union of that state with Venezuela in December 1819. It was, however, a work in progress; pockets of royalists remained in the country, Caracas only fell in 1821, and the Ecuadorean region was not liberated until 1822. In the summer of 1821, however, following capture of the royalist stronghold of Lima by San Martín, the state had been broadened to include most of the above provinces, and called itself Gran Colombia, with its capital at Bogota and Bolívar as president.

Pending Todd's arrival in Columbia, a semi-official channel of communication was opened up in the United States through Manuel Torres. Torres, because of his Colombian roots and long familiarity with the North American scene, had been appointed as consul general shortly after the formation of the new state, and his first task was to take over Lino de Clemente's effort to purchase arms for the struggling new government. Clemente had used Jacob Idler of Philadelphia as his purchasing agent, and Torres continued that relationship. It was a difficult task however; credit was short in the United States due to the 1819 bank crisis, while Venezuelan credit was especially poor and weakened further by the complaints of many unhappy creditors, dating back to Telésforo de Orea's mission.

Torres was able to use his relationship with Henry Clay to obtain introductions to Langdon Cheves, president of the Second Bank of the United States, with whom he opened negotiation for a half million-dollar loan. Torres, recognizing that the bank crisis was caused in part by a severe lack of hard currency, offered what amounted to a futures contract—credit in exchange for a future delivery of South American specie. At Torres' urging when the bank proved hesitant, Bolívar even offered the ownership of a Colombian silver mine in exchange for the credit and assumption of past debts. Torres also appealed successfully to John Quincy Adams to tell the bankers that the administration had no political objection to the proposed deal. However the bankers, finding the proposals beyond their conventional risk threshold, backed off. A still larger second arms deal, negotiated by Torres and Idler with the Dutch firm of Mees, Boer, and Moens for the sale of Belgian muskets in exchange for Colombian bonds (backed by tobacco from Venezuela's Barinas province), also fell through in early 1820, as the proposed exchange foundered when the royalists fought their way back into that province.

The resourceful Torres, however, already had another project underway. Understanding that the peacetime U.S. military had excess stocks of muskets on hand, he had assembled a lobbying group of prominent military and manufacturing officials who would champion a proposal to sell a large quantity—twenty thousand—of the army's surplus rifles to Colombia.[8] The group had considerable clout, and it took a cabinet decision to settle whether the government could be party to such a transaction. The lead in the cabinet discussion was taken by Secretary Adams, who had objections both private and public. Privately, he was protecting his foreign affairs turf from the military's meddling, was in agreement with the president that the proposal was profit-driven and "underhand," and, finally, because he strongly resented the involvement of that persistent and objectionable critic of the administration William Duane of the *Aurora*—who, Adams moreover believed, expected to get a commission from the sale. His argument in the cabinet, though, was based on the public policy issue of whether such a proposal would amount to a sale of arms to a foreign government, and therefore a breach of carefully guarded official neutrality. His argument carried the day, and Torres once more was frustrated in his effort, although he got a polite note from Adams the following day to soften the disappointment somewhat.

And yet Manuel Torres and Jacob Idler, in the spring and summer of 1820, managed to put together two smaller commercial arms sales.[9] The contracts were complicated, in that they involved several merchant houses that would take the commodities offered in partial exchange—chiefly the highly prized Barinas tobacco. Some eleven thousand muskets, gunpowder, foodstuffs, and uniforms were involved—a sizeable supply given the relatively small size of the armies involved in the independence struggle. But Torres' days as commercial agent for Colombia were largely over; his future role would become much more diplomatic.

In early 1821, the Colombians were suggesting that their vice president, Francisco Zea, come to Washington on a diplomatic mission, a prospect that excited Torres because it might open the doors to a high-level dialogue. To his regret, that possibility was never tested, as Zea at the last minute chose to go to London instead. Torres then received new instructions from Juan Roscio, instructing him to open negotiations, himself, for recognition of the Colombian government, and to negotiate a friendship and commerce agreement if possible. Given that there were no other official representatives of the South American patriot regimes in the United States at the time (unless the semi-retired DeForest could be counted).[10] Torres and Colombia had suddenly become the test case for recognition.

Congress took up Henry's Clays motion to appropriate money for United States missions in South America once again, in early February. The congressmen this time were aware of significant and favorable developments in South America. Bolívar was consolidating his position in Venezuela, San Martín in Peru. Moreover, the new constitutional regime in Spain had required the royalist General Morillo to open negotiations with Bolívar; the two previous combatants had even met toward the end of 1820, where they warmly embraced each other before agreeing to a truce. Combined with cancellation of the planned royalist relief force, the truce demonstrated that the tide of battle in the southern continent had turned definitively in favor of the rebels.

In spite of those favorable developments in South America, Clay's bill failed to pass; too many members attacked it as premature or because it did not respect the constitutional separation of powers. The pattern of previous votes persisted: the western representatives favored what they saw as action against Spain, while north-easterners and some southerners, more concerned with keeping friendly relations with the European powers, saw no need to undermine the administration's policy of neutrality. Faced with this situation, Clay lowered his sights. He introduced a nonbinding House of Representatives resolution of sympathy with the South Americans, which concluded that Congress "will give its Constitutional support to the President whenever he may deem it expedient to recognize the sovereignty and independence of any of the said provinces." Weak words, indeed, and yet it passed on February 12 by only 87 to 68, even after most of the speakers avowed that their constituents favored South American independence. The resolution was presented to Monroe several days later, and the president promised to take it "into deliberate consideration." The administration, in short, had finally neutralized Clay's long effort to rally his supporters and utilize the South American issue against their policy and politics.

On the day of the vote, General Vives had finally delivered the Spanish government's instrument ratifying the 1819 treaty. King Ferdinand had finally accepted the reality that Spain, in disorder if not civil war, and he himself a virtual prisoner of the liberals, had no choice but to ratify the treaty. Otherwise, Spain risked losing Florida anyway and having an undefined border between Spanish Texas and American Louisiana. Under the new constitutional procedures, the Cortes had authorized him to sign,[11] and he had done so, however grudgingly. The suspect land grants were explicitly annulled. Vives delivered this welcome news with a glum demeanor, admitting that it had been agreed to only reluctantly in Madrid.[12] That done, the final formalities were quickly dealt with. The Senate ratified the treaty once again to take account of the passed deadline, and the instruments of ratification were exchanged on February 22, 1821, two years after the signing—on what had originally been intended by Onís to be the propitious anniversary of Washington's birthday.

Released from its past disputes with Spain, the United States now had a free hand, limited only by its judgment of the international situation and its responsibilities as a neutral power, to deal with the new governments in Spanish America.

Moreover, there was another self-proclaimed independent state with which to deal. Mexico, which had not followed the path of the South American cabildos and juntas but instead had experienced periodic popular and guerrilla-type insurrections accompanied by brutal military repression, had suddenly become independent by virtue of a political deal between the conservative Church, the major leader of the insurgents, and a creole army officer, Agustín Iturbide. This unlikely coalition was a direct result of the "distress" of Spain, where royal authority had become so weak that the Mexican creole class had come to fear a complete dissolution of the empire in a flood of republicanism. Iturbide, anti-republican to the core, managed to convince the other parties that independence would best serve all their interests. Their February 1821 pact, called the Plan of Iguala, proclaimed the country to be independent, Catholic, and its Spanish origin citizens to be equal; the government was to be a constitutional monarchy under a Bourbon king. By winter Iturbide's army controlled the entire country, and when no prince offered himself to be king, Iturbide would, later in 1822, maneuver himself into the newly created position of emperor. Under his short and controversial rule, the Mexican Empire became fully independent, but far from the liberal republic that its neighboring Americans would have preferred.

The military as well as political situation in Spanish America had begun to firm up by the autumn of 1821. Mexico was independent and the remaining royalist forces there had effectively been coopted by the new government. In the United Provinces of Rio de la Plata, the Buenos Aires government had declared its independence, but its internal political struggles continued. (José Carrera had finally lost his life in those struggles; he was executed in September.) However, the area of the old viceroyalty had effectively been shorn of the provinces of Upper Peru (Bolivia, still in royalist hands), Paraguay (an independent but isolated autocracy since 1811), and the Banda Oriental (which eventually became Uruguay, but was under Portuguese-Brazilian occupation until 1828). Chile under O'Higgins had declared its independence in 1818. Colombia had done so in 1819, but even though Bolívar had won a decisive battle at Carabobo, near Caracas, in June 1821, Morillo's army and other pockets of royalist forces remained to be dealt with before the new state could be consolidated. Only the provinces of Upper and Lower Peru remained as a royalist stronghold, and in spite of San Martín's capture of Lima in September 1821, they would not become fully independent until 1826. Spain also continued to hold onto the Caribbean islands, and particularly the vital island of Cuba. But the patriot regimes were ascendant, Spain itself was in internal turmoil and incapable of further intervention, and the tide of history was clear.

When U.S. congressmen stood on the floor of the House of Representatives, back in March, to declaim that the majority of their constituents favored independence for the Spanish American colonies, they were stating a broad truth. From the president down, most Americans wished the patriots to succeed, that is, to free themselves from Spanish rule. But the stark realities of the fierce ten-year struggle, which had begun with hope that the revolutionaries would follow a liberal, constitutional model, had distinctly lowered expectations. The brutality of the South American and Mexican wars, and the increasingly strong trend among the patriot leaders toward authoritarianism, even monarchy, had diminished the enthusiasm of many American supporters. John Quincy Adams, notoriously skeptical but also insightful, had noted as early as 1817 that he feared that the emerging states would "present to us the prospect of very troublesome and dangerous associates, and still more fearful allies."[13] His caution did not diminish even as the South Americans approached their goal of independence. He wrote in his dairy, at the time of the 1821 congressional debate, that he had told Henry Clay that he could not share the latter's sanguine view about the South Americans. He "wished well to their cause," he wrote, "but I have seen and yet see no prospect that they would establish free or liberal institutions of government. They are not likely to promote the spirit either of freedom or order by their example. They have not the first element of good or free government. Arbitrary power, military and ecclesiastical, was stamped upon their education, upon their habit, and upon their institutions.... I had little expectation of any beneficial result to this country from any future connection with them, political or commercial."[14]

There were other reasons for concern. The excesses of the South American privateers, particularly when American ships became targets of piratical measures, had undermined initial support for the patriots' efforts. Still other favorably inclined observers were confused and alienated by the divisive and publicly fought argument between the supporters of Carrera and those of Pueyrredón (or at least until the exile of the Supreme Leader and the death of Carrera made the debate fade away).[15] In short, many Americans could be both proponents of freedom for the Spanish Americans, and jittery about what kind of neighbors the process would produce.

While Henry Clay, his Western supporters, and other committed enthusiasts like William Duane, Baptis Irving, or William Thornton, continued to object vociferously to an official neutrality policy that Duane called "cold and specious" and blamed entirely on Secretary Adams,[16] the majority of Americans were relatively happy with the government's stance. The policy may have restricted the government, but it allowed the private sector considerable leeway. Merchants and exporters could deal with both sides. Profits from the grain trade with Spain probably outweighed those from privateering, and arms sales to the combatants were open to all who were ready to brave the chances. Neutrality also helped achieve what had been a goal of American policy since Jefferson's time, namely to keep the European powers (and, in the present circumstances, the reactionary powers of the Holy Alliance) from intervening in the Americas.

Careful adherence to the letter (if not always the spirit) of official neutrality had also been of great use to Secretary Adams during the negotiations with Spain. The threat of recognizing the patriot governments had given him leverage with the Spaniards and the British, and it still did. But with the treaty signed and finally ratified, the question of recognizing the new governments could be looked at in a different light; it was no longer a political or diplomatic necessity to stand back. Some three years earlier, Adams had written to President Monroe to suggest that there was a time when the argument for recognition could be based on the prevailing political-military situation, with the requirements of politics and diplomacy secondary in import. "But there is a stage in such contest," he had written, "when the party struggling for independence has, as I conceive, a right to demand its acknowledgement by neutral parties, and when the acknowledgement may be granted without departure from the obligations of neutrality. It is the stage when the independence is established as a matter of fact, so as to leave the chance of the opposite party to recover their dominion utterly desperate."[17]

That the government at Buenos Aires had achieved its independence, "as a matter of fact," had been the argument made by Henry Clay and others for some time. Adams on the other hand had resisted drawing any policy conclusions from those facts out of political considerations, a more critical analysis of the situation on the ground, and purposes of coherency and leverage in his negotiations. But the fact of virtual independence was increasingly clear. And though the situations in Mexico and Colombia were less clear, the historical trend was evident, and the overall tipping point that Adams had described to President Monroe was approaching. And yet, there was at least one more point on which he wanted satisfaction before admitting that the time had come.

A source of Adams's hesitancy about the Buenos Aires regime had been the loopholes in its privateering regime that allowed unscrupulous privateers to victimize neutral ships, and consequently John Forbes had been instructed on assuming his post that pushing a solution to that problem should be one of his priorities. His unfriendly reception during a period of unusual government unrest however created delay, and it was not until almost a year after his arrival that Forbes was able to have a successful exchange with the key minister of government, Bernadino Rivadavia. The timing was favorable. Buenos Aires no longer needed to attack Spanish shipping, for the time being it was tolerant of a Brazilian occupation of the Banda Oriental that had crushed the rival Aritgas regime, and it was eager to remove obstacles to improved relations with the United States. In October 1821, Rivadavia issued a proclamation that removed the thorn: all privateers at sea were ordered to return, disarm, and turn in their commissions, idle commissions were also to be turned in, and new commissions to be issued only for defined purposes. While the loopholes in the Argentine legal structure remained and the government had not given up its right to issue privateer commissions in the future,[18] the decree was designed to placate Washington's concerns, and it did.

Moreover, the United States no longer had disputes with the other patriot regimes over rampant privateering. With Colombia and Chile, such problems as existed arose more from the operations of their navies than privateers, while Mexico had stopped issuing commissions upon declaring its independence. Even the notorious Banda Oriental flagged-privateers had disappeared, along with the Aritgas regime. Piracy of course had not been eliminated; the U.S. Navy conducted anti-piracy patrols of the Caribbean for another generation. Britain's Royal Navy soon joined the effort, and the two squadrons cooperated effectively in squelching a flare-up of Cuban and Puerto Rican flagged corsairs in 1822. But the poisonous nexus between the patriot governments and the out-of-control activities of their proxy navies had effectively gone away, and with it a major remaining impediment to normalization of relations.

Chapter 12

The End of the Beginning

Manuel Torres was a cautious man. He had been appointed to represent the new state of Colombia back in 1819 with instructions to seek recognition from Washington. But he had lived in the United States long enough, and understood American politics well enough, to know that the time was not right. Although Torres was received regularly but informally by Adams, his caution was grounded in his understanding that the United States could take no initiatives toward recognition until the treaty with Spain was ratified. He waited until 1821, two days before ratification, when he tentatively went on record for the first time, in a letter to Adams, pointing out that Colombia would "no doubt" be recognized, but he demanded no immediate response and did not follow up in writing for nine months. His caution was both tactful and tactical; he had informed President Monroe early on that he would not follow the aggressive tactics of Clemente, Aguirre, or Pazos: he "was to press on this government nothing contrary to its wishes or policy." Monroe appeared to be satisfied with this declaration of intent, noting to Adams that the other patriots had made the mistake of allowing themselves to be used by the administration's opponents in Congress. Adams on the other hand was not convinced, reminding the president that DeForest had said the same thing and yet had been among the most troublesome of the patriot agents.[1]

Once the treaty was ratified, Torres did begin to press the issue gently, describing the continued progress of Colombia in a November 1821 letter, and reminding once again that his country sought recognition. Oddly enough, he had by then received instructions to go slow. Pedro Gual, as the recently appointed Gran Colombian minister of foreign affairs, apparently still resented the failure of his earlier efforts as a militant in Philadelphia, since he instructed Torres to concentrate on preparing American

12. The End of the Beginning

public opinion—because little could be expected in the short term from the administration. "The Government of Gran Colombia," Gual had written to Torres in August, "convinced by the indifference which the United States has shown for ten years to the struggle in which we have been engaged, holds no great hope for its inconceivable policy. But should the President, against all hope, show a desire to enter into relations...."[2] Gual's splash of cold water had little practical effect, however, as events finally were moving fairly rapidly.

Since Congress had adjourned in March of 1821, the political and military situations in Mexico and South America had changed rapidly, and in favor of the governments that had declared their independence from Spain. By late autumn, enough reports had come in from South America to indicate that independence, as measured by Adams' criterion that the mother country had no chance of recovering her revolted colonies, was all but assured. And yet there was no rapid move to draw conclusions from the summer's flood of news. Congress would not convene again until December, and would get organized in its usual leisurely fashion. Moreover, Henry Clay would not take a seat at this session, depriving the pro-recognition group of its principal champion. In a January exchange of notes between Torres and Adams, the secretary of state nonetheless gave an indication of the administration's evolving position; Torres' earlier requests for recognition, Adams admitted, were under active consideration.

At the end of the year, Congressmen David Trimble of Kentucky put forth two resolutions recommending the recognition of Colombia and other new governments. But it was yet another congressional resolution, this time requesting information concerning political conditions in South America, that prompted a formal response from the administration.

On March 8, 1822, Monroe and Adams forwarded to Congress a sizeable bundle of recent correspondence with the South American and Mexican governments, as well as reports from the American agents abroad. The volume of documents was considerable, but the significant conclusion was in the covering letter. "When we regard, then, the great length of time which this war has been prosecuted, the complete success which has attended it in favor of the provinces, the present condition of the parties, and the utter inability of Spain to produce any change in it, we are compelled to conclude that its fate is settled, and that the provinces which have declared their independence, and are in the enjoyment of it, ought to be recognized."[3] The House committee to which the president's message was submitted returned a report in ten days, recommending that recognition was both just and expedient. Two resolutions were submitted to debate: the first of which voiced concurrence with the president's recommendation, and the second recommended passage of a bill authorizing funds for any missions sent to the governments that would be recognized. The first resolution passed easily on March 28, the second was passed into law in early May.

The president's statement, predictably, met with a vigorous protest from the new Spanish minister in the United States, Joaquin de Anduaga.[4] Anduaga's angry assertion of Spain's right to "reunite" the provinces at some future date could be seen as pure bluster, given his kingdom's weak situation, but his simultaneous report to Madrid did stimulate a concerted Spanish diplomatic campaign in the capitals of Europe, attempting to refute the new American policy of recognizing de facto governments, defending the Holy Alliance's principle of royal legitimacy, and urging that none follow the American example. The effort was successful in that it delayed European recognition for some years, but the United States' action itself remained unchallenged.

What remained was how to put the recommendation into effect. When the cabinet met in the middle of April, Adams urged, and the other members agreed, that the first step should come from the new governments. Only after a number of envoys' credentials were recognized in Washington should the United States, as senior partner, reciprocate by sending envoys abroad. The follow-on decision was easier. Manuel Torres and David DeForest were the only resident envoys whose applications for recognition were still pending, and the respected Torres clearly was preferred. DeForest made a half-hearted effort to have his credentials accepted, but Adams denied his request in May due to "changed circumstances." The delay caused by De Forest's request, plus the poor state of Torres' health—he had severe asthma and suffered gravely in the spring weather—delayed the presentation of credentials until June.

By that act, the United States would become the first nation, other than Brazil, to offer formal recognition to one of the new nations.

It was a memorable scene, yet a sad one. A quarter of a century after he had come to the United States as a refugee from his own country, Manuel Torres was received by the president as the first official diplomatic representative of a Hispanic-American state. Torres's long campaign, in which he had lost his family and fortune, was finally vindicated. Even that coolly analytical observer John Quincy Adams was touched by the occasion, writing in his diary, "At one o'clock, I presented Mr. Manuel Torres as

12. The End of the Beginning

Chargé d'Affaires from the Republic of Colombia to the President. This incident was chiefly interesting in being the first formal act of recognition of a South American Government. Torres, who has scarcely life in him to walk alone, was deeply affected by it.... The President invited him to be seated, sat down by him, and spoke with kindness that moved even him to tears. The President assured him of the great interest taken by the United States in the welfare and success his country, and of the particular satisfaction with which he received him as its first representative."[5]

Torres returned to Philadelphia, only to die several weeks later in the leafy suburb of Hamiltonville. His funeral was conducted with military honors and attended by some of the city's leading citizens, a mark of the respect with which he was held by all who knew him. He is buried in St. Mary's, the church that was, ironically, also the parish church for many years of the Spanish diplomatic community.

The United States recognized no other representatives that year until December, when José Zozaya from Mexico was received, the delay in his case having been caused by hesitations stemming from Iturbide's assumption of the title of emperor, which did not sit well in Washington. By the end of 1823, and without necessarily waiting for corresponding envoys to arrive in Washington, the United States had named diplomatic agents to the remaining countries envisaged in the congressional resolution: Rio de la Plata,[6] Chile, and Peru.

A bridge had been crossed, and years of informal, exploratory, and sometimes difficult contacts had finally been transformed into more permanent and normal relationships between the United States and the new and nascent states of the hemisphere.

* * * *

A dozen years had passed since the first insecure and tentative South American juntas had sent agents to the United States to seek assistance in defending themselves from either—or both—of Spain's rival monarchs. Events had subsequently driven the juntas into outright rebellion against King Ferdinand, and in time a few autonomous governments were in a position to declare their independence and instruct their agents to seek recognition as well as material assistance from North America. By the end of 1823, five new states had achieved both their independence, and formal recognition by the United States. A watershed had been crossed. The government agents whose activities this study has examined—those sent north by the rebellious patriot governments, as well as those sent south by the United States government—had been part of that journey. But what, exactly was their impact on the evolution of events, and policy?

The South American revolutionaries had won their independence through their own efforts—their leadership, sacrifices, and doggedness in the face of adversity. They had been helped of course by the political disorder of Spain, as well as its military weakness and lack of military allies. The patriots had also received material assistance from abroad. Weapons, munitions, uniforms and other supplies, in addition to volunteers and proxy forces in the form of privateers—much of the stuff needed for their liberation fights—had been imported, largely from Britain and the United States. The patriot agents who had come to the United States had been able to keep war supplies flowing from New York, Baltimore, New Orleans and Philadelphia; they had encouraged merchants to sell arms to the patriots on their own account, and they had also kicked off the privateering war. As the patriot armies had few other supply options available to them, those efforts were sometimes vital.

But the United States, as a neutral, offered a marketplace that was equally open to Don Luis de Onís and other purchasers for the royalist side, and the net effect of supplies from North America on the actual fighting is hard to measure. It was, in any event, inferior to that from Britain, which was, in effect, the patriots' major material supporter during the liberation struggle. Over seventy South American agents had been active in London, Britain's political and cultural model was attractive to them, while British merchants dominated the trade to South America, over five thousand volunteers served in Bolivar's army, and British officers, ships, and crewmen served in the navies of Chile and Buenos Aires.[7]

If the supply efforts of the South American agents in the United States were, on balance, helpful to the liberation struggle but only marginally so, their direct military efforts were distinct failures. Gutiérrez and Toledo's filibustering raid into Texas, the expeditions into Mexico concocted or supported by Pedro Gual and others in the Philadelphia circle, the Amelia Island adventure, were all military and political disasters. All the same, the failures had little effect on the wars being fought in Mexico and South America; they represented opportunities lost rather than key strategic moves. While it is understandable that the patriots blamed the American policy of neutrality for much of their frustration in those efforts, it is clear that without a policy of neutrality they would not have been able to mount the expeditions in the first place. America's policy in effect tied only the government's hands. Private citizens as well as the foreign agents could,

12. The End of the Beginning

and did, find loopholes in the law's application to support the patriots' war effort. The privateer war, often fought by American proxies, was the most successful of these military efforts.

A policy of neutrality had been part of the bedrock of American foreign policy since President Washington had warned against taking sides in Europe's continual conflicts. But like all policy it was subject to interpretation, and had not prevented the United States from an undeclared war against one of the European powers, France, in President Adams's day, or President Madison's war against Britain in 1812. As applied to the struggle between Spain and its rebellious colonies, the policy was interpreted to define the situation as a civil war in which all parties—Spain and the rebels—were viewed as belligerents, to be treated equally. This allowed the U.S. administrations to fend off Spanish objections by protestations that the government itself had taken no actions that compromised its neutrality, while at the same time allowing the private sector to arm both sides, and looking the other way at privateering or filibuster attempts—unless the perpetrators openly broke the letter of the law. This marginally duplicitous position was acceptable domestically because it was favorable to U.S. business interests, and provided an outlet for pro-patriot public sentiment. Most importantly, it served the nation's interest by avoiding a conflict with royal Spain while at the same time allowing the rebels to operate against that government with some impunity.

The political effect of the various measures undertaken in the United States by the patriot agents was to increase the tension between Spain and the United States over alleged violations of American neutrality. That tension might have seemed to serve the patriots' interests, particularly when it contributed to talk of possible war between the United States and Spain, something that would have put the United States squarely on the patriots' side. The administration however was able to manipulate that tension to its own benefit. Given that even the most incompetent military efforts by the patriots served to highlight the reality of Spanish weakness in the borderlands, presidents Madison and Monroe discouraged them no more than they hindered the various American filibusters. John Quincy Adams capitalized on the resultant Spanish anxiety about the security of its colonies to reap the concessions obtained by the 1819 treaty. That treaty was assuredly the major diplomatic victory of the period—not only because of the border changes, but also because it stabilized the United States-Spanish relationship and removed the threat of hostilities that could ensue from U.S. recognition of the new regimes.

It is in this area—their impact on political and diplomatic calculations—that the Spanish American agents may well have had the most important effect. Spanish minister Onís was deeply concerned over their activities, and his anxiety about their imagined collusion with the Washington authorities helped to convince him that only a treaty with the United States could protect the border with Texas and Mexico. He feared, indeed exaggerated, the access to Congress and other opinion makers that was enjoyed by patriot agents like Torres, Gual, Carrera, Aguirre and DeForest, an access that was multiplied by their supporters such as Duane, Porter, Thornton, and Skinner. It is unclear to this writer whether Onís ever realized the degree to which the president and secretary of state were also bemoaning the clamor of that same pro-patriot lobby, demanding, as it did, what the administration considered to be premature recognition.

What is clear is that the broad network of influential contacts established during the long and distinguished residence of Manuel Torres in Philadelphia provided his more radical and militant patriot colleagues an unprecedented platform from which to provide pro-independence information and propaganda to both North and Hispanic American audiences. Profiting from a natural sympathy in the United States for anti-colonial, constitutional movements, the patriots and their American supporters were able to accelerate a pro-independence atmosphere that created momentum and pressure on the administration. Henry Clay's championship of the patriot cause was powerful, and whether it was motivated by personal conviction, or spite, matters little to this discussion[8]; what mattered is that the cause of independence and recognition already had resonance by the time Clay adopted it, and that the administration's actions were influenced by that fact.

In terms of American domestic politics, however, the split between the southerners and westerners (many of them slaveholders) who supported Spanish American independence and recognition, and the east coasters who favored a go-slow position, became another unfortunate facet of the growing North-South divide.

Nor does the fact that the cause of independence had broad acceptance mean that its achievement was not met with numerous disappointments, on both sides.

The creole liberals who had come north in the early years of the struggle, hoping that the United States would readily support their cause out of republican sympathy alone, were the first to have their hopes dashed.

Their successors were in turn disappointed by the harsh credit terms offered by American merchants for risky arms sales, and chose not to understand why the government would not provide aid in the manner that the French had helped the American colonies in 1778.

On the South American side, disappointment in the position of the United States was fed to some degree by the difficulties and frustrations of the agents sent to Washington, but still more by comparison with the greater British military and commercial support for the revolutionary efforts.

American public opinion in turn was disturbed by failure of the independence movements to live up to the initial expectations of liberal constitutionalism. Instead, the reality of brutal and often racially-tinged struggles, the disregard for civil rights by the combatants, and the increasing tendency toward autocratic government on the part of the revolutionary leaders, all left a sour taste for even the most enthusiastic supporters. The pro-rebel press, too, lost its initial uncritical enthusiasm as it learned more about the realities of the Mexican and South American struggles. Even William Duane, that often intemperate champion of the patriots, was chastened and somewhat disillusioned as to the democratic prospects of that continent's governments by a long trip he took to South America in 1822 and 23.[9]

Onís foresightedly saw that the Americans would be in time be disillusioned by South America's course, writing in his 1821 *Memorial* that U.S. political and trade objectives would be frustrated by the fact that in Spanish America "the rebel spirits of the inhabitants were not familiar with a republican regime, and that the result of their independence would be continual conflict between the different parties to obtain command."[10]

Those disappointments were to some degree mitigated by the two sides' voyage from an ill-informed idealism to a slightly more nuanced understanding of each other's social and political realities. The reporting of the United States' early agents in South America, however partial or biased, had contributed to this greater understanding, and laid the foundation for the improved flow of information that followed the opening of official diplomatic missions in the new nations. The Spanish American agents who had come to the United States, some of whom later reached positions of influence in their governments, also promoted a deeper understanding, if not necessarily amity.

Exaggerated prospects for trade between North and South America would lead, in time, to further disappointment. Whereas Torres, Duane, and others had foreseen a prolonged growth in that trade, it turned out that the growth had a natural limit, due to similar product lines, the lack of purchasing power in the South American market,[11] and strong and deep-rooted British competition. American trade, including both exports and the carrying trade of reexported goods, grew rapidly until 1830, but then much more slowly. Even the British, who had replaced Spain as the region's largest supplier, experienced a similar slow growth in their trade to the region.

In late 1822, however, all disappointments were put aside—for a while at least—by general pleasure over the fact that the rebel regimes finally had a measure of international acceptance. But the immediate result of the act was nonetheless limited, and United States recognition had set a precedent that would only be followed slowly by most of the other powers.

Recognition and establishment of more or less normal diplomatic relations with a number of newly independent states also set the stage for declaration of the Monroe Doctrine in 1823. It was by no means a new aim of American policy. Ever since the Jefferson administration, American statesmen had sought to limit intervention by the European powers in the neighborhood. Now that there were new independent states in the western hemisphere that were likely to support such a policy (Brazil, too, had declared its independence from Portugal in 1822), and the United States had earned a position of some respect in the region, it was possible to declare such a policy openly. It also helped that Britain, with its powerful navy and its own reasons for wanting to keep the other European powers at bay, also supported the idea (in fact the British had originally proposed a joint statement of policy, which Monroe and Adams turned down).

The last battles of the liberation struggle in South America were not fought until 1826, in Peru, and that was a South American victory to which the North American contribution was minor. In spite of the military loss of her colonies, Spain remained obstinate and continued to demand that the conservative powers of Europe not recognize the new non-royal governments. King Ferdinand even convinced the other members of the Holy Alliance to intervene in Spain's civil disorder. In 1823, a French Bourbon invasion of his country crushed the liberals and restored Ferdinand to his throne, trashing the constitution of 1812 once again. That draconian step in defense of the principle of royal legitimacy would prove to be, however, the last major intervention of the Holy Alliance. It stimulated Great Britain, which was both unhappy with the reactionary regimes of the

12. The End of the Beginning

Alliance and anxious to solidify its position in South America, to recognize a number of the newly independent states in 1825.

Spain however would not move in that direction until a decade later, after the death of the ever obdurate King Ferdinand in 1833. And it would take still more years of political instability, wars, territorial reconfigurations and autocratic *caudillo* regimes before those states that were newly independent or potentially so in 1822 would reach stability and full international acceptance.

Over a decade of awkward relationships, obliging the United States to deal with a series of unknown, potentially troublesome agents from untested and unstable revolutionary governments, had come to an end. It was a period of mutual exploration, during which the Madison and Monroe administrations tried to maintain the benefits of neutrality, while the South Americans and their American supporters repeatedly probed the weaknesses of the neutrality legislation in their urgent quest for aid. In the end, the frustrations of the process could be put aside because both sides had achieved their major aims. The United States had absorbed Florida, gained an internationally recognized Pacific boundary, and achieved a significant hemispheric role. The patriots had gained some material aid, and an important breakthrough toward legitimacy and universal recognition. But the new relationships were not built on a basis of trust and gratitude, nor should that have been expected. Independence, as the young United States had learned a generation earlier, is better defended by national interest than by sentiment.

Chapter Notes

Chapter 1

1. Jefferson to Archibald Stewart, 25 Jan. 1786, Thomas Jefferson Papers at the Library of Congress, series 1 image 188; http://memory.loc.gov/ammem/collections/jefferson_papers.
2. Jefferson to John C. Breckenridge, 12 Aug. 1803, Jefferson Papers, series 1 image 809.
3. Spanish Minister Del Campo to Foreign Minister Floridablanca, in William Spencer Robertson, *Francisco de Miranda and the Revolutionizing of Spanish America* (Washington, D.C.: Government Printing Office, 1909), 267.
4. Hamilton was eager to strike against Spanish Florida, and even contemplated joint British-American efforts to assist the rebellious Spanish Americans. See John Ferling, *Jefferson and Hamilton* (New York: Bloomsbury Press, 2013), 306–7.
5. Madison to John Armstrong, U.S. Minister to France, 15 Mar. 1806, in William Spencer Robertson, *Francisco de Miranda,* 364.
6. Miranda to Madison, 22 Jan. 1806, James Madison Papers at the Library of Congress, series 1 image 60; http://memory.loc.gov/ammem/collections/madison_papers.
7. Jefferson to Foronda, 4 Oct. 1809, Jefferson Papers, series 1 image 288.

Chapter 2

1. Foronda returned to Spain, where he continued to write works espousing a liberal constitution for his country. Upon the return of the Bourbon monarchy in 1814, he was briefly imprisoned for his views, but was later rehabilitated. He died in 1821.
2. Bernabeu had studied in the United States and married an American woman; as a result Onís never fully trusted his patriotism and did not appoint him consul general. Onís also criticized to Cádiz what he thought was Bernabeau's weak presentation to the U.S. government of the case for accepting his ministerial credentials. Bernabeu died in America in 1835 and is buried at St. Mary's church, Philadelphia.
3. This was of course not a new task; Spanish minister Jáudenes had stressed political reporting in his instructions to the consulates as early as 1795, and his successor José Viar in 1808 had identified and reported on the incognito arrival of a French agent, General Octaviano D'Alvimar, who was arrested in September of that year in Mexico, thanks to Viar's warning.
4. Vicente Rocafuerte, *Ideas Necesarias a todo pueblo Americano independiente, que quiera ser libre* (Philadelphia: D. Huntington, 1821), 1.

5. Miranda's quote is from Manuel H. Gonzalez, "Francisco Caballero Sarmiento, un empressario al servicio de la contrarevolución," *Revista de Indias* 51, no. 2 (1991), 383; Onís's quote of 23 June 1810 to the captain general, Caracas, is from Spanish Foreign Ministry, *Documentos relativos a la independencia de NorteAmérica en archivos españoles* (Madrid, 1976–1985), vol. 3, Legajo 5:636, 131; and that of Mar. 1812 to Mauricio de Onís is from Angel Rio, *La Mission de Don Luís Onís en los Estados Unidos* (Barcelona: Novagrafik 1981), 224.

6. Carlos A. Vilanueva, *Historia Diplomatica de la Primera República de Venezuela* (Caracas, 1967), 478–9.

Chapter 3

1. The American was Robert Lowry, just appointed as U.S. agent to Venezuela; the first citation is from his letter of July10 to Secretary Robert Smith, from Gaillard Hunt, *The Writings of James Madison* (New York: G.P. Putnam, 1908), vol. 8, 106n; the second citation, Onís to the Foreign Ministry, 12 July 1810, is from Spanish Foreign Ministry, *Documentos relativos a la independencia de Norteamérica en archivos españoles* (Madrid, 1976–1985), vol. 3, Legajo 5:636, 137.

2. Robert Smith to Joel Poinsett, 28 June 1810, in Frederic L Paxson, *The Independence of the South American Republics* (Philadelphia: Ferris & Leach, 1903), 108. These appointments, contrary to some commentaries, were not the first official American appointments to unformed and unrecognized states, an honor which should be accorded to Dr. Edward Stevens, appointed to the revolutionary Haitian regime of Toussaint Louverture in 1799, with the title of consul general—with the country however, unspecified so as not to openly disregard nominal French sovereignty over the rebellious colony.

3. Congress subsequently authorized the unilateral annexation of West Florida, up to the Perdido River, in 1812. Following the War with Great Britain, and benefitting from this free access to the Gulf Coast plus the pacification of the Creeks, the population of the Mississippi Territory increased rapidly. Mississippi was granted statehood in 1817, and Alabama toward the end of 1819, by which date Spain had provisionally acknowledged American title to the annexed lands, as well as the rest of Florida.

4. Dorothy Parton, *The Diplomatic Career of Joel R. Poinsett* (Washington, D.C.: Catholic University Press, 1934), 25.

5. Onís to Foreign Ministry, 27 April 1811, in Emiliano Jos, "Juan Vicente Bolívar y su mission en los Estados Unidos," *Revista de Indias* 2, no. 4 (1941), 154.

6. Angel Rio, *Mission de Don Luis Onís en los Estados Unidos* (Barcelona: Novagrafik, 1981), 222 and 81n.40.

7. Onís to the Captain General of Caracas, 2 Feb. 1810. Consul Robert Lowry in Guaira had somehow obtained this acidly critical dispatch, which the Madison administration happily published in an apparent effort to embarrass Onís. *American State Papers, Foreign Relations*, vol. 3, 404.

8. By 1810, Napoleon had realized that the Spanish colonies would never recognize the regime of Joseph (for example, the Marquis de Sassenay, sent in 1808 to Buenos Aires to seek the cabildo's recognition of Joseph, had been placed under arrest as a prisoner of war). French activities were subsequently directed towards encouraging movements to separate the colonies from the regency, or even independence, and French officials in both Paris and Washington occasionally (though fruitlessly) urged direct American cooperation in such efforts.

9. *American State Papers, Foreign Affairs*, vol. 3, 538; *Annals of Congress*, 12th Congress, 1st Session, 14.

10. The nickname of people from Buenos Aires, who will sometimes be called

Argentines in this text, although the official name of the region at the time was the Viceroyalty of Rio de la Plata—subsequently the United Provinces of Rio de la Plata, even though scarcely united as many of the provinces had broken away from Buenos Aires' rule.

11. John B. McMaster, *The Life and Times of Stephen Girard* (Philadelphia: Lippincott, 1918), 171.

12. Miller to secretary of state, 16 July 1812, William Manning, *Diplomatic Correspondence of the United States Concerning the Independence of Latin America* (New York: Oxford University Press, 1925), vol. 1, 326.

Chapter 4

1. Secretary of State James Monroe to Mathews and McKee, 26 Jan. 1811, *American State Papers, Foreign Relations*, vol. 3, 571.

2. Madison to Jefferson, 24 April 1812, *James Madison Papers at the Library of Congress*, image 21; http://memory.loc.gov/ammem/collections/madison_papers.

3. Luís de Onís, *Memoria sobre las negociaciones entre España y los Estados Unidos de América* (Madrid: Ediciones J. Porrúa Turanzas, 1969), 91 and 93.

4. Elizabeth Howard West, "The Diary of Bernardo Gutiérrez de Lara," *The American Historical Review* 34, no. 1 (1928): 73.

5. Ibid., 76.

6. Noroña, a priest from Madrid, had published a liberal periodical there before fleeing to Philadelphia in 1811, where he started a similar periodical, articles from which Duane copied regularly in the *Aurora*. But Onís, knowing that Noroña needed money and admiring his writing, satirical skill, and excellent English, passed him money and tried to recruit him as a publicist (using Sarmiento as a go-between). Cádiz, distrusting Noroña's politics, at first refused, but Onís was able to convince them of the need for a good propagandist and was finally permitted, in February 1812, to hire Noroña.

7. Shaler to Monroe, 13 Aug. 1812, National Archives, Despatches from Special Agents of the Department of State, 1794–1906, vol. 2 (Microfilm Series M37). Roy F. Nichols, in "William Shaler: New England Apostle of Rational Liberty," *The New England Quarterly* 9, no. 1 (1936): 90, posits that Gutiérrez hid his recruitment efforts from Shaler. Most historians (see Lockey, below) believe that Shaler was involved in recruitment efforts from the beginning, but did so secretly so as to hide any violations of the neutrality law. If so, his reports to Monroe may have been designed to hide the truth, in case they were intercepted or published.

8. Onís to his son Mauricio, 12 Mar. 1812, in Angel Rio, *Mission de Don Luis Onís en los Estados Unidos* (Barcelona: Novagrafik 1981), 224. Onís admitted in this letter that he had invited Toledo to a family dinner earlier in his stay, but subsequently discovered him to be a "complete rogue," and was trying to hinder his efforts.

9. Onís to Ignacio de la Pezuela, 7 Oct. 1812, in Joseph B. Lockey, "The Florida Intrigues of José Álavarez de Toledo," *The Florida Historical Society Quarterly* 12, no. 4 (1934): 158.

10. Cogswell's *bona fides* have never been established, but his accusations struck fertile ground with Gutiérrez, who correctly saw Toledo as a rival.

11. The rebuke was without consequence. Shaler went on to a successful diplomatic career, serving on the Ghent peace commission and later as consul in Algiers and, ironically, Havana, where he died in 1833.

12. Poinsett's undiplomatic behavior in Chile was never criticized by the administration, and he went on to lead a successful political career in South Carolina and Congress. In 1823–30 he was American envoy to the new republic of Mexico, where his continued penchant for extra-diplomatic interventions led eventually to his recall.

Chapter 5

1. Matthew McCarthy, *Privateering, Piracy, and British Policy in South America, 1810–1830* (London: Boydell Press, 2013), 35–37.
2. Jerome R. Garitee, *The Republic's Private Navy: The American Privateering Business as Practiced by Baltimore During the War of 1812* (Middletown, CT: Wesleyan University Press, 1977), 219, quotes Henry Didier, Jr. (one of the partners), writing in 1815, "I am in hopes there will be a war between England, France, and some of the continental powers, that we may make use of our fast sailing schooners."
3. Jeffrey Orenstein, "Joseph Almeida, Portrait of a Privateer, Pirate and Plaintiff," *The Green Bag Review of Law* 10 no. 3 (2007): 320. The captain and crew were compensated from the remaining 40 percent. The Argentine government, it appears, was a purely strategic partner in the enterprise. John W. DeForest, in *The De Forests of Avesnes* (New Haven: Tuttle, Moorehouse and Taylor, 1900), 132, claims that his ancestor had already, in 1815, offered a number of commissions directly to American investors, including John Jacob Astor and George Crowninshield.
4. Manuel H. Gonzalez, "Francisco Caballero Sarmiento, un empressario al servicio de la contrarevolucion," *Revista de Indias* 51, no. 2 (1991): 389.
5. Patterson's son, Joseph, however, was involved in the American Concern, and Patterson and the other merchant princes never took action or testified against the privateers.
6. Onís to Monroe, 22 Feb. 1816, *American State Papers, Foreign Relations*, vol. 4, 428.
7. *American State Papers, Foreign Relations*, vol. 4, 184.
8. Ibid., 187.
9. John Quincy Adams, *Memoirs of John Quincy Adams*, Charles F. Adams, ed. (Philadelphia: J.B. Lippincott, 1875–77) vol. 4, 318.
10. Onís to Rush, 2 Feb. 1817, *American State Papers, Foreign Relations*, vol. 4, 188.
11. *Annals of Congress*, House, 14th Congress, 2nd session, 721.
12. *Statutes at Large*, vol. 3, 371.

Chapter 6

1. Onís to Juan José Ruiz de Apodaca, 12 July 1816, in Stanley Fay, "Louis Aury," *Louisiana Historical Quarterly* 25, no. 2 (1942): 630.
2. Picornell would, in 1818, be awarded a royal pardon. In 1820 he removed to Havana, where he continued his medical work as a loyal subject of the king.
3. John Dick to Monroe, 1 Mar. 1816, *American State Papers, Foreign Relations*, vol. 4, 431.
4. One of Patterson's vessels, the *Firebrand*, which was routinely used to escort the arms shipments or provide courier service to Mexican ports for the insurgents, was detained by a Spanish flotilla in the summer of 1816. The incident was blown up in the New Orleans press as a Spanish insult to American sovereignty, but was tamped down by a somewhat embarrassed administration.
5. John Quincy Adams, *Memoirs of John Quincy Adams*, Charles F. Adams, ed. (Philadelphia: J.B. Lippincott, 1875–77) vol. 4, 516 (1 Feb. 1820).
6. Randolf on 20 Jan. 1816, *Annals of Congress*, 14th Congress, 1st session, 728.
7. Carrera to Poinsett, July 20 1816, in Harold Bierck, "Spoils, Soils, and Skinner," *Maryland Historical Magazine* 49, no. 1 (1954): 31.
8. José Carrera Verdugo, *Diario de viaje a Estados Unidos de América*, José M. Barros, ed. (Santiago de Chile: Editorial Universitaria, 1996): 97.
9. Though Correa did send some reports to Onís, he was eventually discovered

and kicked off the expedition. A year later, Correa was petitioning for a royal pardon on behalf of his exiled father Diego, on the basis of his (Segundo's) recent service "attached to Mina."

10. Some historians believe that Toledo had been a royal agent since his defection from the Cortes. The prevailing opinion seems to be that he was an opportunist, who had thought that his best prospects lay with the colonial rebels. If that is the case, he abandoned their cause too early.

11. The investors' heirs were eventually awarded damages in 1890 by an international commission set up by Mexico and the United States to settle citizens' claims. The Mexican Company was awarded compensation of $160,000 plus interest, but final payment was held up by disputes among the claimants' heirs. Smith's award was for $84,000.

12. Graham to Monroe, 12 Sept. 1816, cited in Joseph B. Lockey, "The Florida Intrigues of José Alvarez de Toledo," *The Florida Historical Society Quarterly* 12, no. 4 (1934): 163.

13. Onís to Felix Calleja, Viceroy of New Spain, 14 July 1816, in R. Guzman, "La correspondencia de Don Luis de Onis sobre la expedicion de Javier Mina," *Boletin del Archivo General de la Nation* (Mexico), 2nd series, 9 no. 4 (1968): 517; Carrera, *Diario* 90 (19 Aug. 1816); Servando Mier, *The Memoirs of Fray Servando Teresa de Mier*, Helen Lane, trans. (New York: Oxford University Press, 1998): 192.

14. Gutiérrez remained in the New Orleans-Natchitoches area for several more years and was involved in another filibustering raid into Texas, the Natchez-based James Long expedition of 1819. Gutiérrez returned to an independent Mexico in 1824 and served for several years as a provincial governor and commandant general. He died in 1841.

Chapter 7

1. Gual to Thornton, 12 Nov. 1816, William Thornton Papers, Library of Congress Manuscript Division, reel 2, no. 750.

2. Kristin Ann Dykstra, "On the Betrayal of Nations," *The New Centennial Review* 4, no.1 (2004): 296.

3. *Annals of Congress*, 15th Congress, 2nd session, 1612.

4. MacGregor did provide the administration with a more complete briefing of his plans, in late July, through his main Baltimore contact, Joseph Skinner. See Harold Bierck, "Spoils, Soils, and Skinner," *Maryland Historical Magazine* 49, no. 1 (1954): 39.

5. MacGregor to an unnamed gentleman in Baltimore, 16 July 1817, an attachment to the president's 26 Mar. 1818 message to Congress, 8. The *Annals of Congress* (15th Congress, 1st session, 1523) notes that a number of documents were attached to the president's message (particularly the Pazos memorial, see note 9 below), but not all were published in the Appendix's pg. 1897ff. compilation. This document and the Pazos memorial were accessed July 2013 at http://www.ibiblio.org/pha/USN/1818/18180316Amelia.html#15.

6. MacGregor came to attention once again in London, in 1820, when he launched, to great acclaim, a settlement in Honduras called the Principality of Poyais. He attracted investors and hundreds of settlers, but the project failed and his claim to the land was never proven. In spite of the failure, he persisted in attempts to promote the scheme. He eventually abandoned the effort and returned to Venezuela, where he died in 1845.

7. The Lautaro Lodges in Buenos Aires, Santiago and other cities were secret societies, outgrowths of the Sociedad de Caballeros Racionales, that mimicked some Masonic rituals and took advantage of Masonic connections, but whose aims were patriotic and political. In Venezuela, the Sociedad Patriótica founded by Miranda played a similar role. Many leaders of the patriot movement were members of these societies, including Bolívar, Gual, San Martín, O'Higgins, Pueyrredón, Mier, and Carrera.

8. Gual to Thornton, 22 July 1817, Thornton Papers, reel 2, no. 792.
9. *Annals of Congress*, 15th Congress, 1st session, 14.
10. Pazos Memorial of 7 Feb. 1818, an attachment to the president's 26 Mar. 1818 message to Congress, 31. (See note 5)
11. Adams to Pazos 5 Mar. 1818, Ibid., 50.
12. *City of Washington Gazette*, 10 Mar. 1818.
13. Pazos returned to New York, where his family had joined him, and wrote a book entitled *Letters on the United Provinces addressed to the Hon. Henry Clay* which was a non-political description of South America's history and potential, plus a personal memoir. In late 1818, after the dismissal of Pueyrredón, he and his family returned home.

Chapter 8

1. Kevin Arlyck, "Plaintiffs v. Privateers: Litigation and Foreign Affairs in the Federal Courts, 1816–1822," *Law and History Review* 30, no. 1 (2012): 276.
2. David Head, "A Different Kind of Maritime Predation: South American Privateering from Baltimore, 1816–1820," *International Journal of Naval History* 7, no. 2 (2008): 14–16; John Dick to James Monroe, 1 Mar. 1816, *American State Papers, Foreign Relations* 4, 432.
3. Chew to Secretary of Treasury William Crawford, 1 and 30 Aug. 1817, *American State Papers, Foreign Relations* 4, 134 and 136.
4. Stanley Faye, "Louis Aury," *Louisiana Historical Quarterly* 25, no. 2 (1942): 631.
5. While Herrera's contributions to the republican cause were limited, his persistence on its behalf at least paid off. He survived, and in 1821 became minister of foreign affairs in the first truly independent Mexican regime—ironically, an imperial one.
6. Matthew McCarthy, *Privateering, Piracy, and British Policy in South America, 1810–1830* (London: Boydell Press, 2013), 26.
7. Onís to Rush, 18 Apr. 1817, *American State Papers, Foreign Relations* 4, 193.
8. John Quincy Adams, *Memoirs of John Quincy Adams*, Charles F. Adams, ed. (Philadelphia: J.B. Lippincott, 1875–77) vol. 4, 378 (27 May 1819).
9. By March 1820, with 45 men awaiting execution after condemnation for piracy, the cabinet met to decide on their fate. A decision was taken that two be executed in each of Baltimore, Savannah, Charleston, Richmond, and New Orleans. After much discussion two were hung in Baltimore, two in South Carolina, one in Georgia, three in Massachusetts, and two in New Orleans, but technically the latter were executed for murder—their victim having been Theodsia Burr Alcott, the talented daughter of Aaron Burr, who had been marooned on a coastal island by the two condemned mutineers, and presumed lost.
10. Charles C. Griffin, *The United States and the Disruption of the Spanish Empire* (New York: Columbia University Press, 1937), 142.
11. Adams, *Memoirs*, vol. 4, 318 (29 March 1819).
12. Adams, before the Supreme Court in the Amistad case, 1 Mar. 1841, 92. Accessed March 2014 at http://avalon.law.yale.edu/19th_century/amistad_002.asp.
13. *Poulson's American Daily Advertiser*, 2 Sept. 1817, and *Democratic Press of Philadelphia*, 1 Nov. 1818.
14. Adams, *Memoirs*, vol. 4, 318 (29 Mar. 1819).
15. Skinner was not the only hothead over this issue. The differences between the pro and anti-privateering groups in the business community could become quite heated and often personal. Congressman Samuel Smith, with family shipping interests in Baltimore but not part of the Concern, found it a deep insult when an unused privateer commission was sent to him for possible use. And the differences even resulted in a murder—that of James Stoughton, the son of Thomas Stoughton, the Spanish consul in New

York. James, in his capacity of Spanish vice consul, had caused the arrest of Robert Goodwin, a privateer from Baltimore, who stabbed Stoughton to death in 1819 during a street scuffle over traded insults.

16. *Niles' Weekly Register*, December 19, 1818, 2.

17. Matthew McCarthy, *Privateering, Piracy, and British Policy in South America, 1810–1830* (London: Boydell Press, 2013), 148.

Chapter 9

1. Moreno was a brother of Mariano Moreno, one of the early revolutionary leaders. He and Onís developed an interesting relationship; Onís tried to recruit him to the royalist side but was rebuffed; they nonetheless kept in contact and Moreno served as an occasional source for the Spanish. He stayed in Philadelphia until 1821 and studied medicine while there.

2. John Quincy Adams, *Memoirs of John Quincy Adams*, Charles F. Adams, ed. (Philadelphia: J.B. Lippincott, 1875–77), vol. 5, 56.

3. The bill became the Act of April 20, 1818, which repealed all previous neutrality acts and codified U.S. neutrality legislation, with some new amendments that broadened its scope.

4. Forsyth was rewarded for his efforts on behalf of the administration a year later, with assignment as minister to the court at Madrid.

5. Alberto Palomeque, *Orijenes de la Diplomacia Arjentina: Mision Aguirre a Norte America* (Buenos Aires: Grafico Robles, 1905), vol. 1, 56.

6. Ibid., 209.

7. Monroe to Adams, 13 Aug. 1818, in John Quincy Adams, *The Writings of John Quincy Adams*, Worthington Chauncey Ford, ed. (New York: Macmillan, 1916), vol. 6, 431.

8. Adams to Aguirre, 27 Aug. 1818, in William Manning, *Diplomatic Correspondence of the United States Concerning the Independence of Latin America* (New York: Oxford University Press, 1925), vol. 1, 78.

9. Aguirre also left a debt: three promissory notes, totaling just over $10,000, payable to the U.S. government. Subsequent U.S. efforts to collect those debts in Chile apparently failed.

10. Wooster, who was related by marriage to David DeForest, stayed with the Chilean navy until 1835, with the exception of a short period when he fell out with the colorful Englishman Admiral Thomas Cochrane, who had become the Chilean navy commander.

11. Halsey to John Graham, 21 Aug. 1818, in Manning, vol. 1, 380.

12. Adams, *Memoirs*, vol. 4, 158 (13 Nov. 1818).

13. Thompson never had a chance to clear himself; he died on the voyage home.

14. Delano, with his wife and two sons, settled in Chile where Delano had a distinguished career in the Chilean navy. He was an ancestor of Sarah Delano, Franklin Delano Roosevelt's mother.

Chapter 10

1. Luis Onís, ever alert to perceived threats but not always fully informed, wrote to Madrid in July that the "revolutionary" Poinsett was headed to Chile for suspicious reasons.

2. Poinsett to Monroe, 23 May 1817, William Manning, *Diplomatic Correspondence of the United States Concerning the Independence of Latin America* (New York: Oxford University Press, 1925), vol. 1, 37.

3. Rodney, who was U.S. attorney general at the time, served in 1807 on the government's team seeking to indict Aaron Burr for an alleged plot to lead a filibuster into Mexico. His prosecution however was not spirited, and he subsequently asked to be released from further involvement in the case—which the government lost.

4. Adams to Rodney, Graham, and Bland, 21 Nov. 1817, Manning, vol. 1, 49. Adams had assumed his duties as secretary of state in September; Richard Rush moved on to become the U.S. minister in London.

5. John Quincy Adams to John Adams, 21 Dec. 1817, John Quincy Adams, *The Writings of John Quincy Adams*, Worthington Chauncey Ford, ed. (New York: Macmillan, 1916), vol. 6, 276; John Q. Adams to Rush, 9 Mar. 1818, ibid., 306.

6. John Quincy Adams, *Memoirs of John Quincy Adams*, Charles F. Adams, ed. (Philadelphia: J.B. Lippincott, 1875–77), vol. 4, 106 (11 July 1818).

7. Weeks, 122.

8. Adams, *Memoirs*, vol. 4, 72 (30 March 1818).

9. Adams, *Memoirs*, vol. 4, 388 (4 June 1819).

10. Francisco J. Urrutia, *Los Estados Unidos y las republicas Hispano-americanos de 1810 a 1830* (Madrid: Editorial-América, 1918), 156. Martín Thompson unfortunately died on the voyage home to Buenos Aires.

11. Poinsett was appointed special envoy to Mexico in 1821, and in 1825 became the first U.S. minister to that country. But his continued and undiplomatic propensity for personal involvement in local politics led to his recall in 1830.

12. Manning, vol. 1, 433.

13. *Niles Weekly Register*, October 24, 1818.

14. Manning, vol. 1, 82.

15. DeForest was acting here out of both public and private interest. The case he raised in his note involved a prize of one of the privateers, the *Tucumán*, sailing under a commission he had sold to George Crowninshield of Salem, Mass., an arrangement which entitled DeForest to a cut of the profits. It is unlikely that Adams knew of this conflict of interest.

16. Adams to DeForest, 1 Jan. 1819, *Annals of Congress*, 15th Congress, 2nd session, 1618.

17. Adams, *Memoirs*, vol. 4, 223 (20 Jan. 1819).

18. Quoted in the *Niles Register*, 27 Feb. 1819.

19. Adams, *Memoirs*, vol. 4, 329 and 306 (9 Apr. and 18 Mar. 1819). In referring to Onís's "trickery," Adams probably was referring to his last-minute maneuvers over the land grants in the treaty negotiations.

Chapter 11

1. Onís, due to the changes that took place in Spain during the "Liberal Triennium," was reassigned as minister to Naples, and then to London. He died in 1826.

2. Adams to Charles J. Ingersol, 7 Aug. 1821, John Quincy Adams, *The Writings of John Quincy Adams*, Worthington Chauncey Ford, ed. (New York: Macmillan, 1916), vol. 7, 167.

3. Baptis Irvine remained an agitator for South American independence, putting himself forward as a candidate for the position of special agent to Venezuela—in vain, of course, because of the low esteem in which he was held by Secretary Adams. His next appearance in this story was his foolish involvement in a madcap late 1822 adventure, led by Henri Decoudray de Holstein, to seize the Spanish island of Puerto Rico. Irvine was arrested, condemned to death, but later released. He moved to Venezuela, and eventually became a United States commercial agent in Chile.

4. It might be added that it was also useful to get Perry out of the country at the

moment, as his demand for a court-martial proceeding against one of his Navy colleagues could have been highly divisive.

5. Adams, *Memoirs*, vol. 5, 164 (July 8, 1820).

6. An act to that effect was passed 15 May 1820, conspicuously omitting Baltimore as a port authorized to admit foreign-flagged armed ships.

7. Adams, 19 May 1830 conversation with William Shaler, John Quincy Adams, *Memoirs of John Quincy Adams*, Charles F. Adams, ed. (Philadelphia: J.B. Lippincott, 1875–77), vol. 8, 227.

8. Torres' main supporters for this proposal were George Bomford, the Army's director of ordnance, Kentucky senator Richard Mentor Johnson (a friend of Clay's) and George Mason, owner of the Washington gun foundry.

9. As with many of the private arms sales made by American merchants, payment was slow or nonexistent from the South American governments. Idler submitted claims for $150,000 and received only partial satisfaction before his death in 1856; the claim was not fully settled until international arbitration in 1890, for $70,000 plus interest.

10. A non-official patriotic figure had showed up in Philadelphia however, and was straying at Torres' home. That was José Sevando de Mier, the fiery Mexican priest last seen with Xavier Mina during the ill-fated expedition to Mexico. Mier had escaped from Spanish jail and remained controversial. While in Philadelphia, Mier got deeply involved in a reform effort at St Mary's church, which pitted the patriots against the conservative and royalist Hispanic community. Mier eventually returned to Mexico, opposed Iturbide, was arrested once again, escaped, but died peacefully in 1827.

11. The treaty had been approved by the Cortes in October, a fact that was known in Washington by November. The reason for the delay in delivery, until February, is not clear.

12. Adams to Charles J. Ingersol, 7 Aug. 1821, *Writings of John Quincy Adams*, vol. 7, 168.

13. John Quincy Adams to John Adams, 21 Dec. 1817, John Quincy Adams, *The Writings of John Quincy Adams*, Worthington Chauncey Ford, ed. (New York: Macmillan, 1916), vol. 6, 276.

14. Adams, *Memoirs*, vol. 5, 325 (9 Mar. 1821).

15. Even after the mixed results of the commission, the Carrera supporters had circulated a long pamphlet, "Strictures on a Voyage to South America" attacking Brackenridge's book, which they found too pro–Pueyrredón.

16. Duane to Juan Germán Roscio, 8 Apr. 1820, Charles H. Bowman, Jr., "Correspondence of William Duane in Two Archives in Bogotá," *Revista de Historia de América* 82 (1976): 115.

17. Adams to Monroe, 24 Aug. 1818, *Writings*, vol. 6, 442.

18. Buenos Aires utilized privateers again a few years later, when it went to war with the Brazilians to drive them out of the Banda Oriental.

Chapter 12

1. John Quincy Adams, *Memoirs of John Quincy Adams*, Charles F. Adams, ed. (Philadelphia: J.B. Lippincott, 1875–77), vol. 4, 472 (8 Dec. 1819).

2. Julio Paredes, *La Gran Colombia y los Estados Unidos, 1810–31* (Bogotá: Fundación Francisco de Paula Santander, 1990), 57–8.

3. Monroe to House of Representatives, 8 Mar. 1822, *American State Papers, Foreign Relations*, vol. 4, 819.

4. General Vives had become governor general of Cuba.

5. Adams, *Memoirs*, vol. 6, 23 (June 19, 1822).

6. Caesar A. Rodney, the commissioner from Delaware, was named the first U.S.

minister to the United Provinces of Rio de la Plata in 1823, and died in Buenos Aires in 1824. The Republic of Argentina did not take its present form until 1861.

7. Karen Racine, "This England and This Now: British Cultural and Intellectual Influence in the Spanish American Independence Era," *Hispanic American Historical Review* 90, no. 3 (2010), 423–454. Racine maintains that the British political model of "autocratic reformism," as well as British cultural values, were the dominant external influences on Spanish American patriots.

8. Some historians have argued that Clay's principal motivation was his political ambition, plus anger that he had not been selected for the position of secretary of state. In an interesting twist of fate and politics, President John Quincy Adams appointed Henry Clay to be his secretary of state in 1825, and Clay persuaded the president to take a more positive atmosphere to Western Hemisphere solidarity than Adams had displayed when he was secretary of state.

9. Duane had sold the *Aurora* and undertook the trip partly in memory of his respected mentor Manuel Torres, but also in an effort to recover some of José Carrera's still outstanding debts to Philadelphia figures. In 1826, he published an account of the trip, entitled *A Visit to Colombia in the Years 1822 & 1823*.

10. Luis de Onís, *Memorial Concerning the Negotiation Between Spain and the United States of America*, Tobias Watkins, trans. (Washington, D.C.: De Kraft, 1821), 130.

11. Including Brazil, independent after 1822, and which became a major trading partner.

Bibliography

Adams, John Quincy. *Memoirs of John Quincy Adams,* vols. 5–7. Charles F. Adams, ed. Philadelphia: J.B. Lippincott, 1875–77.
———. *The Writings of John Quincy Adams,* vols. 6–7. Worthington Chauncey Ford, ed. New York: Macmillan, 1916.
Alonso Piniero, Alfonso. *La trama de los 5,000 días: orígenes de las relaciones argentino-norteamericanas.* Buenos Aires: Ediciones Depalma, 1986.
American State Papers, Foreign Relations. Library of Congress. http://memory.loc.gov/ammem/amlaw/lwsp.html.
Annals of Congress. Library of Congress. http://memory.loc.gov/ammem/amlaw/lwac.html.
Barros Arana, Diego. *Historia jeneral de la independencia de Chile,* Vol 4. Santiago, 1854.
Bealer, Lewis Winkler. *Los corsarios de Buenos Aires, sus actividades en las guerras hispano-americanas de la independencia, 1815–1821.* Buenos Aires: Coni, 1937.
Bemis, Samuel F. *Early Diplomatic Missions from Buenos Aires to the United States.* Worcester, MA: The Society, 1940.
———. *The Latin American Policy of the United States: An Historical Interpretation.* New York: Harcourt, Brace, 1943.
Bernstein, Harry. *Origins of Inter-American Interest, 1700–1812.* New York: Russell & Russell, 1965.
Bierck, Harold. *Vida Publica de Don Pedro Gual.* Caracas: Ministerio de Educación Nacional, 1947.
Billingsley, Edward B. *In Defense of Neutral Rights: The U.S. Navy and the Wars of Independence in Chile and Peru.* Chapel Hill: University of North Carolina Press, 1967.
Bornholdt, Laura. *Baltimore and Early Pan-Americanism.* Northampton, MA, 1949.
Bowman, Charles H. *Vicente Pazos Kanki: Un boliviano en la libertad de América.* La Paz: Editorial Los Amigos del Libro, 1975.
Bradley, Edward A. *We Never Retreat: The Texas Filibustering Era, 1791–1822.* College Station: Texas A&M University Press, 2015.
Brooks, Philip C. *Diplomacy and the Borderlands: The Adams-Onís Treaty.* Berkeley: University of California Press, 1939.
Carnicelli, Americo. *La masoneria en la indpendencia de America,* Vol 1. Bogotá, 1970.
Carrera Verdugo, Jose M. *Diario de viaje a Estados Unidos de América.* José M.Barros, ed. Santiago de Chile: Editorial Universitaria, 1996.
Cusick, James G. *The Other War of 1812: The Patriot War and the American Invasion of Spanish East Florida.* Athens: University of Georgia Press, 2003.
Davis, William C. *The Pirates Laffite: The Treacherous World of the Corsairs of the Gulf.* Orlando: Harcourt, 2005.

Bibliography

De Forest, John W. *The De Forests of Avesnes*. New Haven: Tuttle Morehouse, 1900.
De Onís, José. *The United States as Seen by Spanish American Writers, 1776-1880*. New York: Gordian Press, 1975.
Domínguez Michael Christopher. *Vida de Fray Servando Teresa de Mier*. Mexico City: Ediciones Era, 2004.
Fitte, Ernesto. *De la revolution al reconocimiento de las Provincias Unidas*. Buenos Aires: Emecé Editores, 1969.
Garitee, Jerome R. *The Republic's Private Navy: The American Privateering Business as Practiced by Baltimore During the War of 1812*. Middletown, CT: Wesleyan University Press, 1977.
Grases, Pedro. *Obras de Pedro Grases*, vol. 3 *Preindependencia y emancipación: "El Círculo de Filadelfia."* Caracas: Editorial Seix Barral, 1981.
Griffin, Charles C. *The United States and the Disruption of the Spanish Empire*. New York: Columbia University Press, 1937.
Jefferson, Thomas. *Thomas Jefferson Papers at the Library of Congress*. http://memory.loc.gov/ammem/collections/jefferson_papers.
Johnson, John J. *A Hemisphere Apart: The Foundations of Unied States Policy Toward Latin America*. Baltimore: Johns Hopkins University Press, 1990.
Kansil, Joli Q. *John Quincy Adams and Latin America*. Honolulu: South Point Productions,1983.
Keen, Benjamin. *David Curtis DeForest and the Revolution of Buenos Aires*. Westport, CT: Greenwood Press, 1970.
Lewis, James E. *The American Union and the Problem of Neighborhood: The United States and the Collapse of the Spanish Empire*. Chapel Hill: University of North Carolina Press, 1998.
Long, David F. *Nothing Too Daring: A Biography of David Porter*. Annapolis: U.S. Naval Institute Press, 1970.
Madison, James. *James Madison Papers at the Library of Congress*. http://memory.loc.gov/ammem/collections/madison_papers.
Manning, William R., ed. *Diplomatic Correspondence of the United States Concerning the Independence of Latin America*. New York: Oxford University Press, 1925.
McCarthy, Matthew. *Privateering, Piracy and British Policy in South America, 1810-1830*. London: Boydell Press, 2013.
McMaster, John B. *The Life & Times of Stephen Girard*. Philadelphia: Lippincott, 1918.
Mier, Fray Servando. *The Memoirs of Fray Servando Teresa de Mier*. Lane Helen, trans. New York: Oxford University Press, 1998.
Onís, Luís de. *Memorial Concerning the Negotiation Between Spain and the United States of America*, Tobias Watkins, trans. Washington, D.C.: De Kraft, 1821.
Owsley, Frank Lawrence. *Filibusters and Expansionists: Jeffersonian Manifest Destiny*. Tuscaloosa: University of Alabama Press, 1997.
Palacio Fajardo, Manuel. *Outline of the Revolution in Spanish America*. New York: J. Eastbourne, 1817.
Palomeque, Alberto. *Orijenes de la Diplomacia Arjentina: Mission Aguirre a Norte America*, Vol. 1. Buenos Aires: Grafico Robles, 1905.
Paredes, Julio. *La Gran Columbia y los Estados Unidos, 1810-31*, 2 vols. Bogotá: Fundación Francisco de Paula Santander, 1990.
Parks, E. Taylor. *Columbia and the United States*. New York: Arno Press, 1970.
Parton, Dorothy. *The Diplomatic Career of Joel R. Poinsett*. Washington, D.C.: Catholic University, 1934.
Paxson, Frederic L. *The Independence of the South American Republics*. Philadelphia: Ferris & Leach, 1903.
Peterson, Harold F. *Argentina and the United States 1810-1960*. Albany: State University of New York, 1964.

Racine, Karen. *Francisco de Miranda: A Transatlantic Life in the Age of Revolution.* Wilmington, DE: Scholarly Resources, 2003.
Phillips, Kim T. *William Duane, Radical Journalist in the Age of Jefferson.* New York: Garland, 1989.
Rio, Angel. *La Mission de Don Luís Onís en los Estados Unidos.* Barcelona: Novagrafik, 1981.
Rippy, James F. *The Rivalry of the United States and Great Britain Over Latin America, 1808–30.* Baltimore: Johns Hopkins University Press, 1929.
Rivas, Raimundo, *Relaciones internacionales entre Colombia y los Estados Unidos, 1810–1850.* Bogotá: Imprenta nacional, 1915.
Robertson, William Spence. *France and Latin American Independence.* Baltimore: Johns Hopkins University Press, 1939.
———. *Francisco de Miranda and the Revolutionizing of Spanish America.* Washington, D.C., Government Printing Office, 1909.
Ruiz Moreno, Isidoro. *Historia de las relaciones exteriors argentinas.* Buenos Aires: Editorial Perrot, 1961.
Rydjord, John. *Foreign Interest in the Independence of New Spain.* New York: Russell & Russell, 1972.
Sater, William. *Chile and the United States.* Athens: University of Georgia Press, 1990.
Scharf, John Thomas. *History of Philadelphia, 1609–1884.* Philadelphia: L.H. Evert, 1884.
Shurbutt, Thomas R. *United States–Latin American Relations, 1800–1850.* Tuscaloosa: University of Alabama Press, 1991.
Spanish Foreign Ministry. *Documentos relativos a la independencia de Norteamérica en archivos españoles,* vol 3. Madrid: Ministerio de Asuntos Exteriores, 1976–1985.
Stagg, John C.A. *Borderlines in Borderlands: James Madison and the Spanish-American Frontier, 1776–1821.* New Haven: Yale University Press, 2009.
Thornton, William. *William Thornton Papers.* Library of Congress, Manuscript Division.
Urrutia, Francisco J. *Los Estados Unidos y las republicas Hispano-americanos de 1810 a 1830.* Madrid: Editorial-América, 1918.
Vilanueva, Carlos A. *Historia Diplomatica de la Primera Republica de Venezuela.* Caracas, 1967.
Vogeley, Nancy J. *The Bookrunner: A History of Inter-American Relations, 1800–1830.* Philadelphia: American Philosophical Society, 2011.
Warren, Harris G. *The Sword Was Their Passport: A History of American Filibustering in the Mexican Revolution.* Port Washington, NY: Kennikat Press, 1972.
Webster, Charles K. *Britain and the Independence of Latin America 1812–30.* New York: Octagon Books, 1970.
Weeks, William Earle. *John Quincy Adams and American Global Empire.* Lexington: University Press of Kentucky, 1992.
Whitaker, Arthur P. *The United States and the Independence of Latin America.* Baltimore: John Hopkins University Press, 1941.
Wilgus, Alva Curtis. *Some Activities of United States Citizens in the South American Wars of Independence, 1808–1824.* New Orleans, 1931.

Journal Articles

Arlyck, Kevin. "Plaintiffs v. Privateers: Litigation and Foreign Affairs in the Federal Courts, 1816–1822." *Law and History Review* 30, no. 1 (2012): 245–278.
Benedetti, Benedetti. "American Political Parties and the Latin American Policy of the United States, 1798–1826." Unpublished master's degree thesis, University of Colorado at Boulder, 1945.
Bierck, Harold. "The First Instance of United States Foreign Aid: Venezuelan Relief in 1812." *Inter-American Economic Affairs* 9 (1955): 47–59.

Bibliography

———. "Pedro Gual and the Patriot Effort to Capture a Mexican Port." *Hispanic American Historical Review* 27, no. 3 (1947): 456–466.

———. "Spoils, Soils, and Skinner." *Maryland Historical Magazine* 49, no. 1 (1954): 21–41, and no. 2, 143–54.

Bowman, Charles H., Jr. "The Activities of Manuel Torres as Purchasing Agent, 1821–22." *Hispanic American Historical Review* 48, no. 2 (1968): 234–346.

———. "Correspondence of William Duane in Two Archives in Bogotá." *Revista de Historia de América* 82 (1976): 111–125.

———. "Financial Plans and Operations of Manuel Torres in Philadelphia." *Records of the American Catholic Historical Society of Philadelphia* 83, no. 2 (1971): 106–116.

———. "Manuel Torres, a Spanish American Patriot in Philadelphia, 1796–1822." *The Pennsylvania Magazine of History and Biography* 94, no. 1 (1970): 26–53.

———. "Vicente Pazos and the Amelia Island Affair." *Florida Historical Quarterly* 53, no. 3 (1975): 273–295.

Brooks, Philip Coolidge. "Spanish Royalists in the United States, 1809–1821." In A. Curtis Wilgus, ed., *Colonial Hispanic America*. New York: Russell & Russell, 1963, 559–572.

Cox, Isaac Joslin. "General Wilkinson and His Later Intrigues with the Spaniards." *The American Historical Review* 19, no. 4 (1914): 794–812.

———. "Monroe and Early Mexican Agents." *American Historical Association Annual Report* 1 (1911): 199–215.

Cuccorese, Horacio Juan. "San Martín y las sociedades secretas." Instituto Nacional Sanmartíniano, accessed 2/2013 at http://www.sanmartiniano.gov.ar/textos/parte3/texto083.php.

Cummins, Light T. "John Quincy Adams and Latin American Nationalism." *Revista de Historia de America* 86 (1978): 221–231.

Davis, Richard Beale. "The Abbe Correa in America." *William and Mary Quarterly*, Third Series 13, no. 2 (1956): 296–298.

Davis, T. Frederick. "MacGregor's Invasion of Florida, 1817." *Florida Historical Society Quarterly* 7, no. 1 (1928): 2–71.

Dykstra, Kristin Ann. "American Cosmopolitanisms and the Decline of the Spanish Empire, 1800–1832." PhD thesis, State University of New York at Buffalo, 2002.

———. "On the Betrayal of Nations: José Alvarez de Toledo's Philadelphia *Manifesto* and *Justification*." *New Centennial Review* 4, no. 1 (2004): 267–305.

Fall, Vernon W. "William G.D. Worthington: A Study of the Man and His Role in the Recognition of Buenos Aires and Chile." M.A. thesis, Kansas State University, Fort Hays, 1965.

Faye, Stanley "The Great Stroke of Pierre Lafitte." *Louisiana Historical Quarterly* 23, no. 3 (1940): 762–826.

———. "Louis Aury." *Louisiana Historical Quarterly* 25, no. 2 (1942): 625–655.

———. "Privateersmen of the Gulf and Their Prizes." *Louisiana History Quarterly* 22, no. 4 (1939): 1012–1094.

German, Hyman. "The Philadelphia *Aurora* on Latin American Affairs." *Pennsylvania History* 8, no. 2 (1941): 11–130.

Gleijeses, Piero. "The Limits of Sympathy: The United States and the Independence of South America." *Journal of Latin American Studies* 24, no. 3 (1920): 481–505.

Gonzales, Manuel Hernandez. "Francisco Caballero Sarmiento: un empressario al servicio de la contrarevolución." *Revista de Indias* 51, no. 192 (1991): 375–396.

———. "*El Observador Espanol* en Londres, un periodico Fernandino contra la emancipacion Americana." *Revista de Indias* 59, no. 216 (1999): 439–454.

Goren, Yael Bitran. "Servando Teresa de Mier: the Ideological Trajectory of a Mexican *Criollo* in the Times of Independence." Unpublished master's thesis, University of North Carolina, 1994.

Bibliography

Griffin, Charles C. "Privateering from Baltimore During the Spanish American Wars of Independence." *Maryland Historical Magazine* 35, no. 1 (1940): 26–32.

Grummond, Jane Lucas de. "The Jacob Idler Claim Against Venezuela, 1817–1890." *Hispanic American Historical Review* 34, no. 2 (1954): 134–157.

Guzman, José R. "La correspondencia de Don Luis de Onís sobre la expedicion de Javier Mina." *Boletin del Archivo General de la Nation* (Mexico) 2nd Series 9 no. 4 (1968): 509–43.

———. "Una sociedad secreta en Londres al servicio del Hispanoamerica." *Boletin del Archivo General de la Nation* (Mexico) 2nd Series 8, nos. 1–2 (1967): 109–128.

Head, David. "A Different Kind of Maritime Predation: South American Privateering from Baltimore, 1816–1820." *International Journal of Naval History* 7, no. 2 (2008). Accessed 11/2012 at http://www.ijnhonline.org/wp-content/uploads/2012/01/Head.pdf.

Higginbotham, Sanford W. "Philadelphia Commerce with Latin America, 1820–1830." *Pennsylvania History* 9, no. 4 (1942): 252–266.

Hopkins, Frederick. "For Flag or Profit: The Life of Commodore John Daniel Danels of Baltimore." *Maryland Historical Magazine* 80, no. 4 (1975): 392–401.

———. "For Freedom and Profit: Baltimore Privateers in the Wars of South American Independence." *The Northern Mariner* 18, nos. 3–4 (2008): 93–104.

Hoskins, Halford L. "The Hispanic-American Policy of Henry Clay." *Hispanic American Historical Review* 7 (1927): 460–478.

Hyneman, Charles S. "Neutrality During the European Wars of 1792–1815: America's Understanding of Her Obligations." *The American Journal of International Law* 24, no. 2 (1930): 279–309.

Ibaguren, Carlos. "La missión diplomatica de Manuel Hermengildo Aguirre en los Estados Unidos." *Investigaciones y Ensayos* (Academia Nacional de la Historia, Argentina) 30 (1981): 339–366.

Jos, Emiliano. "Juan Vicente Bolívar y su mission en los Estados Unidos." *Revista de Indias* 2, no. 4 (1941): 135–163.

Kanellos, Nicolás. "Hispanic American Intellectuals Publishing in the Nineteenth-Century United States: From Political Tracts in Support of Independence to Commercial Publishing Ventures." *Hispania* 88, no. 4 (2005): 687–692.

Kenway, Mary. "Correspondence Between General William Winder and President Monroe with Reference to Proposals Made by the Government of the United Provinces of South America." *Hispanic American Historical Review* 12 (1932): 457–461.

Lewis, Walker. "John Quincy Adams and the Baltimore Pirates." *American Bar Association Journal* 67, no. 2 (1981): 1010–1014.

Lockey, Joseph B. "The Florida Intrigues of José Álavarez de Toledo." *The Florida Historical Society Quarterly* 12, no. 4 (1934): 145–178.

Lowe, Richard G. "American Seizure of Amelia Island." *Florida Historical Society Quarterly* 45 no. 1 (1966): 18–30.

Mendoza, Cristobal L. "Las premieras relaciones entre Venezuela y los Estados Unidos." *Boletin de la Academia Nacional de la Historia* (Caracas) 37, no. 108 (1944): 346–372.

Narrett, David E. "José Bernardo Gutiérrez de Lara: Caudillo of the Mexican Republic in Texas." *Southwestern Historical Quarterly* 106, no. 2 (2002): 194–228.

Neumann, William L. "United States Aid to the Chilean Wars of Independence." *The Hispanic American Historical Review* 27, no. 2 (1947): 204–219.

Nichols, Roy F. "Trade Relations and the Establishment of the United States Consulates in Spanish America, 1779–1809." *The Hispanic American Historical Review* 13, no. 3 (1933): 289–313.

———. "William Shaler: New England Apostle of Rational Liberty." *The New England Quarterly* 9, no. 1 (1936): 71–96.

Orenstein, Jeffrey. "Joseph Almeida, Portrait of a Privateer, Pirate and Plaintiff." *The Green Bag Review of Law* 10, no. 3 (2007): 307–322, and 12, no. 1 (2008): 36–52. Accessed 10/2012 at http://www.greenbag.org/v12n1/v12n1_orenstein.pdf.

Ortuño Martinez, Manuel. "Javier Mina en los Estados Unidos." *Revista española de estudios norteamericanos*, 17–18 (1999): 183–200. Accessed 10/2012 at http://dspace.uah.es/dspace/handle/10017/5034?show=full.

Perrone, Sean T. "The Formation of the Spanish Consular Service in the United States." In Jörg Ulbert & Prijac Lukian, eds., *Consuls et services consulaires au XIXe siècle*. Hamburg: Dokumentation & Buch, 2010. JZ1444 .C66 2010.

———. "John Stoughton and the '*Divina Pastora*' Prize Case, 1816–1819." *Journal of the Early Republic* 28, no. 2 (2008): 215–242.

———. "The Role of Spanish Consuls in the United States, 1795–1898." In Brian Bunk, et al., eds., *Nation and Conflict in Modern Spain*. Madison: Parallel Press, 2008, 81–102.

Pradells, Nadal Jesus. "La Diplomacia antes de la Guerra." In *Seminario Internacional sobre la Guerra de la Independencia*. Madrid: Ministerio de la defensa, 1996.

Robertson, William Spence. "The Beginnings of Spanish American Diplomacy." In *Essays in American History, Dedicated to FJ. Turner*. New York: H. Holt, 1910, 231–267.

———. "Documents Concerning the Consular Service of the United States in Latin America." *The Mississippi Valley Historical Review* 2, no. 4 (1916): 561–568.

———. "The First Legations of the United States in Latin America." *The Mississippi Valley Historical Review* 2, no. 2 (1915): 183–212.

———. "The Recognition of the Hispanic American Nations by the United States." *Hispanic American Historical Review* 1, no. 3 (1918): 239–269.

Rojas, Manuel. "Traductores de la Liberad, Filadlefia y la diffusion del republicanismo en Hispanoamérica." In Beatriz Zepeda, ed., *Ecuador, relaciones exteriors a la luz del bicentenario*. Quito: Flasco, 2009, 45–76.

Seal-Coon, Frederick W. "Spanish American Revolutionary Masonry." *Ars Quatuor Coronatorum* 94 (1981): 83–106.

Solnick, Bruce B. "American Opinion Concerning the Spanish-American Wars of Independence, 1808–1824." Doctoral thesis, New York University, 1960.

Stewart, Watt. "The Diplomatic Service of John M. Forbes at Buenos Aires." *The Hispanic American Historical Review* 14, no. 2 (1934): 202–218.

———. "The South American Commission." *The Hispanic American Historical Review* 9, no. 1 (1929): 31–59.

Vivian, James F. "The *Paloma* Claim in United States and Venezuelan-Columbian Relations, 1818–1826." *Caribbean Studies* 14, no. 4 (1975): 57–72.

Warren, Harris Gaylord. "Documents Relating to George Graham's Proposals to Jean Lafitte for the Occupation of the Texas Coast." *The Louisiana Historical Quarterly* 21, no. 1 (1938): 213–220.

———. "Documents Relative to the Establishment of Privateers at Galveston 1816–17." *The Louisiana Historical Quarterly* 21, no. 4 (1938): 1086–1109.

———. "The Early Revolutionary Career of Juan Mariano Picornell." *The Hispanic American Historical Review* 22, no. 1 (1942): 55–81.

———. "The *Firebrand* Affair." *The Louisiana Historical Quarterly* 21, no. 1 (1938): 203–212.

———. "Mina's Invasion of Mexico." *The Hispanic American Historical Review* 23, no. 1 (1943): 52–77.

———. "Pensacola and the Filibusters, 1816–1817." *The Louisiana Historical Quarterly* 21, no. 3 (1938): 806–22.

———. "The Southern Career of Juan Mariano Picornell." *The Journal of Southern History* 8, no. 3 (1942): 311–333.

———. "Southern Filibusters in the War of 1812." *The Louisiana Historical Quarterly* 25, no. 2 (1942): 291–300.

Warren, Richard A. "Displaced Pan-Americans and the Transformation of the Catholic Church in Philadelphia, 1789–1850." *The Pennsylvania Magazine of History and Biography* 128, no. 4 (2004): 343–366.

Wellborn, Alfred Toledano. "Relations Between New Orleans and Latin America, 1810–1824." *Louisiana Historical Quarterly* 22, no. 3 (1939): 710–793.

West, Elizabeth Howard, trans. "The Diary of Bernardo Gutiérrez de Lara" *The American Historical Review* 34, no. 1 (1928): 55–77.

Wilgus, Alva Curtis. "Spanish American Patriot Activity Along the Gulf Coast." *Louisiana Historical Quarterly* 8, no. 2 (1925): 193–215.

Wyllys, Rufus Kay. "The Filibusters of Amelia Island." *The Georgia Historical Quarterly* 12, no. 4 (1928): 297–325.

Index

Adams, John 19, 22, 26, 176
Adams, John Quincy 87, 96, 134, 157, 159, 162, 165–6, 187, 180; and privateering 123, 124, 125, 140, 148, 152–3, 160–1; as secretary of state 105, 112, 113, 133, 136, 137–8, 139, 141, 144, 148, 150, 151, 152, 153, 154–5, 172, 173, 174; treaty negotiations 105, 124, 133, 145, 146, 147, 152, 153, 154, 155, 156, 160, 163, 170, 177; views of Spanish Americans 133, 162, 168
admiralty law 118–9
Aguirre, Juan Pedro 53, 77, 86, 132
Aguirre, Manuel 132, 133, 134–5, 136, 137, 138, 139, 140, 141, 142, 144, 172, 178
Aix la Chapelle conference 147
Alabama 184*ch*3*n*3
Allen, Ira 68
Almeida, José 86–7, 121–3, 127
Amelia Island 61–2, 106, 108, 109, 111, 112–3, 114, 115, 130, 134, 144, 145, 151, 152, 176
America Libre 110
the American Concern 81–2, 127, 142
American Philosophical Society 23, 36, 38
L'Ami des Lois (journal) 91
Amistad trial 125
Anáhuac Congress 93, 99, 100, 121
Anduaga, Joaquin 173
Angostura 130, 132, 148, 161
Apalachicola River 20
Aracuano 140
Argentina *see* Buenos Aires
Ariza, Àngel de 91
Arrogante Barcelones 122, 127
Artigas, José 87, 127, 128, 133, 140, 171
Astor, John Jacob 95, 97, 162, 186*ch*5*n*3
Aurora (newspaper) 39, 71, 81, 88, 113, 131
Aury, Louis-Michel 77–8, 83, 94, 101, 102, 109, 110, 111, 112–3, 115, 120–1
Austerlitz 32
Austria 32

Baltimore 21, 37, 38, 40, 56, 73, 88, 89, 93, 98, 107, 107, 176; and privateering 79–82, 86, 96, 119, 125, 127, 148
Baltimore Patriot (newspaper) 81, 133
Bamford, George 191*ch*11*n*8
Banda Oriental 78, 87, 121, 128, 133, 168, 171
Barataria Bay 66, 77, 80, 83, 119–20
Barinas tobacco 165–6
Barnes, James 85, 117, 118, 119
Baton Rouge 47, 48, 61
Bayonne 33
Bello, Andrés 35
Beluche, Renato 77, 120
Bernabeu, Juan 37, 89, 123, 183*ch*2*n*2
Biddle, James 162
Bland, Theodorick 82, 127, 144, 150, 151, 160, 162
Blount, William 12, 17–20, 21, 31, 66
Bolívar, Juan Vicente 35, 40, 43, 47, 50, 52
Bolívar, Simón 35, 39, 46, 52, 71, 76, 93, 94, 103, 105, 106, 120, 130, 132, 143, 148, 149, 161, 164, 165, 166, 168, 176
Bolivia 53, 132, 168
Bonaparte, Joseph 33, 34, 36, 40, 95
Bonaparte, Napoleon 11, 22, 28, 32, 72, 91, 95, 184*ch*3*n*8, 187*ch*7*n*7
Bonaparte, Pauline 91
Boston 37, 38, 89, 117
Bourbon family 36, 73, 74, 75, 164, 168, 180; *see also* Charles IV; Ferdinand VII
Bowers, David 124
Brackenridge, Henry 131, 144, 150, 151
Brazil 32, 71, 87, 141, 168, 171, 174, 180
Brown, Alexander 81
Brown, Noah 137
Brown, Samuel 81
Buenos Aires 24, 34, 46, 49, 53, 71, 72, 76, 77, 778–9, 93, 95, 97, 107, 109, 118, 121, 130, 132, 133–4, 135, 136, 139, 140–1, 143,

148, 150, 152, 153, 160, 161, 164, 168, 170–1, 176; and privateering 78–9, 82, 83, 86, 87, 140, 176
Burr, Aaron 20, 28, 31, 66, 95

Caballeros Racionales 27, 64, 187$ch7n7$; see also Masonic Lodges
Cádiz 33, 34, 35, 55, 159, 163; see also Regency Council; Spain
Calcasieu River 66
Caledonia 98, 101
Calypso 99, 101
Canada 11, 147
Carabobo 147
Caracas 24, 35, 41, 55, 71, 76, 64; see also Venezuela
Caracas junta 45–6, 47
Carrera, José 72, 76, 95, 101, 132, 135, 136, 138, 139, 144, 151, 168, 169, 178, 187$ch7n7$
Cartagena 55, 76, 77, 80, 84, 86, 93, 109, 121, 127
Chacabuco 130
Charles IV of Spain 21, 32, 36
Charleston 82, 107, 110, 111, 112, 115
Chase, John 128
Chasseur 106
Chaytor, James 83
Cheesman, Forman 137
Cheeves, Langdon 165
Chew, Beverly 119–20
Chile 34, 46, 49, 71–2, 95, 109, 121, 130, 132, 133, 135, 136, 137, 139–40, 141, 143, 144, 150, 151, 161, 164, 168, 175, 176
Cienfuegos, José 116
City of Washington Gazette (newspaper) 114
Claiborne, William 64, 66
Clark, George R. 20
Clay, Henry 88, 96–7, 114, 134–5, 139, 145, 151, 156, 165, 166, 167, 169, 173, 178, 192$ch2n8$
Clemente, Lino de 105, 106, 107, 112, 113, 149, 152, 154–5, 165, 172
Clifton 97
Clinton, deWitt 95
Cogswell, Nathaniel 69, 185$ch4n10$
Colombia 24, 39, 76, 164–5, 168, 170, 172, 175; see also Gran Colombia; New Granada
Columbian Centinel (newspaper) 131
Columbus see *Aracuano*
Commission to South America (1817–1818) 143–4, 149–51
Congress 53, 55, 59, 60, 87–8, 96, 103, 114, 133, 134, 135, 139, 144, 145, 148, 151, 153, 155, 156, 160, 162, 166, 167, 168, 172–3, 151, 143, 155, 156, 160, 162, 166, 167, 168, 172–3, 178, 184$ch3n3$

Congresso 82, 86
Correa, Segundo 99, 187$ch6n9$
Correa de Serra, José 87
Cortes of Cádiz 33, 34, 64
Council of Castille 33
Craig, Catherine 41
Craig, John 41
Creek Indians 18, 21, 59, 92, 145, 184$ch3n3$
Cuba 23, 24, 46, 65, 76, 77, 104, 128, 131, 168, 171
Curiacio 138, 141

Dallas, Alexander 37, 65
D'Alvimar, Octaviano 183$ch2n3$
d'Amblimont, Jean 50
Darcy, John 79, 81, 82, 96, 97, 128, 139
Dayton, John 29
DeForest, David 78, 79, 119, 142, 147, 148, 152–5, 166, 172, 174, 178, 190$ch10n15$
Delano, Paul 137, 138, 142, 189$ch9n14$
Desmolard, Captain 38
Devereaux, John 136, 140, 141
Dick, John 94, 119
Didier, Henry 79, 81, 82, 96, 97, 128, 139
Divina Pastora 117–8
Dolphin 99, 101
Dorrego, Manuel 109
Duane, William 39–40, 64, 88, 104, 109, 113, 166, 169, 178, 179–80, 192$ch12n9$
Duncan, Abner 120
Dupuis, Francois 120
Duvall, Gabriel 87, 126

Ecuador 34, 39, 76, 164; see also Gran Colombia; New Granada
Enlightenment and liberal politics 25, 34, 39
Espana, José Maria 25, 57
USS *Essex* 72
Eustis, William 63

Fajardo, Manuel Palacio 56, 98, 131
Fatio, Felipe 115
Ferdinand VII of Spain 32–3, 38, 45, 47, 71, 72, 73, 74–5, 98, 99, 146, 156, 159–60, 162, 167, 175, 180, 181
Fernandina 61, 108, 111
Florida 11, 12, 20–21, 23, 47–8, 59–60, 62, 75, 92, 106, 107, 108, 112, 113, 114, 124, 133, 134, 145, 146, 152, 156, 159, 160, 167, 181, 184$ch3n3$; see also Amelia Island
Folch, Vicente 59, 60, 61
Forbes, John 164, 171
Foronda, Valentin 30, 31, 36, 41, 51, 183$ch2n1$
Forsyth, John 135, 189$ch9n4$
Fourth of July see *Patriota*

202

Index

France: and Spain 32–35, 45; and U.S.A. 11, 21–2, 160, 176, 184*ch3n*8; *see also* Bonaparte, Napoleon

Gaceta de Texas (newspaper) 70
Galveston 78, 83, 101, 102, 109, 111, 115–7, 120–1
General Scott 97, 106
Genêt, Edmond 19–20, 25
Georgia 59, 61
Ghent, Treaty of 73, 75
Girard, Stephen 43, 47, 54
Glenn, Elias 86, 87, 123, 125, 126, 127
Gomez, José 132, 135, 136, 137
Gooding, John 81, 128
Graham, John 63, 64, 100, 144, 150, 161
Gran Colombia 164, 172–3; *see also* Colombia
Gran Reunion Americana 27 *see also* Masonic Lodges
Great Britain: and Spanish America 26–7, 34, 35, 45, 49, 53, 58, 59, 75, 77, 98, 176, 178, 180–1, 192*ch12n*7; and USA 11, 12, 18, 19, 21, 54, 58, 59, 66–7, 71, 73, 75, 77, 92, 152, 154
Grymes, John 120
La Guaira 34, 25, 46, 49, 57, 71
Gual, Manuel 25, 57
Gual, Pedro 56–7, 77, 93, 94, 96, 98, 100, 102, 103, 105, 106, 107, 109, 110, 112, 113, 130, 149, 172–3, 176, 178, 187*ch7n*7
Gutiérrez, José Bernardo 62–8, 69, 90, 92, 101, 176, 185*ch4n*7, 185*ch4n*10, 187*ch6n*14

Haiti 22, 29, 42, 43, 76, 84, 91, 93, 94, 101, 103, 108, 143, 184*ch3n*2
Halsey, Thomas 72, 140, 141, 150, 161
Hamilton, Alexander 25, 26–27, 183*ch1n*4
Havana 18, 38, 48, 50, 89, 116; *see also* Cuba
Herrera, José de 90, 93–4, 110, 121, 130, 188*ch8n*5
Hidalgo, Manuel 34, 48–9, 63, 64
Holstein, Henri de 190*ch11n*3
Holy Alliance 75, 146, 47, 151, 173, 180
Horatio 138, 141
Houston, John 86, 87, 126, 127
Hubbard, Ruggles 107, 108, 110, 113
Humbert, Jean 90, 91

Idler, Jacob 165, 166, 191*ch11n*9
Iguala Plan 168
Indpendencia del Sud 83
Irarte, Juan de 40, 42
Irujo, Carlos de 28, 29, 30, 36, 41, 48, 154, 159

Irvine, Baptis 96, 132, 149, 160, 169, 190*ch11n*3
Iturbide, Augustín 168, 175

Jackson, Andrew 73, 92, 112, 113, 116, 120, 134, 146, 152, 153–4, 156
Jackson, Francis 45
Jáudenes, Josef de 38, 183*ch2n*3
Jefferson, Thomas 11–2, 21, 23, 24, 28, 30, 36, 62, 75, 180
João VI of Portugal 32
Johnson, Richard 191*ch11n*8
Johnston, John 81
juntas: in Spain 33, 25; in Spanish colonies 34, 75

Karrick, Joseph 81, 126–7, 128
Key, Francis Scott 81–2
King, Rufus 25, 26, 27, 28
Knox, Henry 25, 26

Lafitte, Jean 77, 99, 115–7, 120
Lafitte, Pierre 77, 99, 115–7, 120
Lallemand, Charles 116
Lastra, Pedro de la 55
Latour, Arsène 116
Lautaro Lodges 27, 109, 132, 187*ch7n*7; *see also* Masonic Lodges
Leander 29, 30
Ledresench, Louis 50
Lima 164, 168
Livingston, Edward 120
London Convention (1818) 147
Long, James 116
Louisa 122, 123, 125
Louisiana 11, 12, 18, 22, 23, 28, 66, 75, 90, 92, 119–20, 156, 167
Lowry, Robert 46, 47, 49, 51, 71

MacGregor, Gregor 106–8, 109, 110, 113, 130, 149, 152, 187*ch7n*
Madan, Augustine 24
Madison, Dolly 37
Madison, James 12, 28, 30, 35, 36, 48, 53, 56, 58, 59, 60, 62, 63, 65, 70, 80–1, 87, 95, 176, 181
Madrid 32, 33, 72, 74, 89, 124, 156, 159, 162, 167, 173
Magee, Augustus 67–8
Maipú 139
Mangoré 85, 117, 119
Margarita Island 75, 83, 122, 127
Mason, George 191*ch11n*8
Masonic Lodges 27, 57, 64, 86, 187*ch7n*7
Matagorda 109
Mathews, George 59, 60, 61
Mathews, Henry 124

203

Index

McCulloch, James 82, 123
McKee, John 59, 60, 61
Medina River battle 70
Mees, Boer & Moens 165
Mendez, Luis Lopez 35
Mendoza 76
Mexican Company of Baltimore 99, 100, 187*ch*6*n*11
El Mexicano 70
Mexico 12, 22, 23, 34, 38, 40, 46, 48, 50, 63, 65, 67–8, 71, 82, 84, 89, 90, 91, 93, 106, 107, 108, 110, 112, 121, 128, 130, 168, 170, 171, 173, 175; filibusters into 67–70, 98–102, 116, 176; *see also* Texas
Mier, Servando 98, 101, 187*ch*7*n*7, 191*ch*11*n*10
Miller, William 49, 53, 54, 78
Mina, Francisco 97–102, 103, 104, 105, 130
Miranda, Francisco 24–31, 39, 41, 46, 52, 55–6, 80, 99, 106
Misisipi (newspaper) 40
Mississippi (territory and state) 21, 184*ch*3*n*3
Mississippi River 17, 19, 20, 22, 48
Mobile 59
Monroe, James 12; as president 111, 113, 116, 124, 130, 133, 134, 138, 139, 141, 143, 144, 147, 148, 151, 153, 155, 156, 160–1, 162, 167, 170, 172, 173, 176, 178, 180, 181; as secretary of state 51, 54, 56, 60, 62, 63, 66, 68, 70, 85, 90, 100, 123, 140;
Monroe Doctrine 75, 180
Montella, Mariano 98
Montevideo 139
Morelos, José 93
Moreno, Manuel 109, 130, 132, 189*ch*9*n*1
Morgan, Benjamin 120
Morillo, Pablo 75–6, 93, 105–6, 166, 168
Morphy, Diego 90, 91, 92, 94, 101
Morphy, Diego, Sr. 90
Murray, Matthew 81

Nacogdoches 67, 68, 70
Natchez 20, 69
Natchitoches 63, 66, 68, 69
National Intelligencer (newspaper) 126, 131, 134
Neutral Ground 66, 67, 90
neutrality legislation 20, 80, 82, 87–8, 89, 117–8, 124–5, 134, 136, 160, 162
neutrality policy 11, 12, 19, 44, 111, 131, 134, 147, 169–70, 176–7
Neuville, Jean-Guillaume 146, 154, 155
New Granada 34, 55, 71, 76, 93, 103, 107, 161, 164
New Orleans 28, 48, 59, 64, 65–6, 70, 73, 77, 82, 84, 90, 92, 94, 101, 103, 119, 176; smuggling 66, 77–8, 119–20

New Orleans Association 101–2, 115, 120
New York 21, 27, 29, 31, 37, 38, 50, 56, 82, 89, 110, 112, 126, 135, 136, 138, 176
New York Columbian (newspaper) 96
New York Evening Post 131
Niles' Register (newspaper) 40, 81, 114, 121, 126
No Transfer Act 60
Nolte, Vincent 120
Noroña, Miguel 65, 132, 185*ch*4*n*6
Northern Division of East Florida 108

Ogden, Samuel 29, 31
O'Higgins, Bernardo 72, 76, 93, 95, 132, 126, 139, 140, 168, 187*ch*7*n*7
Oliver, Robert 41, 81
Onís, Luis de 36–8, 39, 41, 45, 71, 80–1, 87, 88, 116, 118, 127, 146, 154, 155, 156, 159, 179, 190*ch*10*n*19, 190*ch*11*n*1; as arms purchaser 43, 89, 176; intelligence activities 38, 50, 65, 66, 69, 91, 92, 94, 97, 99, 104, 122, 136, 137, 189*ch*9*n*1; his *Memorial Concerning the Negotiations* 160, 179; protest messages to department of state 70, 73, 75, 84–5, 86, 89–90, 94, 104, 110, 112, 117, 121, 137, 145; his reporting 38, 47, 50, 51, 55, 62, 88, 100; and Republic of West Florida 47–8; treaty negotiations 105, 112, 145, 146, 147, 153, 154, 155, 156, 160, 178
Onís, Mauricio 41, 50, 185*ch*4*n*8
USS *Ontario* 162
Orb see Congresso
Orea, Telesforo de 35, 40–4, 45–6, 50–55, 64, 94, 96, 165
Oregon Territory 147
Orinoco River 103, 105, 161

Paine, Thomas 25, 51
Paraguay 53, 130, 168
Patriota 82, 126, 127
Patterson, Daniel 94, 120, 186*ch*6*n*4
Patterson, Joseph 81
Patterson, William 81
Pazos, Vicente 109, 110, 112, 130, 132, 172, 188*ch*7*n*13
Pearl River 48
Peninsular War 33, 34, 74
Pensacola 20, 59, 73, 92, 100, 101–2, 106, 146
Perdido River 23, 184*ch*3*n*3
Perry, Henry 94, 102, 126
Perry, Oliver Hazard 161, 190*ch*11*n*4
Peru 24, 34, 71, 72, 76, 130, 132, 135, 140, 164, 166, 168, 175, 180
Petit Milan 93
Philadelphia 11, 18, 19, 24, 25, 27, 36, 37,

204

Index

82, 107, 176; "Philadelphia circle" of dissidents 38–9, 40, 44, 51, 57, 64, 68–9, 89, 93, 98, 100, 130, 175, 176; trade with Spain 21, 23, 41
Picornell, Juan 25, 56–7, 68, 69, 70, 91, 99, 115, 186*ch*6*n*2
Pinkney, William 82, 126
Pinkney Treaty 21, 117
piracy 86, 114, 121, 123, 124, 125, 128, 160, 171
Pitt, William 26, 27
Pizzaro, José 154
Plattsburgh, battle of 73
Poinsett, Joel 46, 47, 49, 71–2, 95, 97, 143, 144, 150, 185*ch*10*n*11
Porter, David 72, 95, 113, 132, 178
Portugal 32, 33, 71, 87, 117, 121, 128, 139, 141, 160, 168, 180
Prevost, John 162, 164
Providencia 119
Prussia 32, 147
Puerto Rico 76, 128, 171, 190*ch*11*n*3
Pueyreddón, Juan Martín 96–7, 109, 132, 133, 139, 140, 141, 142, 144, 148, 149, 150, 164, 169, 187*ch*7*n*7
Puglia, Santiago Filipe 25, 39
Purviance, John 123

Randolph, John 97
Ravenga, José 50, 93, 109, 130
recognition of rebel regimes 75, 97, 131, 132, 133, 134, 139, 144, 145, 151, 152, 153, 154, 156, 163, 166, 167, 170, 177, 173, 174–5, 177, 180
Regulus 106
Reindeer 106
Rendón, Francisco 24
Republic of Florida 61, 62, 71, 110
Republic of the Floridas 108, 110, 130
Republic of the Internal Provinces of Mexico 91
Republic of West Florida 47, 59
Republican Army of the North 67, 69, 70, 71, 91
Richmond Enquirer 40, 131, 133
Rio Grande 23, 28, 63–4, 117, 156
Rivadavia, Bernadino 171
Robinson, William 132
Rocafuerte, Vicente 39
Rodney, Caesar 143–4, 150, 151, 190*ch*10*n*3, 191*ch*12*n*6
Romp 82
Roscio, Juan 94, 109, 130, 132, 161, 166
Rush, Richard 85, 86, 87, 90, 107, 121, 135, 136, 144, 145
Russia 32, 147

Saavedra, Cornelio de 53
Saavedra, Diego de 53, 77
Sabine River 66, 156
St. Augustine 20, 59, 62, 108, 110
St. Mary's church, Philadelphia 175, 183*ch*2*n*2, 191*ch*11*n*10
St. Marys River 61, 108, 111
San Antonio 68, 70
San Blas conspiracy 25, 57
San Martín, José 72, 95, 109, 130, 132, 135, 139, 164, 168, 187*ch*7*n*7
Santamaria, Miguel 98
Santiago (Chile) 72
USS *Saranac* 111
Sarmiento, Francisco 41, 42, 80, 185*ch*4*n*6
Sassenay, Marquis de 184*ch*3*n*8
Savage 97
Savannah 107, 109
Scott, Winfield 98
Sedella, Antonio 91–2, 99, 102, 104
Seminole Indians 59, 112, 145, 152
Seminole War 134, 145, 154, 156
Sena, Manuel 51
Sérurier, Louis 55, 56
Shaler, William 46, 47, 48, 65, 67–8, 69–70, 185*ch*4*n*7, 185*ch*4*n*11
Sibley, John 63, 66
Skinner, John 81–2, 96, 97, 107, 126, 132, 133, 137, 138, 144, 151, 178
Skipwith, Fulmar 48
Smith, Alexander 99, 100
Smith, Dennis 99, 100
Smith, Robert 36, 42, 46, 59
Smith, Samuel 81, 188*ch*8*n*15
Smith, William, Jr. 29
Smith, William S. 25, 26, 27, 28, 31
Sociedad Patriotica 27, 57, 187*ch*7*n*7; *see also* Masonic Lodges
Soto la Marina, Mexico 102
Spain 32, 87, 88, 162–3, 176; colonial policy 11, 13, 18–23, 58, 71, 75, 76, 89, 90, 98, 106, 147, 159, 167, 168, 173, 176, 180, 181; dissent in colonies 24–5, 27, 64; French invasion 32–33; the Inquisition 25, 74, 75, 92; liberal 1812 constitution 33, 74, 98, 162, 163, 167, 180; and Louisiana 18–19, 20; Regency Council 33, 34, 35, 40, 45, 55; views on American expansionism 12, 13, 19–20; *see also* juntas
Stevens, Edward 183*ch*3*n*2
Stoughton, James 188*ch*8*n*15
Stoughton, John 38, 89, 117
Stoughton, Matilda 38
Stoughton, Thomas 38, 50, 89
Swartwout, John 29
Swift see *Mangoré*

205

Taylor, Thomas 78-9, 82, 86, 95, 97, 124, 125-6, 127
Tennessee 17-18, 63
Terán, Manuel 94
Texas 12, 22, 28, 63, 66-8, 70, 91, 116, 146, 147, 155, 156, 167, 176, 178; *see also* Mexico; Rio Grande
Thompson, Martín 82, 105, 107, 113, 136, 141, 149, 180*ch*10*n*10
Thornton, William 43, 103, 107, 112-3, 169, 178
Tinoco, Juan 40
Todd, Charles 164
Toledo, José 64, 68, 69-70, 90, 91, 92, 93, 94, 99, 100, 103, 106, 113, 130, 176, 187*ch*6*n*10
Torres, Manuel 39, 40, 43, 51, 53, 54, 55, 64, 94, 105, 106, 109, 112, 131, 165-6, 172, 173, 174-5, 178, 179-80
trade, American: with Latin America 21, 23-4, 35, 71, 72, 105-6, 140, 147, 164, 166, 170, 176, 180; with Spain 35, 71, 170, 176
trade embargo: French, against Britain 32; U.S. 24, 35, 61
Transcontinental Treaty (1819) 155-6, 159, 162, 163, 167, 172
Trimble, David 173
Trinidad 30
Tucumán, congress of 109, 136
Túpac Amaru 24

Umaña, Nicolás 55

United Provinces of Rio de la Plata *see* Buenos Aires
U.S. Navy 61, 80, 94, 96, 111, 123, 128-9, 140, 171
Uruguay *see* Banda Oriental

Valparaiso 72, 162
Venezuela 34, 35, 38, 42, 49, 71, 76, 77, 82, 83, 84, 103, 107, 121, 143, 148-9, 160-1, 164, 166; First Republic 52, 55-6, 58; Second Republic 71
Viar, José 36, 37, 183*ch*2*n*3
Villavincencio, Josef 51
Vives, Francisco 162-3, 167

Washington (city) 37, 42, 63-4, 65, 73, 100, 148
Washington, George 11, 17, 20, 21, 167, 177
Webster, Daniel 118, 124
West, John 120
Whitney, Eli 95
Winder, William 86, 123, 124, 148
Wirt, William 126, 127
Wooster, Charles 140, 189*ch*9*n*10
Worthington, William 140-1, 148, 161, 162

You, Dominique 77, 120
Young Wasp 106

Zea, Francisco 161, 166
Zimmerman, John 78
Zozaya, José 175

www.ingramcontent.com/pod-product-compliance
Ingram Content Group UK Ltd.
Pitfield, Milton Keynes, MK11 3LW, UK
UKHW042004140426
5217IPUK00015B/972